PUBLICATION NUMBER 15
Duke University Commonwealth-Studies Center

Canadian Economic Thought

Canadian Economic Thought

The Political Economy of a
Developing Nation 1814-1914

Craufurd D. W. Goodwin

PUBLISHED FOR THE

Duke University Commonwealth-Studies Center

DUKE UNIVERSITY PRESS, DURHAM, N. C.

CAMBRIDGE UNIVERSITY PRESS, LONDON

1961

© 1961, Duke University Press

L.C.C. card no. 61-6223

I.S.B.N. 0-8223-0072-9

Second printing, 1970

Printed in the United
States of America

To my mother and father

FOREWORD

The history of the development of economic thought may be approached from more points of view than the one usually dominant, namely, that which surveys the filiation of economic ideas in general and which sometimes gives rise to empirico-conjectural arrangements of the milestones that purportedly mark the evolution of theories. One may, for example, group writers in terms of the objectives which they would have economic organization serve, together with the role to be played therein by the state. Or one may focus attention upon the interaction between economic ideas and events. Again one may inquire particularly into why economic ideas sometimes take hold and sometimes do not. Or one may select from among various other points of departure. In fact, some students of the history of economic thought believe that though there is much to be said for the highly focused inquiry of a scholarly Cyclops, it may be more persuasively argued that a Cyclops does best in the end when he has the assistance of a more wide-ranging Argus. And they point in corroboration to the many-facetedness of the historiography of ideas, and to the fact that economic research has manifested so little tendency to progress cumulatively, much less than has research in the fields of natural and life science.

The approach of the present study is unique, though it partially recalls to mind that of scholars who inquired into the spread of Smithianism from Great Britain to the continent and even into Spain. The main concern of Dr. Goodwin, the author, is the transplantation of economic science, such as it was in the nineteenth century, principally from England and Scotland and secondarily from France and the United States, to Canada, and its spread and development within that country during the century preceding the outbreak of World War I and the beginning of Canada's coming of economic and intellectual age. He identifies the men and the works primarily responsible for this inflow of foreign economic thought and shows how it was taken up, modified, and diffused by authors of both foreign and domestic origin. He discloses also how its progress was influenced by various indigenous circumstances, among them the pressing needs of policy-advocates, the underdeveloped state of Canada's university world, and the shortage of her publishing facilities. The author demonstrates, in short, that the growth and development of economics in Canada was greatly influenced—much more, for example than was that of physics—by circumstances present in the economic and the subjective environments of the Canadian people. Improvements in the methodology of Canadian economics were predominantly of external origin. Not until after World War I did Canadian scholars begin to contribute to the progress of economic science in general.

The history of economics in Canada parallels in some measure that of economics in such dissimilar nineteenth-century underdeveloped countries as the United States, Chile, and Holland. The extent to which it parallels the history of economics in Australia will not become clear until Dr. Goodwin has completed his study of Australian economics now under way. In each of these countries a great deal of what was written had to do with questions of policy issuing out of the internal state of the economy as well as out of its position in the world of international commerce. Resident writers brought the views of foreign economists to bear upon these questions, though sometimes only after these views had been considerably modified. The quality of what was written tended to be inferior, in part because the authors lacked both the leisure essential to the conduct of disciplined inquiry and easy access to that milieu of creative stimulus and constructive criticism which university communities sometimes supply. Such research as was undertaken, moreover, was even less cumulative in character than was that carried on by economists in more developed European countries.

Among the more interesting of Dr. Goodwin's findings are those relating to the contributions of Robert Gourlay, E. G. Wakefield, and John Rae (whose works are destined to be reprinted), and those bearing on the development of economics within the English-speaking and the French-speaking university worlds. Of interest also is his assessment of the role of immigrant or temporarily-sojourning economists of foreign birth, among whom the Scots (so important in the development of Commonwealth lands in the nineteenth century) stand out. Of interest too is the similarity of many of the policy issues of concern to Canadian writers to issues of concern to writers in present-day underdeveloped regions.

It may prove illuminating, after Dr. Goodwin has completed his study of the development of economic science in Australia, to contrast his findings respecting newly settled countries with those pertaining to the transplantation of economics from Britain to India and its development in this land of several ancient and integrated cultures. Parallel studies of the transplantation and subsequent development of other branches of social as well as of natural science are indicated. Such studies should disclose the underlying nature of the diffusion process, discover in what respects the process characteristic of the spread of social science differs from that underlying the spread of natural science, and reveal whether the student of the development and spread of economic thought may profitably draw upon the methodology of anthropology and ecology.

Since the Commonwealth-Studies Center is concerned exclusively with the encouragement of research, specific theories or interpretations of Commonwealth affairs appearing in these publications do not constitute an expression of the view of the Center or of the Carnegie Corporation, which has furnished financial support to the Center. The respective authors of the several publications are responsible for the conclusions expressed in them.

Joseph J. Spengler

INTRODUCTORY STATEMENT

Goldwin Smith took stock of Canadian literature shortly after Confederation and remarked that the voice of an infant community is certain to be infantile. This study records a part of the Canadian voice as the country passed from infancy into maturity, when from the Treaty of Ghent in 1814 until the outbreak of World War I a collection of isolated colonies developed into an autonomous Dominion within the British Commonwealth. Concern is with organized discussion of economic problems, with sources of ideas, with modes of expression, and with adaptation of imported theory to a new environment. Although theory and practice were often virtually inseparable, no direct attempt is made to assess the impact of thought upon policy and action.

In mature societies where centers of learning and regular channels of publication are established it is possible to follow the development of scientific thought by observing the work of recognized scholars. In a country such as nineteenth-century Canada, however, where these institutions were developing or were still in the future, it is necessary to look farther, principally to the thought of statesmen and other competent amateurs. The writings covered in this book, therefore, are mainly of a practical character, are concerned with urgent topical matters, and for the most part deal only indirectly with pure theory. As a result, the examination is divided into two parts: the first treats discussion in Canada of three major policy problems—land disposal and settlement, tariffs and international trade, and currency and banking. The second deals with the attainment by economics of scientific status in government, the press, learned societies, and universities. Most of the materials referred to are published works: books, pamphlets, periodicals, and government documents. The writings of important thinkers are examined at some length with a representative selection of less significant works. Certain passages have been translated from French into English with mention made in footnotes.

This study was begun in the summer of 1956 at the suggestion of Professor Joseph J. Spengler. It was intended first as an A.M. thesis to be completed within a period of a few months, but was continued as a doctoral dissertation and was submitted to the Graduate School of Arts and Sciences of Duke University in 1958. I am grateful to the Rockefeller Foundation for assistance during the summer of 1956, and to the Duke University Commonwealth-Studies Center for pre-doctoral fellowships in 1956-1957 and 1957-1958. The Canada Council generously provided a grant in aid in the summer of 1959 to allow the manuscript to be revised for publication. The Editing Committee of the *Canadian Banker* has kindly granted permission to reprint portions of an article by me in the Winter, 1959, issue. I am under obligation for assistance and cooperation to many persons at Duke University and in the libraries and universities of Canada. I am indebted above all to Professor Spengler who for more than three years and through many drafts provided untiring guidance and inspiration. Errors and omissions are my own responsibility.

ABBREVIATIONS

A.A.A.P.S.S.	*Annals of the American Academy of Political and Social Science*
C.H.R.	*Canadian Historical Review*
C.J.E.P.S.	*Canadian Journal of Economics and Political Science*
C.J.I.S.A.	*Canadian Journal of Industry, Science and Art*
C.M.N.R.	*Canadian Monthly and National Review*
E.H.R.	*English Historical Review*
J.C.B.A.	*Journal of the Canadian Bankers' Association*
P.T.R.S.C.	*Proceedings and Transactions of the Royal Society of Canada*
Q.J.E.	*Quarterly Journal of Economics*
Q.Q.	*Queen's Quarterly*
R.E.C.	*Revue Économique Canadienne*
n.p.	No place of publication given
n.d.	No date of publication given

CONTENTS

PART THREE

Economic Thought and Economic Policy

Almost all Canadian economic thought before 1914 was policy oriented, and the division of this study into sections on policy and science is for convenience. Because questions of land settlement, international trade, currency, and banking were discussed most frequently, they are examined in Part One as distinct topics in separate chapters. Writings on economic subjects which were of relatively less interest to Canadians are reviewed in Part Two, where an account is given of the growth of economics as a recognized discipline.

Land Disposal and Settlement

In the century following the conclusion of the War of 1812 the British provinces in North America grew from struggling dependent colonies with less than a million people into an autonomous nation of more than seven million. While the inhabitable portions of half a continent were being settled, problems of land policy were continuous and pressing. In the colonial period immigrants moved into what are now Ontario, Quebec, and the Maritime Provinces, and after Confederation into the areas west of the Great Lakes. The history of Canadian settlement policy will be outlined briefly in this chapter together with the work of men who wrote on the subject.

1. Canadian Land Policy

Governments of the colonies which became the first five provinces made almost no attempt to plan for and direct settlement and colonization.[1] Free grants were made principally as rewards to public officials, Loyalists from the United States, retired soldiers, and anyone with influence either in Britain or America. In the Maritimes the whole of Prince Edward Island was granted to absentee landlords; almost all of Nova Scotia passed into private hands in blocks of from 20,000 to 150,000 acres between 1760 and 1773; and even in New Brunswick where property was usually regarded as relatively undesirable, the pattern was the same. In Lower Canada land along the St. Lawrence became settled seigniories under

[1] See Norman MacDonald, *Canada, 1763-1841: Immigration and Settlement* (London, 1939). One of the best descriptions of land policies in the colonies is still found in Appendix B of Lord Durham's *Report on the Affairs of British North America*. A more recent study of a particular sector is J. Howard Richards, "Lands and Policies: Attitudes and Controls in the Alienation of Lands in Ontario during the First Century of Settlement," *Ontario History*, L (1958), 193-209.

the French regime, but after the conquest in 1760 a profusion of free grants began in the rest of the province. Speculators using a scheme known as "leaders and associates" were able to gain control of as much as an entire township; and six members of one board appointed to dispose of land, after granting 1,425,000 acres to a mere sixty persons, were each awarded more than 10,000 acres for the satisfactory performance of their duties. In Upper Canada land was given mainly to government favorites with most bona fide settlers having to acquire holdings from a prior owner. After widespread criticism of colonial land policies, systematic disposal by sale was attempted in several provinces, particularly in the 1820's; but by this time plans for public sale were in vain because most land of any value had already become private property.

Public land was regarded both by the Colonial Office and by local administrators as a fund for the dual purpose of rewarding persons and encouraging desirable institutions. It was not recognized that in Canada, where most land was still uninhabited, empty estates of absentee landlords and barren wastes of reserves could give small return to their owners and injured the economy by separating inhabitants with stretches of wilderness. Adding to the many large tracts given to speculators who had no intention of settling on them, the Constitutional Act of 1791 provided that in Upper and Lower Canada one-seventh of all public lands should be retained for the support of a protestant clergy. Still another portion was reserved for the future support of the Crown (meaning the appointed Executive Councils), and whole townships were set aside to provide income for schools. Colonists realized only gradually that land in a new country could not become valuable and productive—and therefore a legitimate instrument for reward—until it had first been settled and put to use.

Largely by accident three of the early colonial land grants were administered well. Colonel Thomas Talbot, beginning in 1808, took possession of a large area along the north shore of Lake Erie which he systematically surveyed and sold in small lots. The Huron Tract to the east of Lake Huron was purchased by the Canada Company in 1826 and organized under John Galt on the model of the Pulteney and Holland Land Companies of New York State. The British-American Land Company, chartered in 1834 in the Eastern Townships of Lower Canada and later under the direction of John Galt's energetic son Alexander, made available to immigrants from Europe and to overcrowded French Canadians realistic information, transport facilities, and inexpensive land. Talbot and the two land companies built roads, planned townsites, provided markets and funds for development, and generally afforded a sharp contrast to the apathetic colonial administrators. As a result of the enterprise of their organizers and often in spite of government activity, the settlements were fairly successful in obtaining high quality immigrants; the imaginative practices of Colonel Talbot and the Galts served to highlight the lack of colonization policies on a wider scale.[2]

When the Manitoba Act of 1870 transferred the territory west of Lake Superior from the Hudson's Bay Company to the Dominion of Canada, all ungranted lands, which amounted to five times the area of the original provinces, came under federal control; and for the second time in a century a Canadian government found itself with an enormous region for colonization. Because, however, legislators thought it essential to obtain settlement and railways in the West without delay, they barely paused for examination of methods; most of their "Dominion Lands" policy was patterned after practices in the United States and the rest was a heritage from the eastern provinces.[3] Less than half the land which became private property by 1938 was alienated as free homesteads, and the rest, under a policy reminiscent of colonial days, was reserved for the future support of schools or was given as compensation to railways and the Hudson's Bay Company. Use of the free-homestead system suggested that the government realized that only land under cultivation could add to national income, but large grants and reserves indicated survival of the belief that public lands should be a fund for the disposition of rewards. In the West, as had been true earlier in the East, some recipients of extensive tracts proved to be able promoters of settlement; however, again these cases were fortuitous since cri-

---

[2] See MacDonald, *op. cit.*, pp. 265-311; F. C. Hamil, *Lake Erie Baron: The Story of Colonel Thomas Talbot* (Toronto, 1955), *passim;* and O. D. Skelton, *The Life and Times of Sir Alexander Tilloch Galt* (Toronto, 1920), pp. 21-28 and 46-64.

[3] See the volume containing: A. S. Morton, "History of Prairie Settlement," and Chester Martin, " 'Dominion Lands' Policy," in *Canadian Frontiers of Settlement*, ed. W. A. Mackintosh and W. L. G. Joerg (Toronto, 1938), pp. 229-244 and 356.

teria for the grants had been service to the state and not ability and intention to promote growth.   The Canadian Pacific Railway, acting on the assumption that transport revenues would be greatest in a populated and prosperous West, pursued a far-sighted immigration and settlement program; other grantees, notably the Hudson's Bay Company and several small railroad and land companies, had less enviable records.   Complaints of speculative "land-lock" and separation of inhabitants by expanses of wilderness were voiced as often during the settlement of the West as they had been in the East.

Land policy of the Dominion government was certainly more enlightened than that of the Canadian colonies; nevertheless, there was a distinct continuity of thought.   Throughout the nineteenth century the belief persisted that a portion of arable public land should be kept from settlers, and government was consistently reluctant to assume an active role in land development where there was any chance that a private company might take the initiative.   A policy of laissez faire in connection with land policy was evidenced by an unwillingness to eliminate speculative holdings and to establish orderly practices of disposal.   The discussions of settlement problems and policies in the colonies by Robert Gourlay and Edward Gibbon Wakefield, which are examined below, were in many respects as relevant to western prairie development as to eastern Canada fifty years before.

II. THE WRITINGS OF ROBERT GOURLAY

The earliest systematic analysis of the economics of Canadian settlement came from the pen of Robert Gourlay, an eccentric Scotch immigrant.   Gourlay's methods, theories, and policy proposals are described in this section.

Gourlay's Life

Robert Gourlay was born in Scotland in 1778 of a moderately wealthy farming family.[4]   He attended St. Andrew's University

---

[4] The Hon. W. R. Riddell has provided a well-documented biography of Gourlay in "Robert (Fleming) Gourlay," *Ontario Historical Society Papers and Records,* XIV (1916), 5-133; an account of Gourlay's legal difficulties in "A Canadian Hampden," *ibid.,* XXIV (1927), 500-506; and some amusing anecdotes of Gour-

and the University of Edinburgh, spent some time in military service, operated a farm in Scotland, and about 1800 worked for Arthur Young, Secretary of the Board of Agriculture, on reform of the poor laws. In 1817, after his father's death and a violent disagreement with a British Peer, Gourlay came to Upper Canada. He was characterized through life by an uncontrolled temper, extraordinary conceit, and a marked persecution complex; and while this combination brought misfortune in Britain, it led to disaster in the colonies. He became embroiled immediately in local controversies and made a bitter enemy of John Strachan, the most powerful figure in the province, whom he ridiculed as "a monstrous little fool of a parson," a "villain," and "a contemptible miscreant." Yet Gourlay was able to influence some people and became a popular figure with the dissatisfied farmers of Upper Canada, organizing meetings, issuing proclamations and pamphlets, and calling for public inquiry. Naturally he was viewed with extreme disfavor by the colonial government and in 1818 was twice accused and acquitted of seditious libel. Finally, in 1819 he was banished from the colony following a period of imprisonment during which he suffered great mental and physical hardship.

After Gourlay's expulsion from Upper Canada his characteristic eccentricity neared insanity, particularly in 1824 when following a year breaking flints in order to experience the life of a pauper and exasperated by his failure to obtain recognition in any direction, he went to the extremity of horse whipping Lord Brougham at the gates of the House of Commons. After a stay in prison Gourlay spent the remainder of his life trying to have his reputation restored, and in 1842 was granted an annual indemnity of fifty pounds by the Canadian legislature. He came to Canada for the last time in 1856, was badly defeated in an attempt to obtain a seat in the assembly, and returned to Scotland, where he died in 1862.

Gourlay as a Statistician

On his voyage to Canada in 1817 it occurred to Gourlay that he and other settlers could best become acquainted with their des-

lay's lifetime in "Humours of the Times of Robert Gourlay," *P.T.R.S.C.*, Third Series, XIV (1920), Section II, 69-83. Gourlay's political activities are described by E. A. Cruikshank in "The Government of Upper Canada and Robert Gourlay," *Ontario Historical Society Papers and Records*, XXIII (1926), 65-179.

tined country of immigration from a factual description of its geography and economic conditions. With this in mind, he prepared thirty-one queries, seven hundred copies of which were printed and "sent by post to the public officers of each township." Gourlay's mode and purpose of inquiry were probably influenced by the methods of Sir John Sinclair, who, between 1791 and 1799, had used information supplied by the Scottish clergy to complete *The Statistical Account of Scotland*.[5] Gourlay, like Sinclair, hoped to obtain information for the conduct of government as well as for immigrants; and with his eye always open for controversy, ended his questionnaire with the query "What, in your opinion, retards the improvement of your township in particular, or the province in general; and what would most contribute to the same?"

Back in England Gourlay published the replies to his questions—which had requested data on population, on the quantity and type of public and private capital, and on commodity prices—along with summaries of the information received, an account of his personal misfortunes, and other materials in his *Statistical Account of Upper Canada*.[6] He made an avowed attempt to obtain objectivity and accuracy and insisted he had accepted information only from persons with first-hand knowledge of the facts. The book was in three parts with a total of 2,010 pages. The introductory volume contained most of his theoretical conclusions and policy proposals, Volume I the results and analysis of his survey, and Volume II a variety of political and historical observations. Printing began in 1820 but was not completed until 1822. Later, Gourlay wrote several pamphlets and autobiographical works which contained principally restatements of his earlier views.[7]

[5] Edinburgh, 21 volumes. Sinclair was founder of the Board of Agriculture and a close personal friend of Arthur Young. Gourlay was undoubtedly acquainted with the work of Sinclair and the latter may have known Gourlay through their mutual interest in the rehabilitation of paupers. Gourlay submitted his findings to Young in March, 1801, and Sinclair composed an essay on the subject in May of that year. See John Sinclair, *Essays on Miscellaneous Subjects* (London, 1802), pp. 31-43 and 281-282; and the Hon. W. R. Riddell, "Robert (Fleming) Gourlay," *loc. cit.*, p. 8.

[6] *Statistical Account of Upper Canada, Compiled with a View to a Grand System of Emigration* (London, 1822) (cited hereinafter as *Statistical Account*).

[7] *An Appeal to the Common Sense, Mind, and Manhood, of the British Nation* (London, 1826) (cited hereinafter as *Appeal*); *Chronicles of Canada: Being a Record of Robert Gourlay, Esq., Now Robert Fleming Gourlay "The Banished Briton"* (St. Catherines, 1842); *The Banished Briton and Neptunian: Being a Record*

Gourlay's "Science" of Colonization

Gourlay was led by his study of Upper Canada to the conclusion that methods of colonization ought to constitute an important and separate subject of study. "The *Art of Settlement* in the wilderness," he wrote, "is the grand desideratum, and which should be understood before a penny more of public money is wasted." He explained with his customary lack of modesty that he had obtained a "knowledge of that art, or shall I call it a science, after studying it in all its bearings, its practical process, and its results, for more than four years. . . ." No one else, either in England or America, he added, had grasped correct principles of colonization. "The subject of emigration and settlement has never yet been understood, though it is capable of being reduced to a science."[8] The result of failure to study and plan for Canadian development, he concluded, was ignorance and uncertainty in all phases of settlement.

Emigrants now go out to Canada, only upon a chance of getting land worth acceptance. A thousand doubts torment them: a thousand difficulties and disappointments wait upon their movements. From their native country, and the society of friends, they have to enter into gloomy solitude: they have to cut out the road before them into the wilderness: they have there to take up their abode, while yet unskilled in the art of settlement, and unprepared by experience, to guard against numerous and frightful accidents: they have often to strive, at once, against poverty and sickness. Not one in ten of those who go out to Canada, have, within themselves, the means of making comfortable commencement; and not the half of these can put even sufficient means to speedy and economical account, for want of plan and arrangement.[9]

Colonies, Gourlay claimed, if correctly administered could be doubly useful to Great Britain: as a haven for excess population and as a field for the employment of capital. The rapid rate of population increase which had been explained by Malthus, he argued, could eventually be reduced by a reform of the poor laws leading to a decline in the birth rate; but for a time labor in Britain would still

---

of the Life, Writings, Principles and Projects of Robert Fleming Gourlay (Boston, 1843-1845), in 39 parts. All of Gourlay's writings are extremely scarce, particularly the last two, which were published in serial form. The only complete file of these, to my knowledge, is in the Public Archives of Canada at Ottawa.

[8] *Statistical Account*, Introduction, p. ccc; and *Appeal*, p. 167.

[9] *Statistical Account*, Introduction, p. cxcii.

increase more quickly than the means of subsistence, and a vent for the surplus could be found in the New World.[10]   Moreover, excess capital as well as labor could be employed in the colonies. England accumulated savings each year both from domestic and foreign sources, and although these funds had been used up for many years in wars, in peacetime they could not find employment.

That capital is now running to waste; or worse than waste, it is running on to increase pauperism and idleness; idleness both among the rich and the poor. While this capital is yet at command, England may do wonders, by setting in motion a vast machinery at home and abroad; but let this capital waste itself, as it is now doing, and a little time only will see its end,—a woeful end![11]

Inactivity either of tools or of people, Gourlay believed, was wasteful and dangerous for society; it was his thesis that the empty spaces of Canada offered unlimited opportunities for the employment of British labor and capital. The Empire if organized on correct principles could be drawn tightly together, not only by trade, but by the complementary needs of the developed and less-developed areas. Finally, as an added blessing, when the colonies were populated and prosperous the Mother Country could economize on defense costs, for "who would dare to invade Canada, were it compactly settled?"[12]

Gourlay's Theory of Land Values

The heart of Gourlay's discussion of colonial development was a theory of land values which was novel, received support from the statistical evidence he had gathered, and was at the basis of several suggestions he made for reform. He believed that in a pioneer economy where there were few transport facilities and no metropolitan centers, the prosperity of the community and therefore the value of land was dependent upon the density of population. Becoming more specific, he claimed that the value of land in a new country varied directly with the number of people living upon it and with the density of settlement upon land adjacent to it. Unlike Petty

[10] *Ibid.*, pp. clxxxii and clxxxix.
[11] *Ibid.*, pp. cccxl-cccxli.
[12] *Ibid.*, p. ccccii.

and Smith, who had found returns to land arising from proximity to a market, he attributed land rents to the mere presence of settlers.[13] Because Upper Canada in 1817 had not yet become an important exporter of goods or developed a diversified economy with advanced division of labor, its inhabitants were locally self-sufficient and dependent upon simple exchange among themselves. Land upon the Canadian frontier, therefore, became valuable when the situation and degree of settlement permitted easy co-operation among settlers together with the social contacts desired by civilized men. Gourlay explained:

Land is valuable, according to the degree of convenience attached to it; and other things being equal, increases in value as the density of population increases. A single family planted down on a square mile, as is the case in Upper Canada, can have no convenience—no sufficient strength to make head against obstacles to improvement; and while the settler is held in misery, little value is added to the land he occupies. Plant down two families, twelve, twenty, or more, on the same extent of ground, and each addition, up to a certain proportion, insures greater and greater comfort and convenience to the whole, while an instant and great value is given to the soil.[14]

Land values in Upper Canada, Gourlay insisted, were a result of benefits derived from local division of labor and from social values associated with density of settlement. The price of land depended in but small measure upon what Ricardo had called the "original and indestructible powers of the soil." He observed further that Canadian land was homogeneous as regards physical productivity. "Throughout the whole province nature has wonderfully equalized the value of land. What is better in point of quality, is generally worse in point of local situation; and, at this early stage of settlement, minute differences in this respect are of very little consequence."[15]

[13] Petty argued that total rents increased with population, but that distance from market and transport facilities, together with fertility, explained differences in rent levels. He denied that rents between areas could be determined from the population within the areas. *The Economic Writings of Sir William Petty*, ed. C. H. Hull (Cambridge, 1899), pp. 52, 180, 564. Adam Smith attributed location rent to "local advantage" and to expenditures required for "Good roads, canals, and navigable rivers." *Wealth of Nations* (Modern Library Edition; New York, 1938), pp. 147-149.

[14] *Statistical Account*, Introduction, p. cccxl.

[15] *Ibid.*, p. ccclxxxiii.

Gourlay discussed land values, rather than rent in the sense of a contractual price for the use of land, reasoning that most farmers would accept nothing less than outright possession because the following conditions obtained: land was of approximately uniform quality, uncultivated land was available from the state, ready cash for rent payments was scarce, and land generally was unimproved. In an old country, he pointed out, a tenant was content to farm land, to divide its product with the landlord, and to agree to return the property in the condition in which it had been initially rented. As a result, Gourlay declared, "All land in Britain will bring a clear rent in money. . . ." In a new country, however, such an arrangement was deemed unsatisfactory by settlers. They could always purchase their own land at little cost and were seldom able to exchange products for money wherewith to pay absentee landlords. Furthermore, while living upon rented land, a tenant inevitably and sometimes inadvertently increased the value of his landlord's property, both by carrying out necessary physical improvements such as clearing and building, and simply by adding to the size of the community. In modern phraseology, therefore, so long as a settler in a new country did not actually own his land he did not receive the marginal product of his labor, and agriculture lost attractiveness as an occupation. Hence, Gourlay concluded, "land in America, or in any other new country, can have little value till it becomes private property, and is occupied by the owner. This is an important truth,— a truth which I am anxious should be attended to, not only for the sake of establishing a right principle for the settlement of Canada, but of our immense territories in every quarter of the globe."[16]

Gourlay incorporated his theory of land values into a simple model designed to provide a method of tax assessment in Upper Canada. Given the number of inhabitants in each township Gourlay proposed a means of estimating the value of land. He assumed, first, that the province was divided into townships of 60,000 acres of uniform size and shape; second, that prior inquiry had revealed the population of each township; and third, that the land of a township "A" was worth twenty shillings per acre. Within township "A" there were one thousand inhabitants and within townships on

[16] *Statistical Account*, II, 384.

three sides of "A" there were an additional three thousand settlers. A body of water on the fourth side of "A" was assumed to give the same value to the land of "A" as an adjacent township containing one thousand persons. The population within township "A" and within townships on all sides of it, therefore, totalled five thousand, or .0834 persons per acre (see summary diagram I).

Diagram I

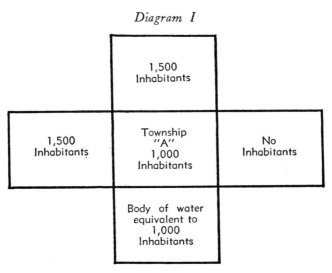

1. Township "A" contains 60,000 acres.
2. Population within Township "A" and within adjacent townships totals 5,000.
3. Effective population per acre of Township "A" is $\dfrac{5,000}{60,000}$ or .0834.

Next Gourlay selected at random a township "E" in which the population had been determined and where he wished to estimate the value of land. He added the population within township "E" to the population of the four townships adjacent to it, and arrived at a total of 7,100, or .118 inhabitants per acre. Following his theory that land values varied directly with the number of settlers, he arrived at the value of land in township "E" by adjusting the value of land in "A" (twenty shillings) by the number of persons per acre for "E" divided by the number of persons per acre for "A"—

$20s \times \dfrac{.118}{.0834}$, or slightly more than twenty-eight shillings per acre.

All of Gourlay's examples have been summarized in Table I, where it may be observed that his theory reduces to the postulation of a linear homogeneous relationship between the two variables "Inhabitants per Acre" and "Price of Land per Acre." This functional dependence is illustrated in Diagram II.

The statistics collected by Gourlay for his *Statistical Account of Upper Canada,* although valuable to the economic historian today, were not accurate or complete enough for him to test his hypotheses. It is evident, however, that the general appearance of these statistics,

Table I

(1) Township	(2) Population of Township	(3) Total Population of Contiguous Townships	(4) Inhabitants Per Acre $\dfrac{(2) + (3)}{60,000}$	(5) Price of Land Per Acre $\dfrac{(4) \times 20}{.083}$
E	1,500	5,600	.118	28s. 4d.
R	0	1,400	.023	5s. 6d.
W	500	1,000	.025	6s.

together with the comments of respondents to his questionnaire, influenced the formulation of his theory. In his illustrative examples the hypothetical values for the size of townships, price of land, and degree of settlement approximate the average values given in the *Statistical Account.*[17] By suggesting a simple method for assessing

[17] In order to obtain some estimate of the relevance of Gourlay's theory to contemporary conditions a simple correlation has been carried out between the price of land and the number of inhabitants per acre in thirty-one townships, using the figures he had collected. (The number of acres in each township was obtained from the *Municipal Directory of Ontario, 1957;* these figures may have changed slightly since 1822). The regression line of this correlation, although not homogeneous, reveals a definite positive relationship. The equation is $Y = 17 + 448X$, where Y is the price of land per acre and X the number of inhabitants per acre. The measure of correlation is significant at .595. The correlation tests a much simplified version of Gourlay's theory, since the effect upon the price of land of

Diagram II

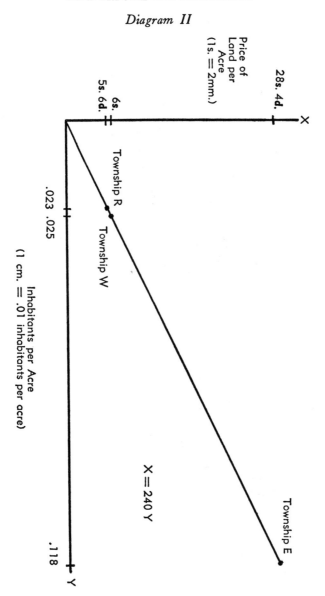

land values for tax purposes Gourlay might have made a useful contribution to Canadian fiscal policy.

settlement in adjacent townships is ignored. The indication is, nevertheless, that Gourlay's fundamental assertion of a positive relationship between population and land values had validity.

Policy Proposals

As corollaries to his theory of land values Gourlay made two policy proposals: first that the settlement of waste lands between inhabitants be accomplished as quickly as possible, and second that transport facilities be constructed to improve the local division of labor. Because he believed that property could not be rented in Canada,[18] he argued that land should never be alienated to anyone who could not actually cultivate it; and in particular, he objected to Crown reserves and to grants for the clergy and absentee landlords:

In Canada large portions of land are set aside for the future purposes of government: large portions are set aside for the maintenance of a dominant church, which has not even a chance of being established; and large portions are given away in favour and for fees of office, to individuals who would never think of cultivating, but who depend on sales at a remote period of time, while actual settlers are, in consequence, removed so far apart, that it is impossible for them to cultivate with economy and profit.[19]

The state should sell all public land at auction, and not restrict purchases by sale at a fixed price. Through accurate surveys and the provision of information the government should assist the legitimate settler and stimulate national growth. Gourlay regarded penal settlement as undesirable; "We have honest men willing to emigrate, and rogues only should be restrained from it";[20] and he expressed the hope that immigration would represent a cross-section of British society: "Is it not possible to create such a tide of commerce as would not only bring with it a *part* of society, but society complete, with all the strength and order and refinement which it has now attained in Britain, beyond all precedent?"[21]

Transportation facilities, and roads in particular, Gourlay declared, were the most badly needed public works in Upper Canada:

. . . good roads are of the first consequence in the improvement of any country; and it is clear that if a fair principle is once fixed upon for the making and support of these, the hand to extort means to such ends may

[18] See above, p. 12.
[19] *Statistical Account*, Introduction, pp. ccccxlviii-ccccxlix.
[20] *Statistical Account*, II, 393.
[21] *Statistical Account*, Introduction, p. cxcii.

be at once relentless and just; for, the greater the expenditure, the greater certainly, will be the gain.[22]

Roads should be built according to their function with main arteries a national responsibility, and smaller roads supported in proportion to the value of land served by them.[23]

A project with special interest for Gourlay was the widening and deepening of the St. Lawrence waterway to the Great Lakes. He maintained, somewhat optimistically, that sufficient capital equipment was available in the form of unused military supplies, and that after completion the increase in returns flowing to adjacent land would be large enough to amortize a loan required to cover labor costs. Finally, the laborers who had been brought from Europe to work on the project "not only reconciled to the novelty of their situation, but pretty well informed as to the various modes of management, and taught to handle the axe" would remain as valuable settlers.[24]

Gourlay counted upon the taxing power of the state to promote both settlement and the building of public works. He proposed financing immigration and construction through the imposition of a tax on the rent of land, estimated from population density as shown above. Land in remote areas would not be taxed as highly as would

[22] *Ibid.*, p. ccclxxxvii. Gourlay believed that the ultimate effect upon national prosperity should be the criterion for any public expenditure. "On the same principle, and with equal confidence, as an individual may proceed, so may a community, and the individuals of a whole nation may yield as cheerfully to taxation, for promoting the general interest, as any company of traders contribute shares to the common stock." *Ibid.*, p. ccccxiv.

[23] Gourlay explained that "roads . . . should rank under three descriptions. Provincial, being those great leading roads which connect together the remotest points, and which should draw from the public fund an absolute sufficiency for their being made and kept perfect. Secondly, district roads, being those connecting less distant points, and which should have support proportionate to the assessed value of the districts through which they pass; and lastly, township roads, which should have their proportion afforded on the same principle." *Ibid.*, p. ccclxxxvii.

[24] *Ibid.*, pp. cccxc-cccxci. It is interesting to note that a similar relationship between transport construction and settlement became very important in Canada long after Gourlay wrote. Professor H. C. Pentland, examining the influx of skilled laborers in the 1850's, writes: "Primarily, it was the railways that provided the market for them, and even imported them. . . . Urban industries encouraged by railways provided for additional immigrants, and contributed to make a genuine skilled labour market, with reserves and alternative opportunities, in the larger cities." "The Development of a Capitalistic Labour Market in Canada," *C.J.E.P.S.*, XXV (1959), 461. Professor Morton, when discussing the impact of railways on the West, explained: "Their construction and organization in an area offered work and good wages to the new settler, and thus the ready money with which to establish himself on a farm." *Op. cit.*, p. 113.

land in heavily populated sections; and because the tax was to be upon land rent—a real economic rent—the margin of cultivation would not be affected. The result of the tax would be twofold. The state would receive increased revenues, and in addition, each landowner would be encouraged either to cultivate his land so as to earn the amount of the tax, or to sell the property in order to escape the tax burden. If a landowner in spite of the tax still preferred to hold his land idle for speculative purposes, he would partially repay with his tax payments the loss incurred by society. A speculator who held uncultivated land in densely populated townships caused the greatest injury but automatically was penalized most heavily. Gourlay regarded the tax as a forced loan from landowners which would eventually be repaid through higher land values resulting from improved division of labor and more dense settlement. He argued that the tax would be profitable even without regard to the immediate revenue received.

Such is the peculiar situation of landed property in this province, that I am fully convinced, were £200,000 or £300,000 raised annually, by taxation, on the principle proposed by me, and thrown into Lake Ontario, it would tend to good. Though at first it would be pinching, by and by it would be less felt, the effect being to force on settlement and cultivation, by rendering wild lands less, comparatively, profitable to hold than cultivated land; and, through this effect, the tax, in the end, would be drawn out of such an increased value in the aggregate, as scarcely to incommode individuals in the least degree. It should never be forgotten, that wild land is the chief bane of this country, and fair means should be left unemployed to lessen it.[25]

Gourlay concluded that a tax on land was peculiarly fitted to a new country. "The idea of raising all taxes from land, is not new. It has often been the subject of political discussion; and often have I mused upon it before my acquaintance with this country. In an old country, many objections start up against its adoption; here I know of none."[26]

Gourlay did not look upon himself, as did his contemporaries, as a political reformer. His primary concern to the consternation of many followers was with economic improvements, and he wrote

---

[25] *Ibid.*, p. ccccxiv.
[26] *Ibid.*, pp. ccclxxxii-ccclxxxiii.

upon his return to Scotland in 1820: "In Upper Canada my efforts had no view whatever to a reform of Parliament. The people there have a perfect representation, and before long they will make a better use of it than they have hitherto done."[27] He considered it more important that Canadian government be efficient than that it simply be representative, and for this reason alone he favored confederation of all the British North American colonies with an annual congress to meet at Quebec City. Colonization could be arranged more conveniently in a large single unit and the credit of the whole in the capital markets of the world would be greater than that of the sum of the parts. Expressing a farsighted faith in the viability of many responsible governments at different levels within the British Empire, he suggested that local legislatures be retained with jurisdiction over regional matters, and that the central congress have independence from Britain in all matters excepting the disposal of waste lands and the formation of commercial policy.[28]

Influence of Gourlay's Ideas

It is not easy to assess the influence of Gourlay's theories and reform proposals. He was for a time very popular with the radical spokesmen of Upper Canada; and from 1829 until 1832 he corresponded with and advised William Lyon Mackenzie, their new leader. However, the essence of much that Gourlay wrote, for example his condemnation of land reserves and appreciation of the need for public works, was already familiar to the settlers before he arrived; he was probably most influential when setting down carefully and supporting by theory these widely held beliefs, thereby mobilizing demands for reform.[29] Gourlay's influence is evident in

[27] "Statement to Editors of British Newspapers, Craigrothie, Fifeshire, January 3, 1820," contained in *Appeal*, p. 6.
[28] *Statistical Account*, Introduction, pp. cccxxxviii and ccccliii-ccccliv.
[29] William Kingsford argued that Gourlay's plan for improving the St. Lawrence was "crude," "visionary," and "a mere echo of a generally expressed opinion"; however, he conceded that "so far as the enquirer can judge by existing records, he [Gourlay] may be mentioned as the first who gave any defined views in writing on the subject. . . ." *The Canadian Canals: Their History and Cost* (Toronto, 1865), pp. 60-61. John Rae (see below, pp. 122-127) reported in 1840 that Gourlay's *Statistical Account* was one of the few works similar in plan to his own proposed *Outlines of the Natural History and Statistics of Canada*. He continued: "Mr. Gourlay's book was published under so unfavourable circumstances that the talent which portions of it evidently display, lies buried under a heterogeneous mass

Mackenzie's famous inquisition in 1835 as Chairman of the Grievance Committee of the Upper Canada House of Assembly; such questions as the following have the distinct flavor of Gourlay's *Statistical Account:* "Does not the inequality of the system of taxation of rateable property, cultivated or uncultivated, afford just grounds of complaint on the part of the people?"[30]

In Britain Gourlay's eccentricity and poor judgment resulted in an unfavorable reception for himself and for his ideas. Furthermore, although his economics was clear and consistent, the disorganization of his published work made it difficult for his contributions to be appreciated. Gourlay's only acknowledged intellectual disciple was J. W. Bannister, a colonist in Canada in 1819 who later became an eminent English jurist and Chief Justice of Sierra Leone.[31] Gourlay's most important influence was upon Edward Gibbon Wakefield, and this will be examined in the next section.

Gourlay's writings are interesting apart from their historical significance for their quality of analysis and particular relevance to Canadian conditions. He was the first to examine in detail methods of settling the country and to exhibit originality in applying economic theory to land problems.

III. THE WRITINGS OF EDWARD GIBBON WAKEFIELD

Edward Gibbon Wakefield can only with qualifications be called a "Canadian economist." He is important in this study, however, for two reasons: first because he composed the portions of the *Durham Report* dealing with land settlement, and second because he

---

of uninteresting matter. . . ." *Hamilton Gazette*, July 27, 1840. This reference was provided by Dr. R. Warren James.

[30] *The Seventh Report from the Select Committee of the House of Assembly of Upper Canada on Grievances* (Toronto, 1835), Minutes of Evidence, p. 12. See also Lillian F. Gates, "The Decided Policy of William Lyon Mackenzie," *C.H.R.*, XL (1959), 187-189. Gourlay printed a letter he wrote to William Lyon Mackenzie concerning emigration in a pamphlet entitled *The Record*, Edinburgh, 1829, pp. 12-13. (The only known copy of this publication is in the author's possession).

[31] There are indications in Gourlay's writings of a friendship with Bannister (e.g. *Appeal*, p. 112); and in 1822, under the pseudonym "A Settler," Bannister restated Gourlay's theories and quoted from the *Statistical Account* in a pamphlet entitled *Sketches of Plans for Settling in Upper Canada, a Portion of the Unemployed Labourers of Great Britain and Ireland* (London, 1822).

was influenced, both in his work with the Durham Commission and in his many publications on colonial policy, by Canadian conditions generally and in particular by the writings of Robert Gourlay. Furthermore, Wakefield was no utopian theorist whose ideas might be simply of academic interest. He was an active colonizer who exerted a positive influence upon British policy; it has been remarked that "there are few political inventors to whom historians would ascribe so large a measure of political success."[32]

Wakefield's Life

Edward Gibbon Wakefield was born in London in 1796 and spent an undistinguished youth in England and with the diplomatic service on the Continent.[33] At eighteen he made a runaway marriage which ended shortly with the death of his wife; and at thirty he became famous, or rather infamous, by abducting a child heiress and contracting a marriage at the Scottish border. After this latter escapade he was overtaken in France and returned to England and Newgate Prison. During his subsequent enforced leisure of three years Wakefield became interested in the problems of the British poor and of the colonies, and he read extensively on these subjects. He quickly developed his own thoughts on colonial policy and expressed them anonymously in 1829 in a series of letters to the London *Morning Chronicle,* later reprinted as *A Letter from Sydney the Principal Town of Australasia.*

In the 1830's, after his release from prison, Wakefield studied the settlements in Australia and New Zealand; and his first book, *England and America* (1833), was a general exposition of his colonial theory.[34] His influence increased steadily; among his converts were Charles Buller and Lord Durham, who persuaded him to accompany them on Durham's mission in 1838. They spent only

---

[32] Professor Graham Wallas, as quoted by R. C. Mills in the introduction to E. G. Wakefield, *A Letter from Sydney and Other Writings* (London, 1929; Everyman Edition), p. xii (cited hereinafter as *Letter*).

[33] See R. Garnett, *Edward Gibbon Wakefield* (London, 1898); A. J. Harrop, *The Amazing Career of Edward Gibbon Wakefield* (London, 1928); and Klaus E. Knorr, *British Colonial Theories 1570-1850* (Toronto, 1944), pp. 269-315.

[34] The American edition of *England and America* (New York, 1834), will be cited here. The book was first published in London in 1833 in two volumes.

part of a year in Canada, and although Wakefield's unsavory reputation did not permit Durham to give his aide official recognition,
Wakefield's influence on the resulting *Report* was extremely important. The *Report* itself was probably the combined work of
Durham, Buller, and Wakefield; but Appendix B "On the Disposal
of Waste Land in the Colonies" was written entirely by Wakefield
and his assistant R. D. Hanson. Buller, who signed the Appendix,
said that "He [Buller] had nothing to do with it, except signing
his name. The merit of this very valuable report was due to Mr.
Hanson and Mr. Wakefield."[35]

Wakefield returned to England in 1838 and became involved,
once again, with the colonies in the Southern Hemisphere. In 1841
he returned to Canada for a short time to look into the formation
of a land company;[36] he became a member of parliament in the new
United Provinces, remaining in office until 1844, and acted as confi-
dential advisor to the Governor-General Sir Charles Metcalfe. Back
in England Wakefield devoted his full attention to Australia and
New Zealand. He died at Wellington in 1862.

The Wakefield Theory of Colonization

Since Wakefield had constructed a theory of colonization before
he came to Canada in 1838, his contributions to the *Durham Report*
must be examined against earlier writings. It is important to note
first that his conception of colonial development was not simply the
increase of productive capacity, either in absolute terms or per capita,
but was rather the creation of a society in the colonies as much as
possible like that of England. He explained the form colonial society should take in an enumeration of "proofs of wealth" in the
settlement at Sydney, Australia. These included, in addition to
towns, roads, and banks, "public hotels, superior to the best in North
America . . . an astonishing number of private carriages built in

---

[35] *Hansard's Parliamentary Debates*, Third Series, XLIX (1839), 503. For
discussion of who wrote the *Durham Report* see: R. Garnett, "The Authorship of
Lord Durham's Canada Report," *E.H.R.*, XVII (1902), 268-275; Charles Buller,
"Sketch of Lord Durham's Mission to Canada in 1838," *Report of the Public
Archives of Canada*, 1923, Appendix B, p. 350; R. C. Mills, *The Colonization of
Australia (1829-42)* (London, 1915), pp. 259-279.

[36] See Ursilla N. Macdonell, "Gibbon Wakefield and Canada Subsequent to the
Durham Mission, 1839-42," *Bulletin of the Departments of History and Political and
Economic Science in Queen's University*, No. 49 (1924-25).

Long-Acre . . . a turf club; packs of hounds; dinner parties, concerts, and balls; fine furniture, plate, and jewels; and though last, not least, many gradations in society, being so many gradations in wealth."[37] Wakefield's enthusiasm for British modes transplanted to Australia was prompted partly by personal taste and sentiment, but also by a conviction that the society of an old country was best for a colony on economic grounds. An English community when established in a new country, he explained, contained wealthy capitalists and entrepreneurs who alone were able to stimulate growth; to support this argument he explained a socio-economic theory of history involving a class division of labor: "Mankind have adopted a . . . simple contrivance for promoting the accumulation of capital, and the use of capital . . . they have divided themselves into owners of capital and owners of labour. But this division was, in fact, the result of concert or combination."[38] Joint-stock companies, he conceded, were able to perform the entrepreneurial function and to replace the capitalist in mature but not in new economies.

A second reason why Wakefield wished colonies to copy Britain was his failure to recognize a need for different technologies in dissimilar environments. He believed that young countries ought to employ the same methods as successful old ones, and that any other practice led to waste. He noted, for example, that on farms in Australia where labor was scarce, a lack of attention to animals resulted in a heavy loss of livestock. "What does all this mean," he asked, "but that there is a constant waste of capital?" He related regretfully, "I could fill pages with an account of the number of things, which would be of great value in England, which would be considered as capital in any densely peopled country, but which we throw away as rubbish."[39] In fact, Wakefield was complaining of activities in Australia which wasted natural resources and capital by British standards, but conserved labor—the relatively more scarce factor in Australia. He did not realize that the use of British techniques and capital forms in Australia, where factor scarcities were different, would have resulted in economic loss to the colony.

Wakefield suggested that the British society he admired be created in the colonies in a unique way—by manipulating the pro-

[37] *Letter*, p. 35.
[38] *England and America*, p. 26.
[39] *Letter*, p. 19.

portions between land, labor, and capital. The relationships between factors, he argued, had determined the character of every society through history: the size and development of towns, capital-forms, and even the culture of the people. In England land had recently become scarce relative to capital and labor, and as a result workers were becoming poor and landowners wealthy—a perilous situation for the empire. In America just the reverse was true; abundant land had caused capital and labor to be spread thinly over a wide area with the consequent neglect of all but land-intensive production. Social customs were reduced to a primitive level because settlers were isolated and without capital: "The effect on the mind of this lonely and monotonous existence," he wrote, "can hardly be conceived by Englishmen generally, to whom the stillness of the country gives fresh and pleasant feelings."[40]   Even slavery in the United States, he concluded, could be traced to the "*super*-abundance of land in proportion to people."

To improve factor relationships in both new and old countries, Wakefield proposed first that capital and labor be moved from Britain to the colonies until the optimum balance with land had been achieved in both; and second, that land be restricted in the colonies and made available only as supplies of other factors arrived. He never specified exactly the amount of land which ought to be released but explained how it could be determined in general terms:

> In order to create and maintain a very high rate of wages in the colony, it is necessary, first, that the colonists should have an ample field of production; ample, that is, in proportion to capital and labour; such an extent of land as to render unnecessary the cultivation of inferior soils, and as to permit a large proportion of the people to be engaged in agriculture; a field, large from the beginning, and continually enlarged with the increase of capital and people. But, in the second place, it is quite as necessary that the field of production should never be too large; should never be so large as to encourage hurtful dispersion; as to promote that cutting up of capital and labour into small fractions, which, in the greater number of modern colonies, has led to poverty and barbarism, or speedy ruin.[41]

A device which Wakefield believed would bring an influx of capital and labor to the colonies at the same time that it restricted

---

[40] *England and America*, p. 193.
[41] *England and America*, pp. 275-276.

land was a "sufficient price" for all lands sold. When combined with assisted immigration, he explained, a sufficient price would make development self-perpetuating. Land sales would yield funds which would be used to bring in laborers who, after working for a time for wages, would buy land themselves and start the cycle again. Workers in the colonies who had not yet earned enough money to purchase land would be an attraction for capital.

> . . . the supply of labour *must* be constant and regular: because, first, as no labourer would be able to procure land until he had worked for money, all immigrant labourers, working for a time for wages in combination, would produce capital for the employment of more labourers; secondly, because every labourer who left off working for wages and became a land-owner, would, by purchasing land, provide a fund for bringing fresh labour to the colony.[42]

Wakefield believed that if his system of land sales were introduced labor would come to the colonies and buy property in the right amount and at the right time. Finally, capital would flow in of its own accord, taking three forms: settlers' effects, funds for speculation in land, and loans to entrepreneurs and the government.

Wakefield, Gourlay, and the Durham Report.

Wakefield's contributions to the *Durham Report* were the most direct applications of his theories to the Canadian situation; they also illustrate clearly the influence of Robert Gourlay's writings. But before discussing the contents of the *Report* it is interesting to examine first the evidence of a personal connection between Wakefield and Gourlay.

It is probable that Wakefield heard of Gourlay when quite young. His father, also Edward, made reference to Gourlay in 1812 in his *Account of Ireland, Statistical and Political.* "From my personal knowledge of that gentleman," the elder Wakefield wrote, "I am inclined to pay very great attention to his opinion, for few have seen so much of England in a practical way as this intelligent North Briton."[43] The father and son were reportedly inti-

---

[42] *England and America*, p. 296.

[43] (London, 1812), II, 812, noted by Gourlay, *Statistical Account*, Introduction, p. lxxxix. The mention of Gourlay came in connection with his work for Arthur Young. Wakefield's intellectual debt to Gourlay was suggested first by R. C.

mate,[44] and it seems likely that Edward Gibbon would have been aware of this high regard. In any event, the evidence of Wakefield's familiarity with Gourlay's work became more concrete in later years. In a pamphlet in 1830 announcing the formation of a colonization society, Wakefield quoted a passage from Gourlay's *Statistical Account,* and obviously paraphrased several others.[45] Also in 1830 Wakefield wrote in an open letter to Lord Howick of having read Gourlay's work:

The fullest information as to the ruinous effects of these Crown and Clergy reserves is to be found in *Gourlay's* account of Upper Canada; but I may observe, that the author, a man who would have done honour to human nature if born under a representative government, has mixed up with much valuable statistical information an account of his own pre-eminent misfortunes, and a picture of his own mental sufferings so distressing—or, if your Lordship should prefer the more aristocratic expression, so annoying—to the reader, that it becomes difficult to extract from his book those parts which are merely useful.

I am informed that Mr. *Gourlay* is still unfortunate. His talents and his honesty no one will question; he was cruelly persecuted, and has had no redress; and his name is popular in Canada. The *Murrays* and *Twisses* would have appointed a footman or a dog, rather than so honest and able a man as *Gourlay,* to some colonial office in which he might be useful. What will Lord *Howick* do, being still young and generous?[46]

In 1833 Wakefield included selections from Gourlay's work in an appendix to *England and America.*[47]

On Gourlay's side there is corroborative evidence of Wakefield's

---

Mills, *The Colonization of Australia* (1829-42) (London, 1915), 136 ff. Mills was incorrect in attributing to Gourlay, as well as to Wakefield, a desire to restrict the quantity of land in use.

[44] A. J. Harrop, *op. cit.,* p. 14.

[45] *A Statement of the Principles and Objects of a Proposed National Society, for the Cure and Prevention of Pauperism, by Means of Systematic Colonization* (London, 1830). The wording of important paragraphs on pages 41 and 62-63 on conditions in Canada and the need for compact settlement is almost identical to Gourlay's *Statistical Account,* Introduction, pp. cccxl and ccccxlviii-ccccxlix. The direct citation of Gourlay is on p. 25.

[46] Letter from P——— to Viscount Howick, Under-Secretary of State for the Colonies, *The Spectator,* IV (Jan. 8, 1831). Wakefield wrote under a pseudonym because of his recent notoriety. He referred to Sir George Murray and Horace Twiss, Secretary and Under-Secretary of State for War and the Colonies from 1828 to 1830.

[47] Pp. 351-356.

acquaintance with his work. Gourlay told of a visit in Canada during 1838 when Wakefield acknowledged an intellectual debt. As Gourlay described it, one evening a man came to see him:

He introduced himself—*Mr. Wakefield:* (the same who had been announced in the newspapers, as accompanying Lord Durham, to instruct as to settling the wild lands of Canada). He told me, that he was the writer of letters which appeared in the *London Spectator*, some seven years ago, regarding me. I called to mind the letters: they were highly complimentary, and intended to draw towards me, the notice of the Grey Ministry. Never before having known to whom I was thus obliged, I thanked Mr. Wakefield, and shook hands with him. He then went on to say, that he was also author of a pamphlet on *colonization*, which was sent me, soon after, under the frank of Lord Howick. This, too, I remembered. It was a very able pamphlet, and contained a quotation from my book on Canada. Mr. Wakefield said, he had taken his ideas on colonization from my book. I replied, that it gave a very imperfect view of my projects: having been altogether an abortion, from distracting circumstances. . . .

Mr. Wakefield added—*"Nevertheless, Government has established a colony on your principles, in Australia."*[48]

It was significant that during his short stay in Canada in the 1840's Wakefield acted on Gourlay's behalf before the Provincial Legislature. In 1843 Gourlay was in Kingston, disheartened at his failure to impress the government; "in this predicament," he explained, "I walked to the Mineral Spring; and, near it, meeting Mr. Wakefield, asked him if he would present, for me, a petition, which he said he would do with pleasure; and perhaps no one else would have done all so well."[49] Wakefield presented the petition and became chairman of a Parliamentary Committee which eventually submitted a report favorable to Gourlay's requests.

In the *Durham Report* as in Gourlay's *Statistical Account* land policy received more attention than any other single topic. Lord Durham wrote: ". . . the disposal of public lands in a new country has more influence on the prosperity of the people than any other branch of Government. . . ."[50] The actual disposal of public land

---

[48] *Neptunian*, pt. 2, p. 27.

[49] *Neptunian*, pt. 14, p. 132.

[50] *Lord Durham's Report on the Affairs of British North America*, edited with an Introduction by Sir C. P. Lucas (Oxford, 1912), II, 242 (cited hereinafter as *Report*). See also I, 153-154.

was no longer an important question by 1839 as the profusion of land grants had already placed most productive land in private hands, but Durham and Wakefield—like Gourlay—went on to identify the existence of privately owned and publicly reserved waste lands between settlers as a significant factor retarding development. Wakefield reiterated Gourlay's belief that in Canada population was the most important determinant of both prosperity and of land values. "Where population is most dense, there invariably the price of land is highest. Any addition to the population of a district must therefore, it would appear, have an influence in raising the value of land. . . ."[51]

The reforms recommended in the *Durham Report* were a combination of earlier proposals by Gourlay and Wakefield. In 1830 Wakefield had opposed Gourlay's suggestion of a tax on land,[52] but in 1839 he reversed his position, noting, "Every witness who was examined upon this subject, concurred in the opinion that the imposition of such a tax was absolutely necessary."[53] He suggested that a fixed annual amount of "a fraction more than 2*d*. per acre" be levied upon all land, and that owners who did not wish to pay in cash be permitted to forfeit the land itself for tax payments at a value of 4*s*. per acre. The returns from the land tax would be spent partly upon subsidized immigration and partly upon the construction of transport facilities. Wakefield asserted in a passage that could have come from Gourlay's *Statistical Account* that the tax would force land into cultivation or would at least have it returned to the state:

The effect of a tax upon wild lands, the whole proceeds of which should be applied in improving the communications and facilitating the

[51] *Report*, III, 98.

[52] In 1830 Wakefield outlined Gourlay's plan for a land tax and admitted it to be "manifestly advantageous to the landowner," as Gourlay had argued; but he concluded "it might introduce some complication into a system, [of land sales at a 'sufficient price'] the great simplicity of which is its chief recommendation." *A Statement* . . ., pp. 53-54. See also *England and America*, p. 277.

[53] *Report*, III, 83. It is not unreasonable to suspect that Wakefield used Gourlay's work extensively when writing his portions of the *Durham Report*. In other writings he usually referred to Gourlay when discussing Canada, and it is not likely that he would have ignored this authority when actually on the scene. Moreover, Wakefield spent a mere six months in Canada before the *Report* was published, and must have had need of as much secondary material as he could muster.

settlement of the country, would be to remove some of the worst evils at present produced by the existence of the immense tracts of wilderness between, and in the midst of, the settled districts, and to diminish the quantity of the land retained in a wilderness state. The former, by opening roads in all needful directions for the transport of produce, and the latter by inducing and enabling the present proprietors of the wild land to settle or dispose of their property. The opening of roads is the one thing, without which it is impossible that a new country can thrive; and the obstacles placed in the way of making and maintaining roads by the waste granted land, constitute the most serious injury that the large tracts of such land inflict upon the province.[54]

The same dual function was attributed to a land tax by Durham and Wakefield as by Gourlay: waste land would be put to use, and the proceeds of the tax made available for public works.[55] One result of Wakefield's tax which would not have followed from Gourlay's formulation, however, was restriction of the total amount of land used. Wakefield reasoned that if the rate were a fixed sum per acre, all land which did not yield a rent equal to the tax would not be worth owning; the margin of cultivation, therefore, would be contracted. In contrast, Gourlay's tax, calculated as a fixed *percentage* of land values, would have burdened property in proportion to its productivity (or potential productivity if unused) and would not have disturbed the margin. Wakefield's tax would have achieved the same end as sale at a fixed rate, and he even specified that all land returned as tax payments would be sold only at a "sufficient price"—rather than, as Gourlay had recommended, at auction. The exact method of calculating land prices was not more clearly specified in the *Durham Report* than in Wakefield's other writings, but he conceded that in the Canadian case the proximity

[54] *Report*, III, 83-84.

[55] It is an interesting sidelight that Wakefield came to Canada in 1841 to investigate a project almost identical to a plan suggested by Gourlay eighteen years before. (See above, p. 17). Wakefield was the head of the North American Colonial Association of Ireland, a group which proposed to build a canal around a series of rapids in the St. Lawrence near Beauharnois. The Association hoped to complete the project and then repay its capital from an increase in the value of adjacent lands. For various reasons the plan was never carried through. See Ursilla N. Macdonnell, "Gibbon Wakefield and Canada Subsequent to the Durham Mission 1839-42," *Bulletin of the Departments of History and Political and Economic Science in Queen's University*, No. 49 (1924-1925).

of cheap American land would have to be taken into account, and he estimated 10*s.* per acre as the highest practical figure.[56]

In addition to reforms in settlement and land policy, political proposals in the *Durham Report* were strikingly similar to Gourlay's recommendations. Of greatest importance, both Gourlay and Lord Durham declared that the colonies should be granted legislative independence at the earliest possible date; in this way, it was argued, they might be retained within the British Empire. Both Gourlay and Durham asserted also that land disposal and the formulation of commercial policy should be retained by the Imperial Government on the ground that these functions could not be performed by the inhabitants of a new territory in the public interest.[57] Both Durham and Gourlay urged colonial governments to provide accurate information and temporary assistance to settlers, and to admit immigrants regardless of their nationality. Durham advocated legislative union of the two central provinces, but Gourlay manifested greater imagination and foresight when he suggested a confederacy of all the colonies with local assemblies having limited powers.

The *Durham Report* was the most important state paper in colonial history because it contained the first expression of policies which led ultimately to the creation of the British Commonwealth. It has generally been assumed that the ideas in the *Report* were the colonial theories of Edward Gibbon Wakefield expressed through his disciples, Lord Durham and Charles Buller. This view is largely correct, but requires recognition that in all his writings, and particularly in the *Durham Report*, Wakefield owed a substantial debt to an earlier colonial theorist, Robert Gourlay.

IV. "COLONIZATION" IN FRENCH CANADA

Early alienation throughout the colonies inhibited discussion of land policy, but in French Canada, where for years the most vital

---

[56] *Report*, III, 110.

[57] *Statistical Account*, Introduction, p. ccccliii; *Appeal*, pp. 33, 34, 146, 151, and 152; *Report*, II, 282. When western Canada was acquired from the Hudson's Bay Company, the disposal of this new land was made a federal function, even though land policy was a provincial matter in the rest of the country. The rationale for this decision was identical to that used by Gourlay and Wakefield. See Chester Martin, " 'Dominion Lands' Policy," *Canadian Frontiers of Settlement Series*, p. 223.

problem remained the continued emigration of native sons, the subject was kept alive. As early as 1830 Pierre de Sales La Tierrière, a physician and seigneur, argued that the British method of land tenure was responsible for French-Canadian stagnation; he claimed that if the seigneurial system were reintroduced on the Quebec frontier the otherwise lethargic "habitants" would be transformed into vigorous pioneers.[58] On several occasions the Provincial Government held investigations, and in 1863 Stanislas Drapeau, a scholarly land agent, reviewed the problem; in the words of Professor Saint-Pierre Drapeau merely "discovered and carried to perfection the art of making a large book by copying page after page of official documents."[59]

The French-Canadian approach to colonization was more idealistic than analytical. In the 1860's a two-part epic novel by Antoine Gérin-Lajoie, entitled *Jean Rivard le défricheur* (1862) and *Jean Rivard économiste* (1864), was the most influential and widely read attempt to portray pioneer life. The books were romanticized descriptions of a fictional settlement, and although the influence of Physiocratic thought may be detected in certain passages,[60] the author probably had little familiarity either with economic literature or with basic principles. Professor Saint-Pierre notes that when Gérin-Lajoie discussed the composition of an ideal library of five hundred volumes ("everything necessary for education") he included no works on economics.[61]

In the 1880's and 1890's propaganda for frontier settlement reached a peak, but still with little analysis of conditions and much Rousseauistic praise of life in the country. Arthur Buies, an improbable advocate of a peaceful existence who had spent part of his

---

[58] *A Political and Historical Account of Lower Canada* (London, 1830).

[59] "La Littérature sociale canadienne-français avant la Confédération," *P.T.R.S.C.*, XLIV (1950), Section I, p. 72 (translation). See also *Report of the Select Committee of the Legislative Assembly of the Province of Canada Appointed to Inquire into the Causes and Importance of the Emigration which Takes Place Annually to the United States* (1849); *Report of the Special Committee of the Province of Canada Appointed to Take Into Consideration the Colonization of Uncultivated Lands in Lower Canada* (1862); and Stanislas Drapeau, *Études sur les développements de la colonisation du Bas-Canada depuis dix ans: (1851-1861)* (Quebec, 1863).

[60] For example, one of the characters in the novel remarks: "Consult for a moment the scholars who are occupied in looking for the sources of the wealth of nations, and you will see that all agree that agriculture is the first source of durable wealth." Quoted in A. Saint-Pierre, *op. cit.*, p. 81.

[61] *Ibid.*

youth in Paris and had served with Garibaldi in Italy, cried, "Let us take possession of the soil" ("Emparons-nous de sol") and graphically described uninhabited parts of the Province.[62] Testard de Montigny, a veteran of the French Foreign Legion and an even more romantic figure than Buies, urged development of the Laurentian Shield north of Montreal and envisioned Quebec as an agricultural complement to industrial Ontario. He explained: "Today when the great social question for our country is to balance the commercial, manufacturing and farming industries, it is of the greatest importance to show that the last is not blocked-up like the others and that it is not less-well understood, appreciated and exploited."[63]

The colonization movement provided much-needed activity for many frustrated provincial patriots. However, with the firm presupposition that agriculture was the only desirable occupation and with little knowledge of methods in economics, these men were seldom realistic in approach and met with little actual success. No important research was carried out and no new analysis evolved. After the turn of the century most of the inspiration for the movement disappeared (in particular emigration and stagnation) and interest declined with industrialization and discovery of minerals in the north.

v. The "Single Tax" on Land

Progress and Poverty, by Henry George, was published in New York in 1879 and achieved worldwide popularity over the next decade. These were the years during which the Canadian West was being opened for settlement, and it was not long before several Canadians had concluded that their fertile prairies were particularly well suited for experimentation with George's "true remedy" for "inequality in the distribution of wealth"—a confiscatory tax on land

[62] For example see *Le Saguenay et la Vallée du Lac St. Jean* (Quebec, 1880); *L'Outouais supérieur* (Quebec, 1889); and *La Vallée de la Matapedia* (Quebec, 1895).

[63] *La Colonisation: Le Nord de Montréal ou la région Labelle* (Montreal, 1895), p. iii (translation). Similar statements are contained in Henri-Gaston de Montigny, *Etoffe de pays, études d'économie politique canadienne* (Montreal, 1901), p. ix.

rent.[64]   George reported in 1880 that W. D. LeSueur, a well-known Ontario essayist, had become one of his first "converts":

I got to-day a letter from Wm. D. LeSueur of Ontario. . . . I gave him a copy of the book when I met him here, and I attach a good deal of importance to his opinion, for he is a man of weight. . . . He started in, of course, all against it, for, in addition to previous predilections, Goldwin Smith, for whom he has a good deal of respect, sat down on it.   But he writes me that he has *never* read a book with so much interest; that during the last few days while he was reading the last part he could think of nothing else; that he is a thorough convert, with the exception that he thinks the men to whom the State has sold lands ought to get some recompense, though he admits that there would be infinitely less injustice in giving them nothing than in continuing the present system; and that now his most ardent desire is to be a co-worker for the destruction of private property in land. . . .   In short he wants to be counted in, and proposes to begin the campaign in Canada.   Now here is a man who in my opinion is worth half the college professors in the United States.

I showed the letter to [Professor E. L.] Youmans, who has a very great opinion of LeSueur. . . .[65]

In 1881 LeSueur defended *Progress and Poverty* from a critic in the *Popular Science Monthly* who had alleged a conflict with the doctrine of evolution; when he praised George, LeSueur took the opportunity to explain the poor regard he held for economics in general:

It was . . . precisely because the point of view taken by Mr. George was never seized by any earlier writer that political economy became "the dismal science,"—a science that could never be reduced to scientific forms; in which everything was at loose ends; and in which, from year to year, confusion seemed only to grow worse confounded.   It is a somewhat significant fact that, up to the present, the regular or professional economists have fought shy of Mr. George.   Prof. Cliffe Leslie is the only English economist of note, so far as I am aware, who has under-

[64] *Progress and Poverty* (Vol. I of *The Complete Works of Henry George* in 10 vols.) (New York, 1904), pp. 326-328.

[65] Cited in Henry George Jr., *The Life of Henry George* (Vol. X of *The Complete Works of Henry George*) (New York, 1904), pp. 340-341.   Perhaps at LeSueur's invitation George made a tour of Canada in 1881.   He lectured at Toronto for a fee of $50 and in Montreal and Ottawa on "speculation."   In Montreal, after one meeting which he described as "a total failure," George gave a second lecture, and reported "Did it.   Best ever have done.   Astonished and pleased them all."   *Ibid.*, pp. 351-352.

taken to criticise the new theories; and he, as every one knows, is not, in his own profession, "of the straitest sect of the Pharisees." If the economists will not notice it, however, the people will; and in that case the heresies of the book, if they are heresies, will only be the harder to deal with in the end for the conspiracy of silence with which they were met at the outset.[66]

William Douglass of Toronto was the most energetic advocate of the single tax, and beginning in 1883 wrote paper after paper which contained both well-reasoned argument and repetitive propaganda.[67] He presented a very carefully prepared article to the British Association for the Advancement of Science at its Montreal meeting in 1884. He noted three "harmonies" which arose from competitive exchange: "Mutual Enrichment, Equality of Reward and Equality of Burden"; but he went on to show that with growing population and improvements in technology two sources of "antagonism" were an increasing share of income going to owners of natural resources and a decreasing share accruing to labor and capital. On grounds of natural justice, Douglass claimed, one portion of society should not have to toil "to supply not only its own wants, but also the wants of the other," and he asked the question "Why are the producers not the possessors?" He proposed that in the West the government either expropriate all natural resources or leave landlords as managers while taxing away rent.

We have a vast tract of unsettled territory of unsurpassed fertility, abounding in coals and other minerals. We are now laying the foundations of

[66] "'Progress and Poverty,' and the Doctrine of Evolution," *Rose-Belford's Canadian Monthly and National Review*, VI (1881), 287.

[67] Douglass was born in England, came to Canada as a youth, and received training at the Toronto Normal School. He spent his life as a teacher, businessman, and ardent supporter of the single tax. He was elected Third Vice-President of the Single Tax League in New York in 1907. See H. J. Morgan, *Canadian Men and Women of the Time* (Montreal, 1912). Douglass' contributions to the publications of the Canadian Institute were: "Land and Labour," an abstract, *Proceedings of the Canadian Institute*, II (1883-1884), 27-28; "Wages," an abstract, *ibid.*, III (1884-1885), 39-41; "Rent, A Criticism of Professor Walker's Work on that Subject," an abstract, *ibid.*, IV (1885-1886), 58-60; "The Antagonism of Social Forces," *ibid.*, V (1886-1887), 136-142; "Study of Economics," an abstract, *ibid.*, VI (1887-1888), 27-29; "A Scheme of Political Economy," mentioned *ibid.*, VI (1887-1888), 41; "Wealth and its Measurement," an abstract, *ibid.*, VII (1888-1889), 7-8; "The Distribution of Wealth as Related to Production," an abstract, *Transactions of the Canadian Institute*, I (1889-1890), 14-17; "The Two Values," an abstract, *ibid.*, II (1890-1891), 7; "Ignored Distinctions in Economics," *ibid.*, VIII (1903-1909), 305-313.

empire. Our actions to-day must affect the fate of millions. By planning wisely, before society is formed and crystallized, we may arrange its forces so that these antagonisms may be minimized. Our opportunity is grand; but unless we cry a halt very soon, that opportunity will have passed away never to return.[68]

In the 1880's the first trade unionists in Canada were influenced by Henry George, and after the editor of one labor journal, the *Labor Union,* described *Progress and Poverty* in 1883 he concluded "Buy it; read it; get its truths by heart and then lend it to your neighbor."[69] Another paper contained an outline of "Henry George's Career and its Lesson" and reported proceedings of the Single Tax Association. Labor enthusiasm reached a peak in 1884 when Henry George spoke to a large and receptive audience in Hamilton; but by the 1890's a land tax seems to have become secondary to other labor reforms.[70]

Several witnesses before the Royal Commission on the Relations of Capital and Labor which reported in 1889 were clearly influenced by the writings of George.[71] Douglass, appearing as the representative of the single tax "Anti-Poverty League" said: "We simply ask that the values caused by the community shall be appropriated by the community for common purposes, and that the individual should be allowed to retain all that he produces except that portion that he would have to surrender for his advantage of location." A. W. Wright, a journalist, declared that the prevailing land system was "a first tax on every man's labor," and he proposed that Parliament "change our land system" so as to "give workmen free access to the source of wealth." John Hewitt, a clerical worker, combined a plea for the single tax with a criticism of income distribution generally:

. . . the great questions that affect labor may be taken on two basic conditions—wealth and monopoly in land. Of course, we have not felt this as severely here, as it has been felt in the old country; but there is one thing certain, and that is, that if the conditions that have produced monopolies in

[68] "Harmonies and Antagonisms in the Social Forces," in *Canadian Economics* (Montreal, 1885), p. 296. Douglass illustrated his theory with diagrams on pp. 292 and 295.

[69] Cited in F. W. Watt, "The National Policy, the Workingman, and Proletarian Ideas in Victorian Canada," *C.H.R.,* XL (1959), p. 18.

[70] *Ibid.,* pp. 11, 22, and 23.

[71] See below, pp. 135-138.

land in the old countries continue to exist here they are going to produce the same results.[72]

Single-tax associations reached a peak of popularity in the late 1880's. In 1888 R. T. Lancefield, a member of the Anti-Poverty League in Toronto, described the purpose of that organization.

The aim of this society is to try and effect such changes in our laws as will result in a better distribution of the products of labor. To attain this object it is guided mainly by this consideration:—

There are certain natural advantages (the chief of which is land) which were provided by the Creator for the sustenance of the human race. These advantages are, by our present laws, given up to the absolute possession of one part of society. . . . The evil effects of this unfortunate and unjust arrangement, we believe can be largely remedied by shifting the taxes from the products of toil to the natural advantages, such as land.[73]

Lancefield emphasized, as had Robert Gourlay sixty-seven years before, that a tax on land by eliminating speculation would fill up Canada's wilderness with settlers; and with true missionary zeal he pictured Christ as an early single taxer and Henry George as a modern prophet of Christianity: "Christ was no mere idle dreamer, and it is possible to bring the Golden Rule within the regime of daily life. But how? We answer: primarily, by freeing all *natural* opportunities, and this will be done by raising all taxes from land values instead of taxing improvements and personality, as we do at present."[74]

Critics of Henry George were aroused by the continuous propaganda of his advocates; William Houston presented an analysis of *Progress and Poverty* to the Canadian Institute in 1888 in which he sympathized with the single tax but deplored the rigor of the supporting theory. Houston believed that within the writings of Ricardo and Mill there was theoretical justification enough for a tax on the rent of land.

[72] *Report*, Ontario Evidence, pp. 16, 300, 324 and 500 ff.

[73] *Why I Joined the New Crusade—A Plea for the Placing of Taxes on Land Values Only* (Toronto, 1888), p. 40.

[74] *Ibid.*, pp. 19-20. In 1887 the Reverend William Burgess of Listowel, Ontario, wished to make a strong case on economic grounds for liquor prohibition, and he cited Henry George for authority as well as the works of Mill, McCulloch, and Fawcett. See *Land, Labor and Liquor: A Chapter in the Political Economy of the Present Day* (Toronto, 1887), *passim*; and below, p. 133.

Mr. George's merit is that he has shown how the unearned increment in land can be appropriated by the community by a sound system of taxation, but he has needlessly weakened a strong case (1) by using words vaguely —a fault which he severely condemns in other writers; (2) by allowing himself to be influenced to some extent by considerations that belong not to sociology but to natural theology; and (3) by assailing certain economic doctrines which, properly regarded, not merely support his main thesis, but are absolutely necessary as a foundation on which it must rest. His position resembles that of a man who not merely draws a sound conclusion from wrong premises but actually goes to great trouble to demolish the right ones. This points to the probability of the conclusion having been suggested to him by circumstances, and of his having gone wrong in his search for reasons, and there is good reason to believe that this is the real history of his mental development.[75]

Houston maintained that Henry George had neglected the role of the entrepreneur and had misunderstood the wage fund, with the result that "his reasoning about rent, wages, and capital must be obscure, as indeed it is." He defended the Malthusian population theory, attacked by George, and insisted that the principles of diminishing returns and of increasing population growth were beyond dispute.

In reality the Malthusian principle is neither more nor less than a well-known biological fact which is as much the basis of Darwin's law of the "survival of the fittest" as it is of the doctrine of the "unearned increment". . . . Mr. George's refutation of the law is no refutation at all, and his citation of the cases of China, India, Ireland are not at all in point. On the contrary, each of these countries is a remarkable proof of the truth of the Malthusian doctrine. That doctrine, taken in connection with the law of diminishing returns from the application of labor and capital to land, is the basis of the Ricardian theory of rent, and also of Mr. George's doctrine of the unearned increment.[76]

Houston's sympathetic yet critical discussion of the single tax was better received by the Canadian Institute than were the repetitive diatribes of Douglass. In 1885 and 1887 several members were skeptical of the single tax; and in 1889 when Douglass had explained "nature's laws" as "produce to the producer only, produce

[75] W. Houston, "The Scientific Aspect of the Henry George Movement," a synopsis, *Proceedings of the Canadian Institute*, VI (1887-1888), 34.
[76] *Ibid.*, pp. 37-38.

limited, produce transitory," discussion became very heated. Finally
in 1889, after still another paper, Arthur Harvey summarized the
views of the critics. It was reported that:

> Mr. Harvey had listened to the paper with mingled sensations of
> pleasure and of pain. Of pleasure, because the author, like others who
> had adopted these new social doctrines, spoke with an air of conviction,
> as if he believed what he was saying, also with the charming air of resig-
> nation and pity which pleasantly distinguished the elect, the *illuminati*, of
> many harmless kinds, and with a grace of diction which might well awake
> envy in less gifted men. Of pain, akin to that which a cat might feel
> when its owner, in a fit of abstraction, was stroking its fur the wrong way.
> Every proposition laid down seemed thoroughly antagonistic to what he
> [Mr. Harvey] had been taught in his youth to believe, and every argu-
> ment made use of seemed to be based on fallacies. He felt that the
> author of the paper was dealing out delusive sophistries, and propounding
> theories, every one of which needed but the touch of experience to burst
> them. . . . The truth was that all commodities possessed different eco-
> nomic attributes. Food, buildings, money, metals, land, all differed; but
> to treat land otherwise than as a marketable commodity surely misled the
> deluded followers of this new school of unpractical dilettanti, *per ambages,*
> into a morass. . . . It had lately happened to him [Mr. Harvey] to cross
> the ocean on the "Servia" with Mr. Henry George for a fellow-passenger.
> On leaving the dinner table one day, during a swell time, Mr. George,
> coming between the rows of chairs, mostly empty, careened against one,
> rebounded from another, and came violently to moorings beside the
> speaker. "Mr. George," he had remarked, "you get on well in smooth
> weather, but this gale upsets your theories." So it was with the extrava-
> gances of single-value men, two (and no more) values men, trade and
> labor union men, citizens of the world, professional negrophilists, soft-
> money men, and the like: they could delude themselves, and obtain more
> or less following for their "views," so long as sober, practical men of com-
> mon sense governed affairs, and peace with honor and prosperity pre-
> vailed.[77]

The Henry George movement declined in the 1890's, partly
because of the hectic prosperity after 1896 which accompanied rapid
settlement of the West, but also because like most panaceas the single
tax eventually went out of fashion.

[77] *Transactions of the Canadian Institute,* II (1890-1891), 8-10.

VI. Summary and Conclusion

During the century covered by this study Canadians peopled half a continent, and were faced repeatedly with questions about methods of land disposal (free grants or sale?), the effectiveness of private development companies and reserves, the optimum size for land allotments, and the correct extent and form for property taxation. By 1914, however, little light had been thrown on the answers to these questions; Canadians accomplished settlement with hastily borrowed, makeshift policies which were not always consistent and were often unsuitable for local conditions. Few persons attempted to analyze land problems critically, and no outstanding contributions were made to the theory of colonization.

Interest in land policy was confined to brief periods and to a handful of enthusiasts. Between 1817 and 1822 Robert Gourlay investigated conditions in Upper Canada, formulated a theory of land values, and proposed reforms. He urged study of development methods and stressed the importance in new countries of efficient government, careful location of settlers, and adequate transport facilities. He suggested a tax on all land in proportion to its value to bring uninhabited wastes under cultivation and to provide funds for public works. Gourlay gathered a few confused followers under his banner of reform and influenced other Canadian radicals; however, he was regarded at the time and is remembered today less as a student of economic problems than as a minor figure in the political turmoil.

Edward Gibbon Wakefield in the *Durham Report* made the only comprehensive study of Canadian land and settlement policies; moreover, much of Wakefield's description and some of his proposals were taken from (or were at least remarkably similar to) Gourlay's work. Wakefield deplored diffuse settlement and reserved lands, and he recommended a land tax to force cultivation and to gather revenue. He differed from Gourlay in wishing to restrict the total amount of land in use; he suggested that all public lands be sold at a "sufficient price" and that the land tax be a fixed money amount regardless of property values. It appeared in 1839, when the work of Wakefield followed that of Gourlay after only seventeen years, that a tradition of study in the field of land problems might be established in Canada; however, this date marked the end of investigation.

Besides the writings of Gourlay, Wakefield, and a few sympathizers, there was little discussion of land problems. French Canadians deplored the continuous emigration of their native sons and called for land "colonization"; however, they were unfamiliar with methods of analysis and were unable realistically to examine the problem. In the 1880's the Henry George movement was imported from the United States and caused a flurry of interest in land policy. In this instance, debate was limited to "single-tax" proposals which were designed less to accelerate growth and prosperity than to counteract the effects of land holding on income distribution. In Canada, where much land lay still unclaimed and where capital and labor—not land—were scarce and highly rewarded, the Henry George panacea found little lasting favor.

Canadian indifference to land problems has several explanations. Discussion of actual disposal methods was meaningful only at the beginning and end of the century during periods when the state had valuable land in its possession, but then conditions were least appropriate for inquiry: in the first, colonial administrators were reluctant to investigate a practice from which they derived substantial profits, and their critics were obsessed with attainment of legislative responsibility; in the second, after the West opened for settlement, an urgent need to create a viable national economy forced debate about land policies into the background and made it appear essential to imitate the successful United States. Canadians who were most interested in land problems were on the frontier, where they had little spare time for writing and where their voices were weak; moreover, critics usually had a relatively small stake in the community and when disaffected simply moved south of the border.

The absence of literature in Europe and America on land problems of new countries inhibited discussion in Canada. When formulating land policy, unlike banking or tariff policy, Canadians found it difficult to turn for guidance to the recorded experience of other nations. In Britain writers had been concerned with such questions as the transition from feudal to free tenure and progress of the enclosure movement; they viewed land in general as becoming increasingly scarce and subject to diminishing returns. These works had little relevance where millions of fertile acres awaited settlement and where capital and labor were relatively scarce. In the United States land problems were similar in many ways to those of Canada; but apart from discussion by social reformers preceding or at the time of Henry George, these problems also received little attention.[78] Canadians were always profoundly influenced by Britain and the United States, and therefore gave little encouragement to writers such as Gourlay and Wakefield who examined matters which seemed to be of strictly local importance. In so doing Canadians missed an opportunity to advance an underdeveloped branch of economic science and perhaps a chance to improve their lot.

[78] See Aaron M. Sakolski, *Land Tenure and Land Taxation in America* (New York, 1957), pp. 198 and 262 ff.

2

Tariffs and International Trade

I. Outline of Tariff History

Import duties were levied in New France as early as 1662, in Nova Scotia in 1758, and in New Brunswick in 1786.[1] Although fiscal autonomy was not granted the colonies immediately, the British government in 1778 agreed to use all revenues for local purposes, and by the Canada Act of 1791 permitted the Provinces of Upper and Lower Canada to impose their own duties supplementary to the Imperial rates. Finally, between 1830 and 1846 Nova Scotia, New Brunswick, and the Province of Canada were given complete control of their tariffs. The colonial duties were usually not higher than 20 per cent and on luxuries only; with the exception of a high rate on spirits in Nova Scotia, the first important protection was imposed in the Province of Canada in 1843 on farm products and in 1847 on selected manufactured articles. At mid-century the average duty on all imports to Canada stood at about 15 per cent up from 8 per cent in 1841. Reciprocity of customs on natural products, maintained with the United States between 1854 and 1866, lowered the average rate to less than 10 per cent; but in the 1850's duties on manufactured articles and luxuries rose once more, and by 1866 the average was again up to 13.6 per cent in Canada and was almost as high in the Maritimes.

Tariffs immediately after Confederation were mildly protective with revenue as their primary purpose; notwithstanding a Liberal administration from 1874 until 1878 committed to a free-trade policy, financial necessity during these years discouraged any sub-

[1] Two histories of commercial policy in Canada are: O. J. McDiarmid, *Commercial Policy in the Canadian Economy* (Cambridge, 1946), and J. H. Perry, *Taxes, Tariffs, and Subsidies: A History of Canadian Fiscal Development* (Toronto, 1955).

stantial reduction. In 1878 a Conservative government came to office with a platform of protection to domestic industry, and by imposing high rates on certain imports raised the average from 14.2 to 16.4 per cent in 1879 and 20.2 in 1880.[2] The Conservatives stayed in power until 1896; and the tariff, although modified from time to time, remained basically unchanged. The Liberals, returned in 1896, altered the rates on certain products but did not change the basic structure of the tariff. A noteworthy innovation under the Liberals was a double schedule affording preference to British goods; otherwise protection was preserved. The Liberals were defeated in 1911 after proposing a reciprocal reduction of tariffs with the United States, and the popularity of protection was confirmed once and for all.

II. ARGUMENTS FOR PROTECTION

The first requests for high tariffs were voiced in the 1820's by farmers seeking protected markets in periods of low prices. Agricultural duties were enacted in the 1840's, but within ten years an increasing population and home market caused farmers to consider them no longer necessary. By this time, however, a growing number of persons were becoming convinced that manufacturing industry was necessary for national development and that tariff protection could achieve this goal; the few existing manufacturers, of course, added their voices to the advocacy. Between 1874 and 1876 the Conservative party adopted the protective "National Policy" as a platform, and lengthy debate preceded its introduction in 1879. Protection remained as an important political issue for the rest of the century, but discussion after 1879 was largely repetition of old controversy. Protectionist arguments are examined here under four headings: tariffs as relief for farmers, as a stimulant to national development, as a benefit for manufacturers, and as a political issue.

A Home Market for Agricultural Products

As early as 1821 farmers in Upper Canada sought commercial protection, and a Select Committee of the House of Assembly urged

---

[2] J. H. Perry, op. cit., II, 672. The duty on manufactured items was raised considerably more than on other goods. See O. J. McDiarmid, op. cit., p. 186.

that tariffs be raised specifically against imports from the United States: ". . . protecting duties should be imposed in Lower Canada, to enable the flour of Upper Canada to maintain itself in the only market to which it can be sent. . . ."[3] In Nova Scotia all goods imported from the United States after 1789 paid an ad valorem rate of 10 per cent, but were brought in duty free if used in the fisheries; a writer in 1833 praised the element of protection afforded farmers by this tariff and recommended its extension to all imports with a bounty instead of a drawback for fishermen: "This will not only enable the native farmers to meet foreign produce with a fair chance of competition, but at the same time give the actual fisherman, that in the shape of bounty which was taken from him in the shape of duties. . . ."[4] In general, requests for protection from farmers and their spokesmen seldom went beyond a protestation of poverty and a prayer for temporary relief.

In the 1830's an element of political unrest was present in requests for duties on agricultural products. Dissident farmers in Upper and Lower Canada advocated tariffs partly for the old reason of security against price fluctuations, but also in the hope of injuring the carrying trade of local merchants from the United States to England.[5] In 1835 a bill "to afford proper protection and encouragement to those engaged in agricultural pursuits and other operations" passed the Upper Canada Assembly but was rejected by the Legislative Council; and in 1840, after a similar bill had again passed the Legislature, resolutions drawn up at a public meeting summarized the arguments and recommendations of the farmers. They said in part:

5.—That almost every article of agricultural produce is now selling in our markets at prices that will not reimburse the cost of production. That this, so far as relates to articles of Home Consumption, is clearly attribu-

---

[3] "First Report of the Select Committee, Appointed to take into Consideration the Internal Resources of the Province in its Agriculture and Exports, and the Practicability and Means of Enlarging them; also, to consider of the Expediency of Granting Encouragement to Domestic Manufactures," reprinted in Robert Gourlay, *Statistical Account of Upper Canada* (London, 1822), II, 670.

[4] A Mechanic, *A Word in Season to the Fishermen and Farmers of Nova Scotia* (Pictou, 1833), pp. 19-20.

[5] See D. G. Creighton, "The Economic Background of the Rebellions of Eighteen Thirty-Seven," *C.J.E.P.S.*, III (1937), 322-334.

table to the supply rapidly exceeding the demand, and to the free admission of like productions from the United States. . . .

7.—That in the opinion of this meeting the remedial measures for the evils complained of, are neither hard to be discerned nor difficult of accomplishment. . . . free admission of wheat and flour of Canadian Growth into Great Britain, the declaration of the Royal assent to the Bill of last session, subjecting American produce to the payment of a duty when imported into Canada for Home Consumption. . . .[6]

Tariffs on agricultural products were imposed in 1843 and were maintained until 1854, when reciprocity with the United States brought free trade in raw materials.[7]

Tariffs for National Development

Beginning in the 1820's writers advocated protective tariffs on manufactured goods as stimulants to growth of a diversified economy. An unidentified author in Lower Canada in 1825 explained the infant-industry argument for protection and believed it applicable to local conditions:

When the chief materials of a manufacture are native or colonial, and when workmen, machinery and capital can be obtained at rates which promise successful competition with foreigners, such manufacture, if not otherwise sufficiently attractive to individuals, should be encouraged by the government.[8]

William Lyon Mackenzie, possibly influenced by his reading of the American economists Mathew Carey, William Gouge, and Daniel Raymond, seems for a time in the 1820's to have favored the use of tariffs to stimulate domestic industry. But Mackenzie's fundamental predilection for agriculture and distrust of wealth, together

[6] Reprinted in H. A. Innis and A. R. M. Lower, editors, *Select Documents in Canadian Economic History, 1783-1885* (Toronto, 1929), pp. 362-363.

[7] For a discussion of the farmers' agitation which resulted in agricultural protection, see R. L. Jones, "The Canadian Agricultural Tariff of 1843," *C.J.E.P.S.*, VII (1941), 528-537; and *History of Agriculture in Ontario 1613-1880* (Toronto, 1946), pp. 122-139.

[8] "Sketches of the Origin and Progress of Manufactures and of the Policy Which Has Regulated Their Legislative Encouragement in Great Britain and in Other Countries. . .," *The Canadian Review and Literary and Historical Journal*, III (1825), 124. It has been suggested by R. Warren James in an unpublished paper presented to the Canadian Political Science Association at its June, 1960, meeting, that this article was an early production of John Rae. See below pp. 122-127.

with a traditional liberal dislike of special interests, quickly overcame this conviction.[9]

In the 1840's well-reasoned pleas for industrial protection were made by R. B. Sullivan, later a prominent jurist, and by Abraham Gesner, a scientist. Speaking before the Mechanics' Institute at Hamilton in 1847 Sullivan declared that capitalists and entrepreneurs would invest and settle in new countries only if encouraged by the state; and Gesner, writing in Nova Scotia in 1849, repeated the infant-industry argument and emphasized the need for relief from the unemployment brought on by fluctuations in the prices of staple products.[10] Both Sullivan and Gesner stressed the importance of the state in national development and the convenience of tariffs for encouraging industry.

After Confederation R. G. Haliburton in Nova Scotia and J. B. Hurlbert in Ontario urged protection for national development.[11] Haliburton declared in 1868 that temporary protective tariffs were necessary to strengthen the new Dominion by fostering trade between the provinces:

As respects free trade in the abstract, few of us will differ. We all like free trade, as we do sunshine and good roads; but sunshine and good roads are not always to be had, and if I should venture to use an umbrella to protect me in a storm, I trust that the man of one idea will not suppose that I am prejudiced against a bright sky, or that I consider that the acme of human happiness consists in going through life with an umbrella over my head. It is a temporary expedient only to escape the effect of a temporary inconvenience.[12]

[9] See Lillian F. Gates, "The Decided Policy of William Lyon Mackenzie," *C.H.R.*, XL (1959), 205.

[10] R. B. Sullivan was the first president of the Council after Union in 1840, a member of the Baldwin-Lafontaine administrations, and a judge after 1848. His speech, which was reprinted in pamphlet form, was reportedly influential and well-received. Gesner, physician and geologist, hoped that protection would bring development of mineral resources in the Maritimes. See Abraham Gesner, *The Industrial Resources of Nova Scotia* (Halifax, 1849).

[11] Three works of lower quality but similar in purpose to those of Haliburton and Hurlbert were: Joseph Wright, *Self Reliance, or A Plea for the Protection of Canadian Industries* (Dundas, 1864); T. H. Grant, *The Future Commercial Policy of British North America* (Quebec, 1867); F. P. Mackelcan, *Labor and Capital; How to Unite Them and Produce Universal Industry and Prosperity* (Montreal, 1872).

[12] R. G. Haliburton, *Intercolonial Trade Our Only Safeguard Against Disunion* (Ottawa, 1868), p. 40. R. G. Haliburton, son of Thomas C. Haliburton (see

Hurlbert in 1870, making good use of the writings of Henry Carey and Friedrich List, emphasized the importance of balanced growth in an economy. He maintained that farmers could not prosper without local markets for their products:

Where all are producers of an article there are no markets. If all, or most, as with us, are farmers, the products of the field find no purchasers —or but few; profits are poor. To have good markets, we must have consumers who are not producers of what is offered for sale. We must have home markets for a hundred products of the garden and the field too bulky or perishable to bear the transit to foreign countries.[13]

Hurlbert listed a series of beneficial developments which would follow protective tariffs: capital and labor would be attracted to the country, competition would increase and prices would fall, employment would be provided for laborers unsuited to farm work, markets would be created for perishable farm products and the consequent rotation of crops would improve the soil, subsidiary industries would grow up beside protected ones, raw materials which had formerly been worthless would become valuable, factories would train youth and would provide a strong and self-sufficient citizenry in wartime. By enumerating some of the external economies of manufacturing Hurlbert presented a convincing case for protection.

Pleas from Businessmen

Before 1850 industrialists pressed for protective tariffs on a few occasions, but without reasoned arguments. A group of millers and manufacturers in Nova Scotia informed the House of Assembly in 1838 "That the principal cause of depression which exists, may be traced to the consumption of articles duty free, or at very low rates of duty," and they asked plaintively that "the Provincial Manufactures may not only receive the protection now sought for, but such

---

below, p. 114), was educated at King's College, Windsor, Nova Scotia, and practiced law in Halifax.

[13] J. Beaufort Hurlbert, *Field and Factory Side by Side; or, How to Establish and Develop Native Industries* (Montreal, 1870), p. 5. Hurlbert was born in Upper Canada and was educated at Wesleyan University, Middletown, Connecticut (A.B. 1835). He was acting principal of Upper Canada College 1839-1841, professor of natural science at Victoria College 1841-1847, and later became a civil servant. In addition to the book mentioned above Hurlbert wrote *Protection and Free Trade with Special Reference to Canada and Newly Settled Countries: History of Tariffs and What They Teach* (Ottawa, 1882).

further encouragement as may seem requisite."[14]   A "Provincial Association" was organized at St. John, New Brunswick, in 1844 to seek tariffs on both agricultural and manufactured products, but it was short lived.[15]   At a meeting of merchants and manufacturers at Montreal in 1849 William Workman, a prominent importer, used example rather than theory to justify tariffs, and pointed to the United States as a country where protection had been conspicuously successful:

I am prepared to show that under the system of protection to home industry which the United States have enjoyed, they have turned the scales against us. But here I will be met by a class of political economists who, although they cannot deny the facts, and they don't like the facts, will, nevertheless, proceed to quote from Adam Smith, and Mill, and Say, and Bastiat, to show that, although there is an apparent advantage, there is no real advantage, that twenty-five cents in Montreal will go as far as sixty cents in Troy; it must, they say, go as far, according to *first principles*. But, *first principles* or not, what are the facts?   The American gets a higher price for his oats, and can buy as many spades, shovels, stoves or scythes for four dollars as the Canadian farmer can buy for six.[16]

In the 1850's the provinces went through a railroad and land boom which brought a growth of industry and renewed demands from manufacturers for protection. It was alleged in *The Canadian Merchants' Magazine and Commercial Review* that with industrial development capital would flow into the country, markets would be provided for agricultural products, and depressions would cease. If protective tariffs were not imposed, one writer cautioned, "a dark cloud will still hang over our poor country, which all the suggestions of our political economists will not be able to dispel."[17]   The "Commercial Views of Eminent Statesmen" were reported as favoring protection, as also were the opinions of Friedrich List, "the great German Economist," and Horace Greeley, editor of the New York *Herald Tribune* "a daily paper of immense circulation."   A banker,

[14] *Journals and Proceedings of the House of Assembly of the Province of Nova Scotia*, 1838, p. 278.
[15] G. E. Fenety reported that this organization had great but temporary popularity. *Political Notes and Observations* (Fredericton, 1867), I, 92.
[16] Cited in William Weir, *Sixty Years in Canada* (Montreal, 1903), pp. 100-101.
[17] II (1858), 92.

Jacob Dewitt, wrote in 1858 that protection to manufactured articles would attract capital and labor, and he argued erroneously that tariffs would shift all the burden of taxation to foreign producers:

> In order to aid the consumer in paying for his goods, it becomes necessary that the revenue, to support an economical government, should be raised by a tariff, so *apportioned* as to give encouragement to the manufacturers of such articles as we can produce or manufacture with advantage in our country. By so doing we induce the investment of capital in machinery, which will enable our manufacturers to compete here among themselves and with foreigners too, by which means the foreign producer must pay the duties into our treasury which we levy, in order to get into our market, which duties he cannot put on the cost of his goods; consequently the price is not increased to the consumer by the duties.[18]

Dewitt repeated the familiar arguments that local industry would give employment to all types of labor and would reduce the trade deficit; and he was one of the first to suggest that tariffs be used to prevent the sacrifice sale (i.e., dumping) of foreign goods in Canadian markets—"why levy any tax? The reason is obvious. It is to prevent the foreign brewer from sacrificing his beer in order to crush our infant breweries."[19] At a meeting in Toronto in 1858 "merchants, manufacturers and others" prepared a memorial to the Legislative Assembly summarizing their arguments for protection. They attributed depression to "unfair competition" from the United States, and asserted that capital and industrial labor would stay in Canada only if tariffs were imposed.[20]

The most vigorous exponent of protection in the business community was Isaac Buchanan, who organized the Toronto meeting in 1858 and was one of the founders in that year of the Association for the Promotion of Canadian Industry, the forerunner of the Canadian Manufacturers' Association.[21] Unlike many protectionists

---

[18] Jacob Dewitt, *Letters to the People of Canada, on Canadian Manufactures* (Montreal, 1858), p. 3.

[19] *Ibid.*, p. 4. See also "Home Manufactures the True Policy for Canada" (a letter to William Lyon Mackenzie from Jacob Dewitt on the tariff), reprinted in Isaac Buchanan, *The Relations of the Industry of Canada with the Mother Country and the United States* (Montreal, 1864), pp. 299-307.

[20] The memorial is reprinted in William Weir, *Sixty Years in Canada* (Montreal, 1903), pp. 107-110.

[21] Buchanan was born in Scotland in 1810 and came to Canada in 1830. He became one of the leading wholesalers and members of parliament; and for a short time he was President of the Legislative Council. See Edward Porritt, *Sixty*

who scorned political economy, he adapted it to his own purposes, distinguishing between free-trade "English Political Economy" and protective "Patriotic or Social Economy." He was well acquainted with protectionist writings and held the views of Henry Carey, Friedrich List, and John Barnard Byles, an English barrister, in particularly high esteem. He described Carey as

> . . . an American Economist, whose writings have raised for him a monument, *Aere perennius.* Of these works I trust there will soon be got up cheap Canadian Editions for the million, through the exertions of the *Association for the Promotion of Canadian Industry.* Social Economy must not hereafter be considered party politics, and I therefore venture to say that if these works now alluded to, were read aloud in Mechanics' Institutes and Debating Clubs, every member subsequently expressing his opinion, it would be the most improving possible of exercises.[22]

Buchanan was able to cite Adam Smith on the value of domestic trade and to quote Joshua Gee "the great authority on trade, a century ago" to prove that it was Britain's natural policy to stifle colonial industry. The publication in Canada in 1859 of a pamphlet by Horace Greeley entitled *Labour's Political Economy* was largely Buchanan's doing, as he said, "for the information of Parliament."[23]

Buchanan was a businessman, but he was also a politician, and he used only those arguments for protection which appealed to voters. Although in his old age he liked to be called "the father of the National Policy," in fact he had little claim to this title. Because in the 1850's Canada as a nation was only a vision in the minds of a few far-sighted statesmen, Buchanan never stressed the importance of tariffs for national development. Instead, beginning his campaign for protection in the depression of 1858, he made his central theme not growth but "that question in Patriotic or Social Economy, which is the only thing of any comparative importance, THE EMPLOYMENT OF OUR OWN PEOPLE." If imports were restricted, he explained, money could not leave the country; the interest rate would stay low, and prices and the level of employment would stay high. Speaking to farmers, he used Carey's arguments that factories

---

Years of Protection in Canada, 1846-1912 (2nd ed.; Winnipeg, 1913), pp. 32-33, and 37; and S. D. Clark, *The Canadian Manufacturers' Association* (Toronto, 1939), pp. 1-5.
[22] *Relations of the Industry of Canada,* p. 74.
[23] *Ibid.,* pp. 115, 123, and 125.

would provide jobs for their children and markets for their crops. He concluded:

TO FIND EMPLOYMENT FOR THE PEOPLE, IS JUST THE VERY THING, WHICH IS SO SUPREMELY DIFFICULT, AS TO BE OFTEN PRONOUNCED IMPOSSIBLE. IT IS THE PROBLEM REMAINING FOR THE TRUE POLITICAL ECONOMIST TO SOLVE; ITS SOLUTION WILL BE AN EVENT NOT LESS BRILLIANT AND FAR MORE IMPORTANT TO MANKIND, THAN THE DISCOVERY OF THE SOLAR SYSTEM.[24]

In a sense Buchanan helped defeat the cause he supported. Because he based his plea for tariffs on the existence of unemployment, with the return of prosperity in 1860 his case disappeared.

After their success in obtaining higher tariffs in the depression of 1858-1859 manufacturers did not press for increased duties in the relatively prosperous 1860's. In 1867, the year of Confederation, however, John MacLean, one of the founders of the Ontario Association of Manufacturers several years later, made the first statement by a businessman of the importance of tariffs not for temporary relief but rather for development of the country. Clearly influenced by List, he described the progress of an economy through stages from raw-material to diversified production; and he stressed the need for protection in the early years:

Now the syllogism presented to the Free Traders, and in which they are challenged to pick a flaw, is that the natural course of progress being *from* the commercial *to* the mechanical or manufacturing stage—which latter is the superior or more advanced stage—the tendency must be, as civilization moves onward, to import less and to manufacture more—that is, relatively, though not always absolutely. The Free Trade dream of one or more great "world's workshops," supported by a number of civilized yet non-manufacturing States, has attached to it a supposition of continued inferiority, on the part of the latter, which is at variance with the very idea of progress.[25]

MacLean argued that foreign producers paid part of the cost of tariffs—"the proportion of import duty paid by home consumers varies inversely as the proportion of the whole home production to the whole consumption," and without explaining further he added, "This view of the case is submitted as affording, in the playful

[24] *Ibid.*, p. 69.
[25] *Protection and Free Trade* (Montreal, 1867), p. 17.

task of its examination, an agreeable recreation for political economists of a mathematical turn of mind."[26]

MacLean made the first direct reference in Canada to the arguments of John Rae in favor of tariffs: "Mill and Rae," he explained, "have said that some comparative advantage may arise simply from having production first. Rae says that trying a good in new circumstances favors invention"; MacLean used the arguments of Henry Carey and others that tariffs prevent sacrifice sales or "raids" by foreign firms, permit a mixed economy and therefore the rotation of crops, and finally lessen business fluctuations by encouraging diversification.[27]   After his own appeals to theory, however, MacLean did not hesitate to ridicule economics as a science.

But take the question out of the circle of concrete private transactions, and put it in print, let us say, giving to it the abstraction and the dignity of a question in the mysterious science of political economy, and straightway the sharp, knowing business man yields himself to the popular, literary weight of delusions which, if presented to him in the shape of actual business, he would instantly repudiate.[28]

In the 1870's manufacturers organized effectively to seek protection, and in 1874 alone twenty-one petitions were submitted to Parliament "praying that the Manufacturing Interests of Canada may be protected by the imposition of certain Import Duties."[29] The Manufacturers' Association of Ontario was formed in 1874-75 "to procure by all legitimate means the aid of both public opinion and governmental policy in favour of the development of home industry." At an organizational meeting in Halifax in 1874 manu-

[26] *Ibid.*, p. 42.
[27] *Ibid.*, pp. 51 and 59. MacLean reflected Rae's influence when he described comparative advantage as "largely or wholly of an artificial character, and capable of transfer" (p. 49).
[28] *Ibid.*, p. 54. In 1879 MacLean pointed to the National Policy as vindication of his protectionist position: "In vain are the arguments of Adam Smith, powerful as they were against certain absurdities prevailing in his time, invoked against Protection as it is shaping itself in ours. He denounced Protection of the few at the expense of the many, but what would he have said had he lived to see Protection demanded by the millions, and resisted chiefly by a few learned *doctrinaires* and by the narrower interests of mere carrying, buying and selling, as distinguished from the broader and more popular interests of actual production?" "The Alliance of Democracy and Protection," *Rose-Belford's Canadian Monthly and National Review*, II (1879), 275.
[29] *Index to the Journals of the House of Commons of the Dominion of Canada, from 1867 to 1876 Inclusive* (Ottawa, 1880), p. 206.

facturers worked up enthusiasm for protection by restating the infant-industry argument and condemning free trade.[30]   Now businessmen stressed repeatedly the importance of tariffs for national growth; and as depression began in 1874 even the Toronto, Montreal, and Dominion Boards of Trade swung over to protection.   Manufacturers concentrated on political pressure as well as public propaganda, and the Manufacturers' Association of Ontario actually assumed responsibility for drafting parts of the tariff legislation of 1879 and later revisions.   The Canadian Manufacturers' Association replaced its provincial parent in 1887, and with a correlation between its activity and need for "tariff education" it grew until World War I.

Protection as a Political Platform

Tariffs on manufactured products were considered by colonial legislatures at an early date, as for example when a Select Committee of the Upper Canada House of Assembly concluded in 1821:

. . . it is deemed sound policy in every country to protect domestic manufactures, provided it can be done without making too great a sacrifice of other objects.

Domestic manufactures give a value to our raw materials, and serve to retain, within the Province, capital, of which it must be deprived for the payment of similar articles when imported.[31]

So long as Imperial sanction was required for all duties, however, colonial legislation threatening discrimination against the Mother Country was out of the question.   Legislators were limited to other means of stimulating local industry including the free import of raw materials; in particular, the Inspector-General of the Province of Canada said in 1845: "Every encouragement will be given to home manufactures; and for this purpose the duty upon raw materials will

[30] One speaker in Halifax "ridiculed the idea that because Adam Smith and other theorists of political economy had convinced themselves that free trade was the grand panacea for the world's ills; that the practical facts of every day life should be ignored, and the theories of these men accepted as gospel truths." *Report of the Meeting of Manufacturers, held in Argyle Hall, on Thursday, 26th March, 1874* (Halifax, 1874), p. 7. See also S. D. Clark, *op. cit.*, p. 5.

[31] "First Report of the Select Committee, Appointed to take into Consideration the Internal Resources of the Province in its Agriculture and Exports, and the Practicability and Means of Enlarging them; also, to Consider of the Expediency of Granting Encouragement to Domestic Manufactures," reprinted in Robert Gourlay, *Statistical Account of Upper Canada* (London, 1822), II, 679-680.

be reduced to one per cent merely for statistical purposes."[32]   A committee of the New Brunswick House of Assembly was only slightly less cautious when it reported in 1847 that

> . . . the principle of protection to home industry, irrespective of Revenue, should be recognized, by levying Duties on those productions and manufactures of Foreign Countries which the people of this Province are capable of producing and manufacturing themselves, making a just discrimination between raw materials and manufactured articles, and as a general rule admitting raw materials Duty free.[33]

After the colonies had obtained tariff independence in the 1840's, Clark Gamble, a Toronto lawyer, in 1852 gave the first unqualified political support to protection of manufacturing industry.   In a speech before the Canadian Legislative Assembly he accused the British Government of keeping the colonies hewers of wood, drawers of water, and purchasers of "clothing and other necessaries from them"; he began the myth, perpetuated by Buchanan and others, that the policies of the Colonial Secretary (Lord Grey) were taken from the writings of an eighteenth-century mercantilist, Joshua Gee.   Indisputable proof of the importance of protected manufacturers in a new country, Gamble asserted, was the economic success of the United States.[34]

Other members of parliament endorsed high tariffs in the 1850's and in 1857 a Special Legislative Committee on Emigration concluded that unemployed capital and labor were streaming from Canada because of unprotected industries.   With a vivid description of a sad future awaiting the country, the Committee concluded that if domestic manufacturers did not receive "that encouragement . . . which the laws of the United States still accords to them, they will perish in their infancy, our resources will become of no avail, capital will be banished from our country, and the energies of our countrymen will be paralyzed by the want of that occupation which they need."[35]   A parliamentary committee in Nova Scotia, taking a more

---

[32] *Mirror of Parliament*, March 3, 1845.

[33] *Journals of Assembly of New Brunswick*, 1847, p. 190, cited in O. J. McDiarmid, *op. cit.*, p. 114.

[34] Gamble cited the address by R. B. Sullivan on protection in 1847. See Edward Porritt, *Sixty Years of Protection in Canada 1846-1912*, pp. 166 and 174-179.

[35] *Journals of the Legislative Assembly of the Province of Canada*, 1857, Appendix 47, unpaged.

positive approach, declared that tariffs would correct an adverse balance of payments, increase the number of local firms, improve competition and lower prices, attract and provide employment for capital and labor, arrest emigration, retaliate against foreign duties and provide domestic manufacturers with equivalent advantages, alleviate depressions, and develop infant industries. The committee, after emphasizing that both the United States and Great Britain had reached maturity through protection, acknowledged the heresy of their views and ended with incongruous apologies to free trade:

> . . . we are not in any manner reduced to the necessity of maintaining the position that perfect freedom of trade is not, in a politico-economical sense, sound in principle. Without in any manner offending the most fastidious advocates of free trade, we can, nevertheless . . . demand for our manufacturers . . . the same encouragement and protection of the home market as is awarded to their competitors.[36]

Before Confederation the seemingly unimpeachable logic of free trade and its popularity in England discouraged important Canadian statesmen from giving more than grudging support to protection. After the tariff increase of 1859 Finance Minister Galt explained that his government still upheld "the true principle of political economy"—revenue first and protection as an incidental benefit.

> The policy of the present Government in re-adjusting the tariff has been, in the first place, to obtain sufficient revenue for the public wants; and, secondly, to do so in such a manner as would most fairly distribute the additional burthens upon the different classes of the community; and it will undoubtedly be a subject of gratification to the Government if they find that the duties absolutely required to meet their engagements should incidentally benefit and encourage the production, in the country, of many of those articles which we now import.[37]

John A. Macdonald, who in 1879 introduced the highly protective National Policy, in 1861 barely endorsed Galt's incidental protection: "It is," he explained, "as I have often said before, useless to discuss the abstract principles of Free Trade and Protection, but it is matter for consolation that the Tariff has been so adjusted as incidental to

---

[36] *Journal and Proceedings of the House of Assembly of the Province of Nova Scotia*, 1853, Appendix 45, pp. 359-362.
[37] A. T. Galt, *Canada, 1849 to 1859* (Quebec, 1860), p. 30.

encouraging manufacturing industries here."[38] The finance ministers of the Maritime Provinces, like Galt and Macdonald in the Province of Canada, favored incidental protection; and for a time this position even posed a barrier to Confederation. After a meeting in 1863 to discuss intercolonial trade the Maritimers reported: ". . . it would not have been just to existing interests, hastily, and without sufficient notice, to bring the larger and more advanced manufactures of Canada into competition with the limited and infant productions of the maritime Provinces. . . ."[39]

The years from 1867 to 1874 were prosperous, and high tariffs were not advocated either by the government or the opposition. Arguments for protection, which still centered on relief from depression and encouragement to selected industries, rang hollow in good times. Only a few members of parliament suggested half-heartedly that tariffs might stimulate interprovincial trade, prevent foreign firms from dumping, and serve as a weapon to force renewal of the Reciprocity Treaty.[40] Macdonald, the Prime Minister, held to incidental protection rejecting both extreme tariffs and doctrinaire free trade. He implied in 1870, however, that his position on commercial policy was not finally settled:

The hon. gentleman [Luther Holton] thinks that Free Trade, after the fashion of Jeremy Bentham, John Stuart Mill, and John Bright is the bible, the catechism, the creed, and the paternoster of the political belief of Canada. . . . He (Sir John) believed we had a policy of our own, and that we would have a policy of our own, notwithstanding the remarks of the hon. gentleman.[41]

In French Canada protection received some attention in the press immediately after Confederation as a possible solution to the eternal problem of emigration.[42]

The Conservatives were defeated in 1873, and thereafter while in opposition formulated the "National Policy." They began by

---

[38] *Address of the Hon. John A. Macdonald to the Electors of the City of Kingston, with Extracts from Mr. Macdonald's Speeches Delivered on Different Occasions in the Years 1860 and 1861* (n.p., n.d.), p. 61.

[39] *Journal and Proceedings of the House of Assembly of the Province of Nova Scotia*, 1863, Appendix 62, p. 1.

[40] *Debates*, 1870, pp. 273-275.

[41] *Ibid.*, p. 1202.

[42] J. I. Cooper, "Some Early French-Canadian Advocacy of Protection: 1871-1873," *C.J.E.P.S.*, III (1937), 530-540.

simply criticizing free trade, until in 1876 Macdonald proposed a "re-adjustment of the tariff, which will not only tend to alleviate the stagnation of business . . . but also afford encouragement and protection to the struggling manufacturers, and industries as well as the agricultural productions of the country."[43]   In a memorable speech he defended his plan with an imposing array of arguments: that trade which was not reciprocal could not be free; that John Stuart Mill, John Rae, and other economists approved tariffs in new countries; that large revenues were needed for public works; that farmers needed a home market for their perishable products; that manufacturing alone could attract capital and provide varied employments for labor; that tariffs would prevent "slaughter" sales of foreign goods—either of leftovers or to obtain a monopoly; and finally that relief would be given to depressed industries.[44] The most important characteristics of Macdonald's address were an emphasis on the relation of tariffs to national development, and use of the argument expounded by John Rae that comparative advantage changed over time and could result merely from a head start.   Macdonald explained:

The collective interests of a nation must be considered.   They are various, and a nation must stand on its own ground.   Theorists, with regard to free trade, have laboured under a misapprehension, and have advocated a false science, opposed to the protection of the industries of a country under any circumstances. . . .   We are a young country, just emerging from the first struggles with the forest.   We have but little realized capital as yet; the manufactures of the country, with a few small exceptions, having scarcely taken root.   They are lying alongside of a country which has had the advantage pointed out by Mr. Mill, of having commenced first . . . .   our manufactures have the same right to be encouraged that the child has to look to the parent for guidance until able to walk alone. . . .[45]

In 1877 and 1878 Conservative demands for protection increased, although they were not usually as well prepared as Macdonald's and were for the most part without references to political economy.[46]

[43] *Debates,* 1876, pp. 489-490.   [44] *Ibid.,* pp. 488-497.
[45] *Ibid.,* pp. 490-491.
[46] A few Conservatives did cite authorities, but they were the exception.   Dalton McCarthy read from "Prof. Cairnes' Work on Political Economy"; Charles Colby referred to McCulloch, Mill, and Cairnes; and James Domville quoted Cairnes, Mill, Byles, Adam Smith, List, and others. *Debates,* 1878, pp. 550 and 1030-1058.

One spokesman categorically rejected all discussion of theory:

Of the 250 volumes in the library, it would be found that each had, in some degree, a special theory of its own. There were gentlemen in this House who also held such theories, but, when they argued upon subjects that came home to the great body of the people, the people did not care to come there and read through those 250 volumes to see which theory was right. They wished to know how far the theories of Free-Trade and Protection affected their pockets, and of this they were able to judge without considering musty theories.[47]

In all protectionist statements after 1876 there was an increased appeal to nationalism, and Macdonald spoke for a large following when he explained in 1878 that although tariffs would bring about a temporary financial loss, this would· be a small price to pay for creating a national identity: "There are national considerations . . . that rise far higher than the mere accumulation of wealth, than the mere question of trade advantage; there is prestige, national status, national dominion,—and no great nation has ever risen whose policy was Free-trade."[48]

The Conservative party returned to office in 1878 and the National Policy was introduced in 1879.[49] Because the election had been fought over protection, tariffs were increased without much additional discussion. Finance Minister Tilley did emphasize that in addition to the long-run plans for national development there was an immediate need to diminish imports to combat depression: "I think, then," he explained, "without entering into a discussion here of Free Trade and Protection, . . . we should turn our attention to the best means of reducing the volume of our imports from all parts of the world."[50] After 1879 tariffs continued as an extremely controversial political issue, were often debated in Parliament, and were

[47] *Debates*, 1878, p. 773.
[48] *Ibid.*, p. 855.
[49] Between 1876 and 1878 numerous pamphlets were published supporting protection with the arguments used by politicians. Representative works were: A. Baumgarten, *Industrial Canada: The Duty of Development and How to Accomplish It* (Montreal, 1876); A Freeholder, *To the Freeholders of Canada: Political Facts for Consideration with a Short Treatise on Free Trade and Protection* (n.p., 1877); R. W. Phipps, *Free Trade and Protection, Considered with Relation to Canadian Interests* (Toronto, 1878); J. R. Lithgow, *Tariff Literature, Letters to the People* (Halifax, 1878); *La Protection combattue et refusée par le gouvernement libéral* (n.p., 1878).
[50] *Debates*, 1879, p. 414.

crucial in the elections of 1891 and 1911. Protectionists, however, depended primarily on restatements of old arguments with the only added note as the economy developed that industries fostered by protection could not subsequently be abandoned to the perils of free trade.

III. ARGUMENTS FOR FREE TRADE

Free trade did not become a possibility in the British North American colonies until the 1840's when Britain lowered imperial preferences and gave tariff independence.[51] Merchants and financiers who hoped to develop an *entrepôt* traffic between Europe and the American West were the first to support free trade, and they were assisted by writers under the influence of classical economics who preached a general policy of laissez faire. Finally, in the 1870's commercial policy became a major political issue and low tariffs the platform of the Liberal party. Arguments for free trade are examined here by dividing the advocates into three groups: the business community, apostles of classical economics, and politicians.

Stimulus for Businessmen and Merchants

W. H. Merritt, a promoter of the Canadian canal system and member of the Legislative Assembly, was one of the most vigorous free-trading merchants; he was eager to see the St. Lawrence developed as a trade route to the West, and he argued in 1847 that the tariff on agricultural products, made permanent in 1847, should be removed:

It would ensure the Western Trade, and the Revenue on our Public Works; and from the general prosperity which would become visible,

[51] Before 1840 a few writers supported free trade while criticizing the colonial system; for example, Robert Gourlay wrote: "If the corn of America could be exchanged for the manufactures of Britain, the consequences would be glorious. Every hand in this country would find employment; every rational desire would be satisfied; every murmur would be stilled." *Statistical Account of Upper Canada* (London, 1822), Introduction, p. clxxix, and see chap. i, above. The rebellious leader William Lyon Mackenzie complained in 1832: "With regard to trade generally, England declines to give the colonists a monopoly of her markets for their produce, and she declines to permit them to supply themselves with such things as they want from abroad at the cheapest market." Reprinted in Edward Porritt, *The Fiscal and Diplomatic Freedom of the British Oversea Dominions* (Oxford, 1922), p. 422.

the continuance of our connexion with the Mother Country would be firmly established. If those reasons are sound, it is clear that *a necessity exists for the removal of Import Duties.*[52]

In the 1850's Thomas C. Keefer, a brilliant engineer and author, explained that on the one hand imperial preferences were undesirable because of their uncertain duration, and that on the other domestic protection raised costs of transporting Canadian goods by excluding Americans from the St. Lawrence and thereby reduced the scale of canal operations.[53] The only protective duty that could wisely be imposed in any new country, Keefer declared, was upon carefully selected partly manufactured goods:

A moderate, and therefore permanent, encouragement—for those manufactures only which require little manual labour, and of which we produce the raw material,—is all that could be attempted and would tend most to the manufacturers' true interest; because high tariffs produce ruinous local competition, and invite attacks which are sure to be made, and a crisis must then ensue.[54]

Keefer used a theory of economic growth similar to that of Friedrich List to defend free trade and discourage premature protection. Canada, he maintained, should have low tariffs because the country was still in an agricultural stage of development:

. . . we foresee a future gradual resort to manufactures, in order to employ the idle months, as well as to support our commerce. The one cannot long flourish without the other—but as we must have Commerce *before* we can have Manufactures—all restrictions upon the infancy of that commerce, by needless and premature legislation, should be avoided.[55]

After repeal of the Corn Laws in 1846 merchants in Montreal established a Free Trade Association and began the *Canadian Econ-*

[52] *Letters Addressed to the Inhabitants of the Niagara District, on Free Trade, &c.* (Niagara, 1847), p. 18. Similar statements by Merritt can be found in: H. A. Innis and A. R. M. Lower, editors, *Select Documents in Canadian Economic History, 1783-1885*, pp. 187-188; and *Report of a Special Committee of the Legislative Assembly of Canada, on the Subject of a Free Trade with Great Britain and of a Protection to those Productions from the Competition of Foreigners in the Colonial and Home Markets* (Kingston, 1842).

[53] Keefer said, ". . . few reflecting men, of whatever shade of political feeling, will desire the return of the old system of alternate protection and restriction, attraction and repulsion, and vacillating legislation." *The Canals of Canada: Their Prospects and Influence* (Toronto, 1850), p. 28, also pp. 33-35.

[54] *Ibid.*, p. 39.

[55] *Ibid.*, p. 43. Keefer did not cite List.

omist as their organ.[56] Writers in this journal argued that protection, whether in the form of colonial restrictions or domestic tariffs, distorted the allocation of resources and increased costs to consumers. They made a single exception for infant industries:

Protection to any branch of agriculture, manufactures, or commerce, involving as it does the manifest injustice of taxing one class of a community for the support of another, can only be indicated under the plea that the interest, so to be protected, labours under some temporary disadvantage, which can only be combatted by such protection. We designedly say *temporary*, because if the disadvantages be permanent, it is contrary to the maxims of sound policy, that encouragement should be afforded by the state to any branch of industry, which, instead of adding to the sum of national wealth, will detract from it.[57]

Merchants stated explicitly at a meeting reported in the *Canadian Economist* in 1846 that the best commercial policy for Canada was tariffs for revenue only:

. . . in order to render the application of Free Trade principles thoroughly effectual, it is necessary to embrace them in all their comprehensiveness in this Colony . . . protection and regulation in every form should be repudiated, and the commerce of the Colony approximated as nearly to perfect freedom as the exigencies of the Public Revenue will permit.[58]

The *Canadian Economist* contained numerous references to classical economics, and one writer who treated political economy as synonymous with free trade optimistically described the influence of "the science":

Gradual approaches towards the sound principles of trade have been made at various intervals since the war: it is only of late, however, that the advancing intelligence of the age has obtained for the science of political economy what it well deserved,—a careful investigation, and a favorable reception by all classes. The advocates of sectional interests continue to denounce the system as visionary and theoretical; but they forget that sound theory and sound practice are inseparable, and that it is vain to pro-

[56] The *Canadian Economist* was operated and controlled by John Young, a prominent merchant, and William Bristow, a journalist. It ran from May 2, 1846, to May 8, 1847. See W. Notman, "John Young," *Portraits of British Americans* (Montreal, 1867), II, 231; and H. J. Morgan, *Bibliotheca Canadensis* (Ottawa, 1867), pp. 48, 49, 405-406.
[57] *Canadian Economist*, I (1846), 49.
[58] *Ibid.*, I (1846), 5.

pose to regulate commerce without referring to certain principles which constitute its true theory.[59]

The Toronto Board of Trade gave lip service to free trade in 1846, but apparently because of British example rather than the conviction of its members. A spokesman explained:

To attempt the establishment, in a colony of the Empire, of that restrictive system of commercial policy which has been so thoroughly abandoned by the mother country, would be a retrogression in the science of government, ill becoming a people who claim distinction because of their fraternal connection with that nation, whose improvements in every department of knowledge are with avidity adopted by the civilized world; and whose institutions have served as a model to every government that has sought to improve the condition of its subjects.[60]

For some businessmen the prospect of increased trade along the St. Lawrence was no compensation for the depression which followed the end of British preferences; and a group of Montreal merchants issued a manifesto in 1849 favoring annexation to the United States. Annexationists denied that free trade would restore prosperity because, "If obtained, this would yield but an installment of the many advantages which might be otherwise secured."[61] Good times did return, nevertheless, and the Reciprocity Treaty of 1854 answered most of the prayers both of the free traders and of the would-be annexationists.

The Influence of Classical Economics

Beginning in the 1840's, several writers who were neither merchants nor politicians but converts to classical political economy eloquently expounded free trade. James Buchanan, a civil servant, denounced agricultural protection as "injustice to the community at large," and continued, "I ask, upon what principle can such be claimed? save to retaliate for the imposts upon our produce on importation into the United States. So that *injustice* begets *injustice*;

[59] *Ibid.*, p. 2. One writer remarked: "It is impossible for any man attentively to read Smith and Ricardo and not feel convinced that the principles laid down by them are natural truths, just as much so as are any truths in the natural sciences. . . ."

[60] *The Globe*, Toronto, January 6, 1846.

[61] *Circular of the Committee of the Annexation Association of Montreal* (Montreal, 1849), p. 4.

yet it is called by both—*protection!*[62] Arthur Harvey, another civil servant, statistician, and untiring critic of all plans which conflicted with classical doctrine, urged Canadians to reject "the exploded fallacy that it is possible for a Government, by imposing vexatious duties on all articles of import, to benefit all classes of its subjects" and to make it clear that they were "imbued with, and know how to support, the principles of a more enlightened political economy."[63]

The Reverend William Hincks, Professor of Natural History at the University of Toronto, held forth on the wonders of free trade in the 1860's to the Canadian Institute at Toronto.[64] He said that commerce was the divine method of making different areas of the world complementary, and that any nation suffered by making itself artificially self-sufficient.

> Commerce is an appointment of the All-wise and infinitely benevolent Author of Nature, for equalizing, as nearly as may be, the advantages of different climates, soils, mineral productions, and other variable circumstances in the world's condition, by each region sending the superabundance useless to itself, of what it best produces, to other parts, and obtaining in return what is there best produced, thus at once conferring and receiving blessings and extending civilization, knowledge and enjoyment.[65]

Hincks rejected the arguments of protectionists that prosperity was determined by the balance of trade, that tariffs were effective as retaliation, and that a duty could be both protective and revenue yield-

[62] *Letter on Free Trade, and Navigation of the St. Lawrence* (Toronto, 1846), p. 7.

[63] Harvey explained further: "The demand for other than the 'incidental protection,' which may be necessary to raise revenue and satisfy the public creditor, implies conscious weakness—a feeling of which, with our climate, our soil, our geographical position, our wonderful resources, and the acknowledged energy of our constantly increasing population, we who dwell on this portion of the Western Hemisphere ought to be ashamed." *First Prize Essay: The Reciprocity Treaty: Its Advantages to the United States and to Canada* (Quebec, 1865), p. 29; and see also below, p. 115.

[64] John MacLean, a noted protectionist, identified Hincks as one of the most influential free traders in Canada. *Protection and Free Trade*, p. 48; and see below, p. 118.

[65] "Notes on Some Practically Interesting Questions in Economical Science Bearing on the Prosperity of Countries Situated as Ours Is," *C.J.I.S.A.*, XI (1868), 99.

ing. Having made the customary exception for infant industries, he made a plea for tariffs to provide revenue only:

Our's [*sic*], I trust, will continue to be the policy of unrestricted freedom of trade. Let duties be imposed for revenue only on as many different articles as are worth their collection, but cautiously kept within such bounds as not to limit consumption, and they will reach their highest productiveness with least inconvenience or injury.[66]

Hincks hit upon his real source of disagreement with protectionists when he said: "No one can, I think, attempt to establish any difference between the case of nations, which are but collections of individuals, and that of individual members of one nation."[67] This assumption that national interest was the sum of private interests was at the basis of most free-trade thinking, and was the principle challenged in theory by John Rae in 1834 and in practice by Sir John Macdonald through the National Policy.

Etienne Parent was the first staunch defender of free trade in French Canada. Speaking to the *Institut Canadien* at Quebec City in 1846 he applauded reduction of imperial preferences on the ground that all trade restrictions led to conflict:

Is it not well known that the old prohibitive and protective system had the effect of making all people enemies of each other, making them regard themselves as interested in the ruin of others? The new system, on the contrary, has the effect of interesting all people in the prosperity of others. . . .[68]

Parent criticized tariffs on agricultural products and justified protection exclusively for "newly-born" or "decrepit" industries:

. . . nothing is better established in political economy than that protection is an absurd and disastrous system, except perhaps in certain particular cases where it would be a question of supporting the first steps of a new industry, appropriate for the land, the climate and the situation of a country, or for moderating the decline of an old industry. . . .[69]

[66] *Ibid.*, p. 113.

[67] "An Inquiry into the Natural Laws which Regulate the Interchange of Commodities between Individuals and Nations, and the Effects of Interference with Them," *C.J.I.S.A.*, VII (1862), 185.

[68] "Importance de l'étude de l'économie politique," *Le Répertoire National*, IV (1850), 35 (translation). Parent cited Say and McCulloch in support of his views. See also below, p. 145.

[69] *Ibid.*, p. 40 (translation).

Free Trade as a Political Platform

All respectable politicians before Confederation professed at least grudging approval of free trade—even Alexander Galt, who brought tariffs to a high point in 1859. It was only after 1876 when the Conservatives became doctrinaire protectionists that the Liberals found it necessary actively to defend free trade. When the Liberals took office in 1872, their tariff policy had not been clearly formulated, and a legislative committee in that year even reported that a tariff would be justified on the products of Canadian infant industries and American firms which used Canada as a "slaughter-market."

This disturbing element in the manufacturing industry of the Dominion [dumping] arising out of our geographical position, and out of the trade policy of our neighbours, should induce even those who may regard free trade as a correct principle, in the abstract, to recognize the necessity for a modification of that principle as a measure of self-protection. . . .

It appears to be well established that the cost of manufacturing decreases as the quantity of goods manufactured increases. Thus a large manufacturing establishment can afford to sell its products at a lower rate than a smaller one. If, therefore, Canadian industry is relieved from the pressure of such undue competition . . . the effect will be that the manufacturing establishments will be worked to their full capacity, and the cost of production, and the consequent cost to the consumer will be proportionately reduced.[70]

In 1875 Prime Minister Alexander Mackenzie firmly rejected protection and announced that the Liberals would not use tariffs for any purpose other than revenue:

Protection as a principle will never prevent a stagnation in trade or a reduction in prices, because in the United States, the most thoroughly protected manufacturing country in the world, the manufacturers have not been able to hold their own, and their manufacturers have for the last year been in the greatest distress of all. . . . The Government having adopted the policy which we always held in Opposition, that the revenue of the country is to be raised by the imposition of import duties, and heavy duties as far as possible on whisky and spirits distilled in this country. We cannot depart at present from that principle.[71]

---

[70] "Report of the Committee to Enquire into the Manufacturing Interests of the Dominion," *Journals of the House of Commons*, 1874, Appendix 3, p. 1.

[71] "Speech at Sarnia," in *Speeches of the Hon. Alexander Mackenzie during His*

David Mills, Minister of the Interior, whom Macdonald always called derisively "the philosopher of Bothwell," was a chief architect of Liberal commercial policy.[72]   Author of a parliamentary report in 1876 on methods of ending the current depression, Mills declared that tariffs would only injure merchants, reduce competition, slow technological advance by hindering international competition, raise prices to consumers, and distort the allocation of capital.   He rejected the argument that tariffs were an effective diplomatic weapon and claimed that protected industries were a cause of depressions, that the United States had grown strong in spite of high tariffs, and that protection would diminish not increase government revenue.[73] Although protection might create jobs for immigrants, he conceded, the cost to the Dominion would be far greater than the gain; he estimated that if the average duty were raised from 17½ to 25 per cent 150,000 additional immigrants could be employed, but with an increase in import costs of $12,500,000.   Mills concluded in good liberal fashion that it was never fair to tax the many to benefit the few.

Richard Cartwright, the Liberal Minister of Finance, when defending free trade made the politically dangerous assertion that Canada might be destined never to become an urban and manufacturing nation:

> . . . there are but three great sources of wealth in Canada—our farms, our forests, our fisheries and our ships; and . . . although others may

---

Recent Visit to Scotland, with His Principal Speeches in Canada since the Session of 1875 (Toronto, 1876), p. 154.

[72] Mills was born in western Ontario and educated at the University of Michigan. He was successively school teacher, inspector of schools, editor, and barrister. O. D. Skelton, *Life and Letters of Sir Wilfred Laurier* (London, 1922), I, 172 and 340.

[73] Mills blamed depression in the United States on past protection: "The unhealthy stimulus that was there given by a highly protective tariff during the past twelve years to various branches of manufactures, diverted the capital of the country from its natural channels into those enterprises which promised through Government interference a larger profit. The consequence had been the production of larger quantities of certain kinds of goods than can be disposed of in the United States markets, and which cannot at the high cost be sold abroad at remunerative prices. The result has been that production has been disturbed by legislation. Trade has become depressed." "Report of the Select Committee on the Causes of the Present Depression of the Manufacturing, Mining, Commercial, Shipping, Lumber and Fishing Interests," *Journals of the House of Commons*, 1876, Appendix 3, p. v.

be and are important in their degree . . . at present these are the things from which our wealth mainly comes, and . . . in regulating the policy of this country we must look first and foremost to see how any policy will affect the welfare of the men who are actually engaged in adding to the real and substantial wealth of the country.[74]

The most vocal exponent of doctrinaire laissez faire among the Liberals, Cartwright claimed that too much capital had been devoted to public works and that Canadians should be satisfied to remain farmers forgetting their fanciful notions of industry. Citing Adam Smith and Mill, he explained that protection was always unfair to some segment of the economy and that it made "honest and economical" government impossible.[75]

Plans for unrestricted reciprocity with the United States received some attention in Canada in the 1880's, and brought the last great defense of free trade. Goldwin Smith became president of the Commercial Union Club in Toronto and repeated the familiar arguments for laissez faire, blaming every misfortune and inconvenience on protection—even the high price and poor selection of books which, he predicted, "must have its effect on the tastes and the intellectual progress of our people."[76] Under the auspices of this club experts on specific sectors of the economy explained how division of labor improved with size of the market, and how misallocation and inefficiency as a result of protection caused prices to rise. The advocates of unrestricted reciprocity and commercial union underestimated the nationalism and anti-Americanism of Canadians, and the apathy of Americans; and the movement met with no success.

While in opposition from 1878 until 1896 the Liberals continued to support tariffs for revenue only, although they expressed some reservations. Edward Blake, leader after Mackenzie, preferred to attack particular aspects of the tariff schedule rather than the principle of protection, and he said in 1882: "Free trade is, as I have repeatedly explained, for us impossible; and the issue is whether

[74] Cited in J. R. Long, *Canadian Politics, with Speeches by the Leaders of Reform and Progress in Canadian Politics and Government* (St. Catherines, 1903), pp. 87-88.
[75] *Debates*, 1876, p. 580. See also *Reform Government in the Dominion: The Pic-nic Speeches Delivered in the Province of Ontario during the Summer of 1877* (Toronto, 1878), pp. 82-83.
[76] *Handbook of Commercial Union* (Toronto, 1888), p. xix.

the present tariff is perfect, or defective and unjust."[77]   Wilfred Laurier, who followed Blake as leader, confirmed his party's faith in free trade in 1893: "I say the policy should be a policy of free trade, such as they have in England. . . ."[78]   After winning the election of 1896, however, the Liberal Finance Minister Fielding declared that, desirable as free trade was, it had become impossible because of firmly-established protection.

The evil of protection, like most other evils, is wide-reaching in its influences, and it has become so blended and interwoven with the business of Canada that if we should attempt to strike it down to-day, we should do harm not only to the protected interests, which have no claim on us, but to other interests which are not directly connected with the protected interests.   It would be folly not to remember that we are dealing not with the protected manufacturer only, but that the interests of labour have to be considered as well as the interests of capital.[79]

For fifteen years after 1896 the Liberals professed free trade without lowering tariffs, until finally in 1911, under pressure from western farmers, Laurier revived the old issue of reciprocity with the United States.   In the subsequent election the same arguments were used as in 1878, although with fewer appeals to principles; and again the popularity of protection was confirmed by defeat of the Liberal party.

IV. SUMMARY AND CONCLUSION

Commercial policy was a controversial topic in Canada as early as the 1820's but did not become a really important issue until the 1840's, when the colonies obtained tariff independence.   Protective tariffs were advocated first by farmers on agricultural products and then on manufactures by businessmen and proponents of a diversified economy.   Free trade was defended by merchants, by transportation promoters who expected an increase in traffic along the St. Lawrence, and by exponents of doctrinaire laissez faire.   Tariffs became a vital political question in the 1870's and 1880's but de-

---

[77] Cited in *Canada: An Encyclopedia of the Country*, ed. J. C. Hopkins, pp. 312-313.

[78] *Official Report of the Liberal Convention* (Ottawa, 1893), p. 33.

[79] *Debates*, 1897, p. 1106.

clined in the 1890's after argument had given way to tiresome repetition and free traders finally recognized the futility of their case. A revival of controversy in 1911 did not lead to any new analysis and ended in another victory for protection.

Protective tariffs were suggested most frequently as shelter for infant industry, but also for a variety of other purposes: as a means of strengthening national ties, providing a home market for agricultural products, reducing the severity of depressions and raising the long-run average level of employment, retaliating against foreign tariffs, preventing "dumping," increasing government revenue, and generally of stimulating economic growth. The most able protectionists cited writings of North American economists: Henry Carey, Rae, and List (whose work may be considered a product of the American environment);[80] but because these authorities were viewed by most people at best as heretical, and hardly respectable, tariff defenders came to mistrust economics as a "science." The widely-held conviction that orthodox political economy was no more than laissez faire propaganda became for more than half a century the most powerful check on the development of Canadian economics.

Defenders of free trade took their arguments from classical economics; they explained that division of labor and total national product both increased with the size of markets and were greatest where there was complete freedom from commercial restriction. They claimed that protective tariffs misallocated resources, took from one group and subsidized another, injured merchants, fostered monopolies, diminished government revenue, and generally retarded national development. Free traders were able to quote the scholarly pronouncements of the Physiocrats, Smith, Ricardo, Say, Mill, and later classical writers; they were able also to call upon the polemics of Cobden and the Manchester School. Finally, free traders claimed an essential similarity between commercial and political liberty which they argued should be regarded as desirable not merely as means but as moral ends in themselves.

The weight of old-country authority behind free trade probably weakened its case in Canada. As the colonies gradually broke from the Imperial orbit, like adolescents leaving the family group, they

[80] See J. A. Schumpeter, *History of Economic Analysis* (New York, 1954), p. 505.

selected the more imaginative and rebellious policy of protection ahead of the reasonable and at-first-sight defensible practice of free trade. A genuine conviction that protectionist theories were valid was undoubtedly the reason why many persons gave support to high tariffs; for others it was convenient to jump on a popular band-wagon. Most Canadians, however, came to regard protection as an ambitious gamble for success and free trade as stoical acceptance of continued dependence on Great Britain and the whims of world markets. In the environment of a new country it was not surprising that the selection was of a policy which promised independence and the means to achieve an impressive national destiny.

3

Currency and Banking

Currency and banking were discussed in Canada almost exclusively by government officials and by bankers themselves. Because monetary questions were not often widely controversial and were by their nature highly technical and complex, few persons were interested or had enough understanding to make intelligent comments. Writing on the subject was not plentiful, was usually upon some current problem, and seldom dealt with principles.

To place discussions of currency and banking in perspective it has been necessary to provide a more detailed historical account than is included with other chapters. The division into sections on currency and banking is for convenience and does not deny the existence of related and parallel lines of development.

1. CURRENCY

Coinage and the Unit of Account

When Great Britain acquired Canada in 1763, the monetary system was in great disorder;[1] under the French, playing cards signed by government officers and other constantly depreciating notes had caused the disappearance of coin. The British quickly eliminated this paper currency, however, and Spanish, French, and other coins began to circulate at official rates. It was thought desirable that the Spanish dollar be overvalued because of its great popularity in the United States, and it soon become predominant. But the British by no means settled on a single medium of exchange; for almost a

[1] For histories of Canadian currency, see C. A. Curtis, "Currency," *Encyclopedia of Canada* (Toronto, 1935), II, 159-167; "Canada's Monetary System," *Canada Year Book*, 1924, pp. 784-791; Bank of Canada, *The Story of Canada's Currency* (Ottawa, 1955); and R. Craig McIvor, *Canadian Monetary, Banking and Fiscal Development* (Toronto, 1958), pp. 12-85.

century whenever any coin through wear or tear or even debasement became unacceptable elsewhere it usually arrived in Canada. Professor Adam Shortt has described the situation thus:

... the office of a Canadian currency broker was a veritable curiosity shop, exhibiting the remnants of several national currencies in the last stages of demoralization. There, from a currency point of view, the halt, the blind and the disowned of many mints foregathered in shabby company. Their thin, worn and battered faces mutely witnessed to a long and busy life with much travel and hard usage.[2]

The testimony of one irate Nova Scotian in 1820 was representative of the criticism during the period.

Our currency is now like a Scotch haggis, made up of contradictions, of things good and bad, oatmeal, onions, hog's lard, butter, crumbs of bread, salt, pepper, garlic, leeks, parsley, &c. &c.

I tell you the "Haggis will burst, and scald many who are little expecting it."[3]

After the conquest, to establish generally accepted units of account, foreign coins were related to English monetary units with two forms of overrating known as York Currency (employed in Upper Canada) and Halifax Currency (also called Quebec Currency and used in parts of Lower Canada and the Maritimes). These units were only a standard of value, had no equivalent in coin, and were different both from British and from American denominations. Robert Gourlay in 1822 expressed what must have been the feeling of many when he urged abandonment of this inconvenient system and adoption of American decimal units.

... could prejudice be got over, it would be well to adopt dollars and cents as the standard. They would tally as well with our sovereigns as Halifax currency, and in transacting business with the United States, would be advantageous. In the State of New York much confusion is kept up by individuals adhering to pounds, shillings, and pence, New York currency, instead of uniformly reckoning by dollars and cents. In Canada dollars and cents, Halifax, and York currency, are all resorted to, confusing and confounding.[4]

[2] "Currency and Banking, 1760-1841," *Canada and Its Provinces* (Toronto, 1914), IV, 619-620.

[3] *Acadian Recorder*, Oct. 21, 1820, reprinted in H. A. Innis and A. R. M. Lower, editors, *Select Documents in Canadian Economic History 1783-1885*, p. 433.

[4] *Statistical Account of Upper Canada* (London, 1822), II, 370. See above, pp. 6-20 ff.

In 1825 the Lords of the Treasury set out to reform the currency and money of account of the colonies by making British silver coins (shortly before made token in England) the only unlimited legal tender, and by issuing bills of exchange for payments in England. The Spanish silver dollar was to be devalued in terms of sterling and would eventually cease to be legal tender. When Lord Dalhousie, the Governor-General, attempted to implement this plan, however, he met strong local opposition.[5] A decimal system of accounts using the Spanish dollar was becoming popular, and considerable sentiment continued to be attached to the variety of old coins, particularly by French Canadians. The British government hesitated to infringe on Canadian law which fixed rates of foreign coins, and instead, hoping to teach by example, shipped quantities of silver into the colonies to be used for payments. But with other coins still rated above the British silver and the discount rate on bills of exchange fixed at a high level, "bad money drove out good" and the new currency quickly returned to England. Continued refusals by the colonial legislatures to raise the rating of British coins, to make them exclusive legal tender, or to use sterling units of account, led the British to abandon attempts at reform and leave the colonies to work out their own monetary destinies, meanwhile continuing with their complicated overrating and hodgepodge of miscellaneous coins.

Some persons suggested in the 1830's, perhaps with reason, that the recently established commercial banks were partly responsible for

[5] Commissary-General R. I. Routh explained the proposed reforms in the currency to a Special Committee of the House of Assembly of Lower Canada:

"In order to give effect to the intentions of His Majesty's Government, I venture to propose the following measures for His Excellency's consideration:

"It is expedient to fix the corresponding values of the English coins and to make them a legal tender at these rates.

"It is expedient to establish sterling money as the money of account, and exclusively recognizable in Courts of Law.

"It is expedient to restrict the bank notes on the renewal of the several charters to sums of five pounds sterling, and to prevent their issue under that amount.

"It is expedient to repeal the Provincial Act of Parliament which fixes the rate of the Spanish dollar at 4s.6d. sterling, establishing it for the purpose of calculation at 4s.4d. sterling, which is found to be the intrinsic value of that coin, whilst such coins shall remain legally in circulation.

"It is expedient to fix the rates at which the old French coins and pistareens are to pass, and to name a period from which that regulation shall commence.

"It is expedient to name a period after which Foreign coins shall not be considered a legal tender, or otherwise than bullion."

blocking the British attempt at currency reform. Although bank-notes were nominally redeemable in specie at par, the banks could give constancy to their issue by holding their most underweight and disreputable legal tender for redemption. One anonymous writer, criticizing this practice, argued that the debased coinage did not really benefit the banks because public confidence alone determined demands for redemption and confidence was dependent on a bank's general stability rather than the state of its coin. The only effect of overvaluation, he explained correctly, was inflation in terms of the favored coins; he concluded that reform of the currency would injure the banks little and benefit the economy much:

> . . . our Provincial crowns and half-crowns should be reduced to their real intrinsic value, and allowed to take their chance in the circulation with the paper currency of our Banks, which is a uniform value throughout the Provinces, and even at but a trifling discount in the neighbouring States. A large sum, in coin is confined here, only to enhance the price of all consumable articles,—for that is invariably the effect of raising the denomination of the local coin. It does not add any thing to the stability of our Banks, or the credit of their paper. In the Province, the holders of Bank notes rely on the character and conduct of the Directors of the Banks and the large capital, and widely-diffused interests involved in them. And among our neighbours, the notes are received, or goods sold to us, from a confidence in the great natural resources of the country, and its means of meeting demands against it, with an export of its products, and not from any reliance on the quantity of debased coin it possesses.[6]

After the Union of the Provinces of Upper and Lower Canada in 1840 the question of the currency again came up for review. The business community in particular had become increasingly critical of the many coins which passed current at different rates in various parts of the provinces.[7] Leading bankers and businessmen were questioned by the Legislature and were found to favor adoption of the American decimal system and the rating of fewer coins as legal tender; but the act which was passed in 1841 was still only a partial reform in this direction.[8] British and American gold coins to-

---

[6] *Considerations on the Uses of Paper Money* (Montreal, 1836), p. 37.

[7] In 1840 a meeting was held to protest the situation. See Adam Shortt, "The Hon. Adam Ferrie, Reformer, Merchant, and Financier," *J.C.B.A.*, XXXII (1924-1925), 59.

[8] See "First Report of the Select Committee on Banking and Currency," *Journals of the Legislative Assembly of the Province of Canada*, I (1841), Appendix O.

gether with American and French silver were made legal tender at fixed rates, and other coins were valued as bullion. Halifax Currency was retained as the official unit of account although, informally, dollar accounting became increasingly widespread in the 1840's.

Finally, in the 1850's the coinage question was settled. Following the end of imperial protection in the 1840's the Provinces turned first to trade among themselves and then to increased trade with the United States; to aid this swing away from the Mother Country it seemed necessary to issue Canadian coins with denominations corresponding to the American dollars. A legislative committee concluded in 1851:

> . . . it is extremely desirable that there should be an uniform currency throughout British North America, especially as there is a prospect of an extensive inter-colonial trade between the said Provinces, and likewise a common system of postage. The Committee of Council entertain no doubt that it would tend much to facilitate the growing commercial intercourse between all the Provinces, and the neighbouring states of the American Union, if the currency were assimilated as much as possible to that of the United States.[9]

In 1852 J. B. Cherriman, Deputy Professor of Mathematics and Natural Philosophy in the University of Toronto, made an interesting and characteristically Canadian attempt to reach a compromise between British and American traditions. He proposed that Canada mint a coin with decimal units but British denominations.[10] Despite Cherriman's plea, however, the Province of Canada in 1853, and the Maritimes slightly later, passed acts which stated that accounts could be kept in dollar terms, that gold alone was standard with silver token, and that the American eagle and the British sovereign would both be unlimited legal tender. After Confederation the Uniform Currency Act of 1871 repeated these conditions for the new Dominion.

Metallic currency in Canada in the first half of the nineteenth century was very similar to that of the United States; various gold and silver coins circulated and were recognized as legal tender.[11] But

---

[9] *Journals of the Legislative Assembly of the Province of Canada*, X (1851), Appendix Y. Y.

[10] "On Provincial Currency," *Canadian Journal*, I (1852-1853), 177-180.

[11] See N. Carothers, *Fractional Money: A History of the Small Coins and Fractional Paper Currency of the United States* (New York, 1930), pp. 69-137.

dispute over the coinage ended in Canada in 1853 with adoption
of the gold standard. Metallic currency never became the controversial political question that it was in the United States in the latter
half of the nineteenth century when bimetallism was an issue in one
national election after another. A statement by Professor John
Davidson about conditions in 1896 holds true for the whole century:
"There has been," he remarked, "a large measure of agricultural
discontent in Canada; but the remedy has been persistently sought
in a reform of the tariff, and not in a reform of the currency. The
majority cannot pin their faith to more than one panacea at a
time."[12]

Government Issue of Redeemable Paper Currency

The first government notes in British North America were issued
by the Province of Nova Scotia in 1812, and in the same year wartime emergency led to circulation of "Army Bills" in the other colonies, which were payable by the British Treasury on demand but
which passed from hand to hand without frequent redemption.[13]
Both of these issues, however, were designed for government finance, and any improvement they brought in the currency was incidental. The Nova Scotia Treasury continued to issue notes in
moderate quantity until Confederation, and the Army Bills were discontinued at the end of the war. A new issue of government bills
was discussed for a few years; but the notes of the commercial banks,
which increased steadily after 1817, answered most demands for
paper money.

The first serious attempt to have large amounts of paper currency issued by a provincial government came during and after the
economic depression and civil rebellions which began in Upper and
Lower Canada in 1837. While the crisis was at its height, Francis
Hincks[14] recommended to a legislative committee on banking in
Upper Canada that the government lend a quantity of legal-tender
debentures to the banks to prevent suspension of specie payment
and speed recovery from depression. His proposal was rejected and

---

[12] "Canada and the Silver Question," *Q.J.E.*, XII (1898), 142-143.
[13] See J. S. Martell, "A Documentary Study of Provincial Finance and Currency
1812-1836," *Bulletin of the Public Archives of Nova Scotia*, II (1941), No. 4.
[14] See below, p. 113.

the banks suspended, but Hincks was not without support. One anonymous author wrote:

We may remark that we have heard it suggested that the government should issue debentures for small amounts, say as low as four or five dollars, not bearing interest, which should be a legal tender. This proposition would in some respects answer better than allowing any description of Bank paper to be a legal tender, as such debentures would command greater confidence in the country, and it is therefore well worthy the serious consideration of the Legislature.[15]

Lord Sydenham, the first Governor-General after the Union of the Provinces in 1840, had reform of the currency as one of his primary aims. He had been a member of the group in England known as the "Currency School" and his biographer reported that, when in Canada, "he hoped to establish a system of currency in that colony, which should prove a model for other countries."[16] Sydenham confided to Francis Hincks in 1841 that what he wished, in brief, was "the establishment of a perfectly sound paper currency by means of a single bank of issue" adding "the principle, in short, for which I contended in the Cabinet, in the first instance in 1833, and which Sam Loyd has since so ably advocated in a pamphlet."[17] Sydenham condemned the issue of notes by commercial banks as contributing to undesirable price fluctuations, such as had occurred in the crisis of 1837:

No conditions of any kind can prevent numerous banks of issue in competition one with another, and in great ignorance of each other's proceedings, from at one time flooding the country with paper, and at another being compelled, if their notes are made convertible, suddenly to withdraw all accommodation, and reduce the general circulation far below its natural limits.[18]

Sydenham's reform proposal was for a Provincial Bank, with one-quarter of its assets to be held in specie and three-quarters in govern-

[15] *Thoughts on the Banking System of Upper Canada and on the Present Crisis* (Toronto, 1837), p. 15.

[16] G. Poulett Scrope, *Memoir of the Life of the Right Honourable Charles Lord Sydenham, G.C.B.* (London, 1843), p. 68. For a description of Currency School principles, see Lloyd W. Mints, *A History of Banking Theory in Great Britain and the United States* (Chicago, 1945), p. 75.

[17] Sir Francis Hincks, *Reminiscences of His Public Life* (Montreal, 1884), p. 69.

[18] "Memorandum on the Paper Currency Suggested for Canada by Lord Sydenham," Appendix IV to G. Poulett Scrope, *op. cit.*, p. 386.

ment securities. Initially the issue backed by securities would be limited to three-quarters of a million pounds but could be extended with growth of the economy. One-quarter of a million pounds would be backed entirely by specie and additional notes would be issued pound for pound of gold. Need for an increase in the issue backed by securities, Sydenham declared, would be indicated by a continuous flow of gold into the Bank. He explained to the Canadian Legislature that there would be three advantages to the "Bank" (which would, in fact, have been identical to the Issue Department of the Bank of England after 1844): a safe and stable currency, an annual profit for the Provincial Treasury, and an immediate sum for construction of public works.

To bring about the passage of his reforms Sydenham sought the confidence of the colonial legislators; and it is reported that he virtually turned the Assembly into a classroom, lecturing on economics and finance.[19] One of his first converts was Francis Hincks, who was chosen as Chairman of a Select Committee on Currency and Banking and, according to Hincks, became "one of a very few members of the House who, in Lord Sydenham's opinion, thoroughly comprehended and approved of his views."[20] Hincks probably required little conversion to "Currency School" principles, for he reported in his *Reminiscences* that he had read a pamphlet by Samuel Loyd several years before Sydenham's mention of it "and had been much struck with the soundness of the views therein advocated. . . ."[21] Hincks's clear and well-prepared statements on the importance of a government currency in 1841 are worth repeating at length. He argued that the proper functions of banks were the granting of loans and the holding of currency on deposit—but never the issue of notes.

Banks are established because the public convenience requires them, and it is quite evident that they must obtain a remunerative profit. Under the present system a portion of this profit is derived from the public at large, who hold their notes. If they were deprived of the right of issue they would obtain precisely the same profit, but it would have to be paid *by their customers*, as it is in England, where the most profitable business is done

[19] R. S. Longley, *Sir Francis Hincks* (Toronto, 1943), p. 85.
[20] *Reminiscences*, p. 69.
[21] *Ibid.*, p. 70. Hincks probably referred to a work by Loyd entitled *Reflections suggested by a Perusal of Mr. J. Horsley Palmer's pamphlet on the causes and consequences of the pressure on the Money-Market* (London, 1837).

by Banks of Deposit and Discount alone. So far, then, as the Banks are concerned, they would be paid under the proposed system by their customers, instead of, as at present, by the community at large. It is said that if the banks were suddenly called on to redeem their present circulation they would have to contract their loans, and thus bring distress upon their debtors. This difficulty has undergone serious consideration, and we have no hesitation in stating that it may easily be overcome. Even, however, admitting that some temporary inconvenience might be experienced, it should weigh nothing in comparison with the permanent good that would be effected for the country. Every additional charter to issue paper money increases the difficulty of changing the system.[22]

The proposed bank of issue never passed the legislature. Opposition came from commercial bankers who stood to suffer from the loss of note issue, and also, according to Hincks, from legislators who recognized the plan's merits but feared the transition from bank notes to government circulation. If the commercial banks had been permitted to reduce their issue very slowly, as was arranged for in England under the Peel Bank Act three years later, Hincks believed that the Provincial Bank would have received approval.[23] Hincks went on to become Inspector-General (as the position of Minister of Finance was then known), and in 1848 he sold interest-bearing government debentures in small denominations ostensibly as an emergency financial measure but also reflecting his continued fondness for a government currency. His critics were not fooled and condemned the issue for its inflexibility and again for the loss it caused the commercial banks. The debentures were not continued after 1850.

Sydenham's plan for a central bank of issue, although unsuccessful, never quite died in Canada. For example, one enthusiast (George Wilkes of Brantford) described the merits of the scheme again in 1858. "The coinage of money," he wrote, "either of gold, silver, copper, leather, wood, or paper, rightfully and properly belongs in all countries to the soverign [sic] power, and the increase or profit therefrom likewise belongs thereto, and cannot be diverted,

[22] Cited in *Reminiscences*, pp. 72-73. Hincks reported he was influenced in 1841 by the writings of Condy Raguet, an American writer on banking and commercial policy.
[23] *Ibid.*, p. 71.

without injury to the people and a derangement of commerce."[24] A government issue of notes, he explained, if perfectly convertible into specie, would vary in quantity with the flow of gold.

By a central point of issue and redemption, the most perfect barometer is gained; when the currency is too great, it returns upon the issuer for gold; when it is not sufficient for the purposes of trade, gold is brought in for it, and thus a proper equilibrium is established.[25]

Canada was fortunate during the nineteenth century in having several ministers of finance who, besides achieving business success, had great breadth of vision and wide knowledge. The second of these, after Francis Hincks, was Alexander Galt,[26] who interestingly enough also favored a government issue of notes. Galt suggested in 1860 that a Provincial Treasury Department be formed to issue a redeemable legal-tender paper currency. The commercial banks would lose their issue rights but would receive government notes "on delivery of one-fifth the amount in specie, one-fifth in government securities, and three-fifths in the shape of a first lien upon their general assets, and they were to pay a tax of three per cent on circulation up to half their paid up capital and of four per cent on the excess."[27] Galt's description of the virtues of his plan to the legislature could have been a speech either by Hincks or by Sydenham. He explained:

Up to this time, in Canada, the paper money circulation has been created and controlled by the Chartered Banks, and the idea has widely obtained that there is a necessary connection between banking and currency, but this is simply a misapprehension; for the currency of any country is, of all things, the one most properly belonging to the State, and in this respect there is no difference between paper money, and gold, or silver coin, which latter, every one admits, it is the business of Government to watch over. . . . I hold, then, that it is as imperative upon the Government to watch over the paper circulation, and to ensure its soundness, as it is to prevent the coin circulation from being alloyed. . . . I propose to separate currency

---

[24] "Banking and the Currency," *Hunt's Merchants' Magazine and Commercial Review*, XXXIX (1858), 193.

[25] *Ibid.*, p. 195. Wilkes praised the theories of the Currency School and referred to the "leading political economists of the last fifty years" as "Lord Liverpool, Mr. Ricardo, Mr. Huskisson, Sir Robert Peel, C. P. Thomson [Lord Sydenham], Lord Overstone [Samuel Loyd], &c., &c. . . ."

[26] See below, p. 113.

[27] O. D. Skelton, *The Life and Times of Sir Alexander Tilloch Galt*, p. 282.

from banking. . . . I think that the circulation of the country, should be kept entirely separate from its commercial relations, and that the public should have as much money as they really want, with the assurance that it will be always convertible into specie, and that the security of the whole country will be bound for its redemption.[28]

In 1865 a much modified version of Galt's proposal was accepted and with it the principle that government and the banks should at least share the issue privilege.

Galt hoped to achieve two ends from the issue of government notes—safety and stability in the money supply and a ready market for public debt. He was a good politician and in 1860 when people still remembered the credit restriction of 1857, and two major bank failures which occurred in 1859, emphasized the monetary improvements which would follow. In 1866, after confidence in the banking system had been restored, he described the issue of notes as a loan from the public and not as an addition to the money supply. The government, he explained, "merely proposed to authorise the Receiver-General to issue a new kind of debentures, a different class of securities to that formerly issued. They did not wish to control the banks, nor to be lenders or traders in money, but to use the machinery of one bank to effect a loan with our own people."[29]

After Confederation the Dominion Notes Act of 1870 repeated the terms of Galt's earlier legislation. A limit of nine million dollars (which was increased steadily over the years until World War I) was stipulated for the government fiduciary issue with a 20 per cent reserve in specie, all notes above the limit to be backed 100 per cent by gold. The denominations of Dominion Notes were not to exceed four dollars, which pleased the banks because small notes were judged most likely to be brought in for redemption during a run. The legislation was passed with Francis Hincks (now Sir Francis) again Finance Minister, back in Canada after a long absence as a colonial governor in the West Indies. After thirty years Hincks finally saw a shadow of his Currency School principles come into effect, and he was at last able to say with pride, "The Canadian

[28] *Thompson's Mirror of Parliament*, March 27, 1860, No. 21, p. 8, and No. 22, pp. 1 and 2.
[29] Ottawa *Times*, Aug. 3, 1866.

Dominion notes are redeemable in gold, and are issued on much the same principle as those of the Bank of England."[30]

Plans for an Irredeemable Paper Currency

Reform proposals are usually received most enthusiastically during depression; and after the financial crisis of 1857, Isaac Buchanan, a merchant and member of the Legislative Assembly from Hamilton, was able for the first time to gain support for a scheme to have the government issue irredeemable notes. Buchanan's argument, which contained both excellent insight and pedantic nonsense, was that the tie between money and gold placed the Canadian economy at the mercy of fluctuations in foreign trade, and despite the fact, he added, that "the internal transactions of a country are calculated to be at least twenty times the amount of its exports. . . ."[31] A decrease in exports relative to imports led to withdrawals of specie from banks, which were then forced to reduce loans, causing panic and even more demands for specie. Soon credit became unobtainable except at exorbitant rates of interest.

The rule is, no gold, no paper; no paper, no money; no money, no discounts, except on terms of extortion. This is the reason why interest rises; this is why the trading world are compelled to pay 10 per cent., and a commission of 20 to 30 per cent.; and it is clear that they are forced to pay it, under penalty of bankruptcy, not for the fair and legitimate use of money, but on account of its artificial scarcity—a scarcity created by Act of Parliament for the benefit of usurers.[32]

The shortage of money after the outflow of gold also caused a fall in prices, which, together with high interest rates, caused depression and unemployment.

Buchanan proposed to the legislature in 1857 that:

Whereas the present Money Law of Canada, being utterly erroneous in principle, is most fatal in practice or operation to the industry of the province, sacrificing its home trade and labor, which are *necessities*, to foreign trade and imported labor which are only INCIDENTS. . . . *Be it*

---

[30] "The Bank of England and the Act of 1844," *C.M.N.R.*, III (1873), 177-188.

[31] *The Relations of the Industry of Canada with the Mother Country and the United States* (Montreal, 1864), p. 100.

[32] *Ibid.*, pp. 93-94.

enacted &c., &c., that in addition to the coins which are at present the legal tender of Canada, and with the view of practically dispensing with these except for small change, the Government of this province are hereby authorized and required within three months from the passing of this act to have arrangements completed for issuing its own notes. . . .[33]

In addition to increasing employment and lowering the interest rate, Buchanan explained, the notes would provide government revenue and make taxes unnecessary. In reply to those who alleged that irredeemable notes would cause overissue and inflation, he argued, erroneously, that any excess issue would return to the government. "The air we breathe exists in SUPERFLUITY around us, but the *lungs* only appropriate the necessary quantity, so trade *could* only absorb money to the extent of its *transactions,* which are the *lungs* of trade."[34] Buchanan's proposal did not pass the legislature, and the return of prosperity together with the unhappy American experience with "greenbacks" discouraged its revival. In fact, when Alexander Galt was defending the issue of a redeemable government currency in 1866, he was very careful to deny any similarity to Buchanan's scheme. He explained: ". . . the introduction of Provincial circulation on a specie basis, instead of being an encouragement to an issue of greenbacks, such as that which had taken place in the United States, and captivated many of our own people, would be a positive barrier in the way."[35]

The depression of the 1870's and the subsequent decline in prices which lasted until the 1890's led to new proposals for an irredeemable paper currency. W. A. Thomson, speaking to the House of Commons in 1878, declared that the "want of harmony" resulting from the development of "mechanical science" could be eliminated by the establishment of "Agricultural Banks" which, in return for interest-bearing government securities deposited with the Treasury, would receive irredeemable Dominion notes to be loaned for agricultural development. It was hoped that the net effect would be a reduction in interest rates to farmers and an addition to national revenue sufficient to "reduce the public debt ten per cent, annually, carry on . . . public works, make free trade and increase the pro-

[33] "The Question of Money," *Canadian Merchants' Magazine,* I (1857), 127-128.

[34] *Relations,* p. 102.

[35] Ottawa *Times,* Aug. 7, 1866.

ductive power of the country."[36]   A further result, not mentioned by Wallace, would of course have been inflation to the extent of the new issue.[37]   There were some very enthusiastic supporters of Agricultural Banks outside Parliament, notably Thomas Galbraith of Port Hope;[38] but although the measure attained some popularity, it was never adopted.

A second proposal during the 1870's was for an irredeemable national currency patterned directly after the "greenbacks" of the United States.[39]   William Wallace, the foremost advocate of this scheme in Parliament, explained that gold was needed only for foreign exchange, and that the tie with domestic currency had caused shortage of funds and depression:

Only the importer or the man leaving the country wanted gold, others never thought of it; the legal tender answered all their purposes, and if there was no gold to-day, that confidence would not be impaired in the least. . . . He contended that the depression we were suffering from was not from a legitimate cause, but simply from the fact that we had too little money in circulation, and credit was at present destroyed. . . . Why insist that the measure of value—which money was—should be made of gold any more than a yardstick. . . . He understood depression brought on by the forces of nature, such as storm, inflicting untold misery by destroying the food of the people, but he could not understand depression

[36] *Debates*, 1878, pp. 1211-1218.

[37] It is interesting to note that the terms of the proposed Agricultural Bank Act were very similar to the Finance Act of 1914. See McIvor, *op. cit.*, pp. 102-103.

[38] Galbraith reiterated his arguments for Agricultural Banks many times. He was contemptuous of the monetary theories of the classical economists whom he called "the best writers of fiction."   John Law, he declared, "accomplished a thousand times more for the world's industry than did the author of the *Wealth of Nations*."   *A New Chapter Added to Political Economy: Pointing Out A 100 Million Dollars Capital that May be Made Available to Canadian Industries by the Establishment of a Mortgage Bank of Issue* (Toronto, 1882), p. 4.   See also *New Monetary Theory. The Absolute Depreciation of Gold Demonstrated to the Extent of 50 per cent; The Prevalent Monetary Theory Overturned; The Nature of Money Defined* (Montreal, 1863); *Bensalem; or The New Economy.   A Dialogue for the Industrial Classes on the Financial Question* (New York, 1874); and comments to the Canadian Institute, *Proceedings of the Canadian Institute*, IV (1886-1887), 60.   Some trade union supporters advocated irredeemable notes at this time. See below, p. 129.

[39] Greenbacks became popular in Canada only when they were disappearing in the United States.   Specie payments were resumed on American national bank notes in January, 1879, although agitation for more greenbacks continued. See Chester W. Wright, *Economic History of the United States* (2nd ed.; New York, 1949), pp. 664-665.

bringing severest misery in its train without apparent cause. . . . If it was not due to natural causes, it must be due to false regulations imposed on society. He believed that the cause of the depression from which we now suffer was due to the present system of money. They had idolized gold, placed it on a throne, made it master of the world, and, to-day, it was crushing the life out of capital and destroying labour.[40]

Walter Arnold, an Ontario barrister, supported proposals for a national currency, wishing to see a restriction of banking functions. "The proper office of banks," he declared, "is simply to lend their own capital, borrow money and lend it, taking care the loan on their part falls within the terms of their borrowing, facilitate exchanges and hold money on deposit."[41] Others praised the plan, which critics called derisively the "rag-baby," but like the "Agricultural Banks" it never passed Parliament and, as in the 1850's, lost popularity with the return of prosperity and rising prices.[42]

Discussion of an irredeemable paper currency mobilized defenders of a gold standard and the existing currency system. G. Manigault of London, Ontario, employed a simple quantity theory of money and argued that any addition by government to the present note issue would simply cause inflation.

A Government issuing paper money, may increase the nominal amount of the currency *ad libitum;* it can double it, quadruple it, make it twentyfold what it was, but it cannot permanently increase the purchasing power of the currency in the slightest degree. It can only raise the nominal prices of all commodities to any height. But the twenty-fold millions

[40] *Debates,* 1879, pp. 1552-1554 and 1560.

[41] *Money and Banking* (Ottawa, 1880), p. 2. Arnold condemned the use of bank credit as money: "Did warehousemen of flour and wheat bank as those of money do, they would occasion great ups and downs in the flour and wheat market, but their practices would affect little else than flour and wheat; but those treating money in the same way making it cheap at one time and dear at another, periodically upset the whole business of the country. If therefore, the flour and wheat man deserves three years penitentiary for issuing a promise to deliver on demand what he has not got, the banker when he does the same thing, on account of the widespread misery he occasions, ought to be sent to the penitentiary for life." *Ibid.*

[42] Other writings containing arguments for an irredeemable paper currency were: Robert Bradford, *Addresses Delivered at Agincourt, April 2nd and May 7th, 1878* (Toronto, n.d.); G. D. Griffen, *Important Information on Banking, Exchange, Interest and the Value of Bank Stocks, Showing the Causes of Financial Crises and How to Prevent Them* (Hamilton, 1883); A Husbandman, *Money and the Money Question in Canada and Some Considerations Arising Therefrom* (Toronto, 1897).

of the new issue will buy no more commodities than the original millions did.[43]

Manigault used the fallacious "Banking School" argument that a "natural" volume of currency could be obtained only when competing commercial banks issued notes redeemable in specie, and he argued that any government currency, redeemable or not, was unsound in principle. He exempted "small bills" from this rule as they were already issued by the government.

No people can safely confide in a currency of promises to pay on demand, issued by the Government; for there is no higher authority to be appealed to for the enforcing of the fulfillment of these promises; and this easy mode of raising funds, perpetually tempts the administration to improvidence, extravagance, and corruption. But the Government may safely permit banks to issue promises to pay money (but not small bills), for it can provide safe-guards to enforce the keeping of these promises. The natural law controlling trade, and the rivalry of the banks with each other, will assist in keeping their issue within bounds.[44]

John Charlton described at length to the House of Commons a history of the use of precious metals as the basis for circulating media, and after condemning the proposed "National Currency," remarked that he "hoped it would be long before any considerable portion of the Canadian people would listen to such fallacious arguments with regard to the paper currency system of this country."[45] As it turned out, Charlton's hopes were fulfilled; and it was not until the 1930's that an irredeemable paper currency was seriously contemplated again.

[43] "What is Money?," *Rose-Belford's Canadian Monthly and National Review*, V (1880), 412. Manigault wrote further: "The whole theory of a National Currency, which is to banish gold and silver from circulation, and abolish them as the standards of monetary value, seems to me to be a complicated tissue elaborately woven out of a confusion of ideas as to values, as to the nature of trade and contracts, and as to what things Governments can, and what they cannot, do." P. 412.

[44] *Ibid.*, p. 418. A similar defense of the currency status quo was made by G. E. Casey, a member of Parliament, in *Money and Paper Currency, A Study for the Times* (Ottawa, 1880).

[45] *Debates*, 1879, pp. 1561-1571.

II. BANKING

The First Commercial Banks: Their Exponents and Critics

Before the establishment of regular banking facilities in the British North American colonies merchants performed many of the customary functions of banks. They bought and sold foreign exchange, held money on deposit, discounted commercial paper, and even issued their own notes, called *"bons."*[46] The export sector of the economy, dependent first on furs and later on timber and grain, was financed with British credit through local firms. The first banking enterprise was the Canadian Banking Company, established in Montreal in 1792, whose promoters were representatives of three large commercial houses, two in Montreal and one English partnership having a large trade with the colonies. Its history is not well documented but it appears to have been formed to take over the banking functions of the merchants. The outbreak of war in Europe discouraged the supporters of the scheme, and after less than a year its operations ceased.

Canadian banking began under commercial auspices and it continued in this way for some time. Merchants in Lower Canada in 1806, and again in 1808, attempted to establish a bank, but unsuccessfully because of government skepticism and growing friction between Britain and the United States. A project for a bank in Upper Canada was put forward at Kingston, but the supporters of this plan were discouraged by the expiration of the charter of the Bank of the United States in 1811 and by increased tension abroad. Following the War of 1812, after new and unsuccessful attempts had been made by Montreal merchants to obtain a charter, the Bank of Montreal was established as a private corporation with articles of association published in 1817. In 1818 three more corporate banks patterned after the Bank of Montreal were established: the Quebec Bank at Quebec City, the Bank of Canada at Montreal, and the Bank of Upper Canada at Kingston. In 1821 bills to charter the three

---

[46] See Adam Shortt, "The Hon. Wm. Allen, Merchant and Banker," *J.C.B.A.*, XXX (1922-1923), 159, and "The Hon. John Richardson, Merchant, Financier and Statesman," *J.C.B.A.*, XXIX (1921-1922), 23 ff. For an excellent brief account of the early history of Canadian banks, drawing on the work of Shortt, Breckenridge, and others, see R. Craig McIvor, *Canadian Monetary, Banking and Fiscal Development* (Toronto, 1958), pp. 12-85.

banks in Lower Canada passed the Legislature and became law in 1822. Between 1824 and 1831 the Bank of Canada was absorbed by the Bank of Montreal, leaving three banks in the two provinces. The Bank of Upper Canada at Kingston was superseded by the Bank of Upper Canada at York (now Toronto) under the control of the ruling oligarchy (later dubbed the "Family Compact") and received its charter in 1821. Banking began in the Maritimes at the same time as in Upper and Lower Canada; the Bank of New Brunswick was chartered in 1820 and the Halifax Banking Company began private operations in 1825.

In the 1830's several new banks, similar to the older ones, received charters: the City Bank of Montreal, the Commercial Bank of the Midland District at Kingston, and the Bank of Nova Scotia at Halifax in 1832, and the Gore Bank at Hamilton in 1836. Unchartered joint-stock banks were also established and helped to meet demands for increased facilities. The Agricultural Bank opened at Toronto in 1834 and the Farmers' Bank and People's Bank in 1835; in Lower Canada the Banque du Peuple became a French-Canadian competitor to the chartered banks. The Bank of British North America, incorporated in England and in the Colonies, opened branches at Quebec, Montreal, Toronto, St. John, Halifax and St. John's Newfoundland.

The example of American institutions was very important to the first banks. The bank bill of 1808 in Lower Canada was an almost exact copy of the charter of the Bank of the United States in 1792; and the Articles of Association of the Bank of Montreal and all charters after 1820 were derived from this model. Principal requirements of the charters, which were renewable every ten years, were that banks could not deal in any securities other than commercial paper, that all outstanding liabilities could not exceed triple the amount of specie paid up as capital or deposited (because capital could be loaned out this was not a reserve requirement), that all notes would be payable on demand, that branches could be opened, and finally, that the government had the right to inspect banks.[47]

The Scottish influence upon the early banking system of Canada, as well as the American, was probably significant. A large number of the first bankers were immigrants from Scotland who had been

---

[47] McIvor, *op. cit.*, p. 27.

trained before they left the old country.[48] But the most important
determinants of the system were conditions in the provinces and the
fact that banks were founded primarily by merchants for the purpose of facilitating trade. It was in the interests of the merchants to
require convertibility and limitation of the note issue and to demand
the restriction of bank lending to commercial paper. Any extra inflation which would have resulted if the banks had followed a less
conservative policy might have discredited banking and hindered
trade.

Merchants, when trying to convince the public of the importance
of banks, emphasized the need for improvement in the quantity and
quality of the currency; in particular they pointed to the unsatisfactory character of coins and "*bons.*" They argued that as the economy developed and commerce increased, the money supply had to
grow in proportion; evidently they believed the fallacy that, regardless of changes in the price level, a certain quantity of money is
required for any number of transactions.[49] One advocate of a bank in
1806, after noting that "never yet, to my knowledge, have any remarks, on such a measure been offered to the public," explained:

In all countries the circulating medium should be proportionate to the
wants and useful purposes of the inhabitants; where commerce does not
exist no other is required than hard money as it is wanted for few other
purposes than procuring the necessaries of life, and, comparatively speaking, little will suffice; but where commerce takes her busy stand money
is its life, and must there be more easily and abundantly procured. . . .

Because, the writer continued, the quantity of coin was not "sufficient. . . . Different mediums of intercourse must be resorted to,
of which none is so safe, so convenient, and so adapted to the purpose as the notes of a Bank, authorized and supported by the monied
interest of the country."[50]

[48] R. M. Breckenridge has laid great stress upon the importance of the Scottish
experience in Canadian banking. See "The Canadian Banking System 1817-1890,"
Publications of the American Economic Association, X (1895), 34-35, and *passim.*
Adam Shortt, on the other hand, minimized this factor. See "*The Canadian Banking System 1817-1890.* Some Critical Observations," *J.C.B.A.*, III (1895-1896),
100-106.

[49] McIvor, *op. cit.*, pp. 25-30.

[50] A. T., letter dated Dec. 1, 1806, Quebec *Mercury*, Jan. 5, 1807, reprinted in
H. A. Innis and A. R. M. Lower, eds., *Select Documents in Canadian Economic
History*, *1783-1885*, pp. 370-371.

John Richardson, one of the founders of the Bank of Montreal in 1817, explained the merchants' position in detail in a statement of "the general principles of banking" to the Lower Canada House of Assembly in 1808.[51] Citing "Dr. Adam Smith, who, upon the subject of political economy has written with an intelligence and profundity of observation, beyond any person," he observed that banks had been formed in other countries, with "increasing industry, confidence and credit" to issue notes as supplements to scarce coin. Richardson believed, as did Smith, that so long as loans were on bona fide commercial paper and notes were convertible into specie, overissue was impossible.

Circulation is like a sponge, which can imbibe only a certain quantity of water, and when full, any excess must immediately return to the reservoir from whence it was drawn. So it is with paper. The moment the circulation is full, the excess will return upon the Bank, and be exchanged for Specie.[52]

Richardson declared that the state should require convertibility of bank notes and might keep a paternal eye on bank operations, but should never dictate what reserves were to be held in specie against notes. "What *disproportion* may safely be admitted between such paper and such gold and silver? This is a question, to which no precise answer can be given, as the disproportion must fluctuate according to a great variety of circumstances."[53] Richardson regarded banks as institutions which, if properly constituted, would provide the correct increase in the money supply with growth of the economy. As a disciple of Smith he made no attempt to argue that banks caused growth but only that they facilitated transactions which resulted from man's propensity to "truck, barter and exchange." Other merchants and financiers acted as apologists for banking, but Richardson's comments were representative.[54]

[51] For biographical material about Richardson and comments on this address, see Adam Shortt, "The Hon. John Richardson, Merchant, Financier and Statesman," *J.C.B.A.*, XXIX (1921-1922), 25-26 and *passim*.

[52] Quebec *Mercury*, IV (May 2, 1808), 138.

[53] *Ibid.*; compare this passage with Adam Smith, *The Wealth of Nations* (Modern Library Edition; New York, 1938), p. 284.

[54] See Adam Shortt, "Horatio Gates, Wholesale Merchant, Banker and Legislator," *J.C.B.A.*, XXX (1922-1923), 34-47; "Austin Cuvillier, Merchant, Legislator and Banker," *ibid.*, XXX (1922-1923), 304-316; "The Hon. Peter McGill, Banker, Merchant and Civic Leader," *ibid.*, XXXI (1923-1924), 297-307; "The

Critics accused banks of a multitude of sins: too much credit and too little, debasement of the coinage, monopoly practices, and favoritism. William Lyon Mackenzie, with the support of farmers in Upper Canada, proclaimed the dangers of inflation and evils of monopoly, and in 1830 announced that if the Bank of Upper Canada were not restrained, products would soon be exchanged for mere "paper rags."[55] Only four years later John Langton, a recent immigrant from England, expressed the opposite view also held by many people that the notes of the Bank of Upper Canada were inadequate, although he agreed with Mackenzie that the fault lay in monopoly.

The bank issues are not half sufficient for the wants of the country, and they are under great restrictions in this respect from Government, but above all they are a monopoly. When they are refusing discount to everyone else, the directors and their friends find favour in their sight; they are a monopoly, not by statute but by the circumstances of the country.[56]

Langton's complaint of inadequacy and favoritism was echoed by French Canadians in Lower Canada and by others throughout the colonies in demands for private or joint-stock corporate banks.[57]

Many of the demands for more banks and an increased circulation resulted from confusion over the difference between money and capital, as for example, when the Montreal *Gazette* explained to the citizens of Kingston in 1836 how easy it was to build lumber mills with bank paper.

If the people of Kingston wish to increase the trade of their town

---

Hon. Adam Ferrie, Reformer, Merchant, and Financier," *ibid.*, XXXII (1924-1925), 50-63; "The Hon. Wm. Allen, Merchant and Banker," *ibid.*, XXX (1922-1923), 154-166; "John S. Cartwright, Banker, Legislator and Judge," *ibid.*, XXX (1922-1923), 475-487; "The Hon. George Moffatt, Merchant-Statesman and Banker," *ibid.*, XXXII (1924-1925), 177-190.

[55] "Report on the State of the Currency," *Journal of the Upper Canada House of Assembly*, 1830, Appendix. See comments upon Mackenzie and this report in Bray Hammond, *Banks and Politics in America* (Princeton, 1957), pp. 652-656. Mackenzie reprinted portions of pamphlets by the American hard-money economists James Ronaldson and William Gouge in support of his position. Lillian F. Gates, "The Decided Policy of William Lyon MacKenzie," *C.H.R.*, XL (1959), 193.

[56] *Early Days in Upper Canada: Letters of John Langton from the Backwoods of Upper Canada and the Audit Office of the Province of Canada*, ed. W. A. Langton (Toronto, 1926), pp. 100-101.

[57] See H. A. Innis and A. R. M. Lower, eds., *Select Documents in Canadian Economic History 1783-1885*, pp. 373-374; and *Thoughts on the Banking System of Upper Canada and on the Present Crisis* (Toronto, 1837), pp. 3-4.

why not enter into this valuable lumber trade with New York themselves? Why not raise a Joint Stock Company, for the express purpose, and if money be wanting, what is easier than to apply to Parliament for Banking privileges; and should that be refused as it probably might, what can prevent them from issuing their own notes, in the same way as the Farmer's and Peoples Banks do, or as the Bank of British North America intends to do? We have been asleep too long—it is time to get up and be stirring, and not suffer the Yankees to engross our trade, while we stand and look on with our hands in our pockets.[58]

In contrast to those who viewed banking as a panacea, some held just as exaggerated views of its inherent evils. It was even alleged in Halifax in 1835 that banks caused emigration from Nova Scotia.

The introduction of Banks, the *Recorder* [a Halifax newspaper] conceives, has tended to this result; acquiring an intimate acquaintance with the affairs of every individual in the community, which, by the way, is of limited extent, they, it is asserted, use the power thus acquired to the detriment and hindrance of many, who, although not rich might yet, by a judiciously applied confidence, become useful and valuable members of the community.[59]

Neither the arguments supporting banks nor criticisms of them exhibited great perception or imagination. Merchants and bankers stressed improvements in the circulating medium. Less realistic advocates foresaw a magical increase in capital. Critics talked of inflation, monopoly, and a variety of often ill-defined evils. The best analysis of the importance of banking came surprisingly from a man who was neither an active exponent nor critic of banks, but was rather a remarkable school teacher living in Upper Canada.

The Banking Theory of John Rae[60]

In his *New Principles of Political Economy*, written in Upper Canada in the 1830's, John Rae, unlike the Canadian merchants, argued that banks had more important functions than simply the issue of notes, and that they were institutions causing, not merely as-

---

[58] Reprinted in H. A. Innis and A. R. M. Lower, eds., *op. cit.*, p. 255.

[59] From the Montreal *Gazette*, reprinted in H. A. Innis and A. R. M. Lower, *op. cit.*, p. 397.

[60] Rae's general contributions to economics are examined below, pp. 122-127. Portions of this section first appeared in my article "John Rae: Undiscovered Exponent of Canadian Banks," *Canadian Banker*, LXVI (Winter, 1959) 110-115.

sisting, economic growth: "the popular notion, that the advantages of banking are limited to the substitution of paper for specie, and the creation to that amount of fictitious capital, is altogether erroneous."[61] The scarcity of currency and prevalence of barter in new countries, he explained, were the result, not as some people alleged, of a small supply of coin or spendthrift habits of the users, but rather of the great scarcity and high productivity of capital. In recently settled areas capital goods gave high rates of profit and were purchased abroad, and therefore money quickly left to pay for imports. Because the returns from having liquidity did not equal the yield from capital the inhabitants made do with barter; and if all the banks did was add to the money supply, as most of their advocates suggested, this in itself was no reason why the use of money would increase. Rae went on to show that banks, by the provision of services and not only by the issue of notes, encouraged exchange and raised the demand for money at the same time that they increased its supply.

To illustrate the state of commerce where there were no banks, and to indicate ways in which banks led to improvements, Rae described conditions in remote parts of Upper Canada at the time he wrote. His description would have applied to most parts of the colonies a few years before. Trade, he explained, was carried on by balancing purchases against sales with a single merchant and by making up any difference with book credit.

Every dealer provides himself with a general assortment of all sorts of commodities in demand in the settlement he inhabits, and reckons on being paid for them in the shape of grain, potash, pork, beef, and other commodities, in the formation of which his customers are engaged. But in this sort of barter, one article will generally fall short or exceed the value of the other, a pound of tea will not exchange for a hog, nor a quarter of wheat for a dozen pounds of sugar. To obviate the difficulty, the merchant opens an account with each of his customers, charging him with the goods furnished, and giving him credit for the produce received, and in this way perhaps all the transactions between the two are managed, either by barter or credit, without the assistance of a dollar of cash.[62]

These barter transactions usually involved compensation for deferred

---

[61] *New Principles*, p. 411.
[62] *Ibid.*, pp. 183-184.

payment as well as for the articles sold when merchants, lacking other means of providing credit for their customers, were compelled to add the cost of waiting to prices. The average storekeeper was not able to determine the trustworthiness of each customer and often, wishing to increase his sales at any cost, extended credit to those he knew did not deserve it. He then raised the prices of all his goods—according to Rae by as much as 30 per cent—to take account of the delay in payment. This penalty for those who paid immediately discouraged transactions and thereby the division of labor.

Capital loans, as well as the exchange of goods, were complicated and difficult in the absence of banks. For example, Rae wrote, ". . .it is a common practice in many parts of North America, especially in new settlements, to sell cattle and sheep on trust, the terms being that double the number thus transferred, is to be returned in four or five years, as the agreement may be made."[63] If, however, the lender of the animals wished to make the loan for an irregular period of time, or if the borrower were a stranger, the loan could not be contracted. Because of the obvious necessity that the borrower and lender have exactly opposite needs with regard to cattle and sheep, and that the lender have an intimate knowledge of the prospective borrowers, many loans did not take place and capital accumulation was restricted.

Banks in a frontier economy, Rae explained, increased exchange and the use of money, first, because the extension of credit was kept distinct from the merchandise trade, and both, thereby, were improved and enlarged. The banker, able from experience to assess credit worthiness and not "urged on by the dread of stocks lying on his hands too long" provided funds only to deserving borrowers at market rates of interest. Because the storekeeper no longer had to wait for his receipts, he lowered the prices of his goods to their actual costs; and with charges to customers both for credit and merchandise accurate and fair, transactions and the division of labor increased. In addition to improvements resulting from the specialized handling of credit, the accessibility of loan facilities made other exchanges possible. Rae gave the example of a farmer who, in the absence of banks, was unable to buy a team of horses because the loss of income in holding money idle until a horse dealer happened by

[63] *Ibid.*, p. 194.

raised their cost to a prohibitive level. With a bank in his community the farmer was able to obtain a loan at the time a dealer arrived and to liquidate property after the purchase. Because the farmer acquired horses he was able to produce more efficiently, the horse dealer was able to extend his business, and the existence of banking facilities again had increased the demand for and use of money, making the country more productive.

Rae was particularly impressed by the potentialities of deposit banking, which was increasing in Canada at the time he wrote. (Total deposits of the chartered banks in the Province of Canada were almost as great as their notes in circulation in 1841, and by 1851 deposits exceeded notes). Primarily, he stated, it was necessary for any growing economy to have an institution to collect savings and to make them available to investors. But, apart from the savings function, he also understood how fractional-reserve demand deposits were created, and he treated them legitimately as a component of the money supply. He explained the use of checks on deposits as an improvement in the efficiency of currency: "When a man wants cash, he goes to the bank for it, when he has cash, he carries it to the bank. Money never lies idle."[64] When notes and coins were loaned by banks and returned as deposits they remained in each hand a shorter length of time and experienced an increase in what he called their "celerity of motion." Because, he added, bank deposits could do some of the work of currency, "it follows that the more perfect as an art deposit banking becomes, the less, other circumstances being equal, is the amount of the circulating medium required, and the greater the saving to the community."[65]

The rate charged bank borrowers for money which would in large part return to the banking system as new deposits, Rae explained, made it possible for interest to be paid to depositors. (Interest on deposits was an innovation brought to Canada in Rae's time by the Agricultural Bank and was greeted with little enthusiasm by the other firms which were forced by competition to follow suit). Deposit interest, he believed, was desirable for three reasons: first because

[65] *Ibid.*, p. 411. It is interesting to note that this last statement by Rae was well borne out by history. When he wrote, bank notes and coins constituted more than half the money supply, whereas today, after an enormous growth in deposit banking, currency has fallen to approximately one-tenth.

[64] *Ibid.*, p. 187.

payments brought currency back to the banks to be loaned out again; second because the use of money was made more attractive if people lost less earning power than when holding cash; and finally because the deposit rate, with the loan rate, could be used to control the flow of currency out of a bank. Deposits, and particularly those paying interest, Rae concluded, were another service whereby banks stimulated exchange, increased the demand for money, and improved the division of labor.

In contrast to the allegations of some bank critics that all bank notes were inflationary and therefore contrary to the public interest, Rae showed clearly that a larger money supply as a result of the introduction of banking and consisting in part of bank issue could be taken up by increased exchanges encouraged by banks, and need not cause a rise in prices. Although one bank note, backed itself only in part by specie, led to the creation of several times that amount in new demand deposits, all this additional money did not have to bring inflation—"in the same way," he explained, "as when a road is much improved, though one horse may be sufficient to transport what three did before, yet the commodities transported so increase, that there are, notwithstanding, thrice the number of horses employed." Rae believed that when banks were formed, the quantity of money rose with the addition of notes and deposits, but at the same time the number of transactions increased, and therefore the price level could remain constant or even fall.

Rae was careful to point out that dangers as well as benefits could accompany banking. Because notes and deposits were backed by the credit of borrowers, errors in judgment or dishonesty of bankers could result in loss to the note and deposit holders, and might even cause a general collapse. In new countries, he remarked (probably referring at this point to the United States more than to Canada), the danger was particularly serious—"there is a great temptation to divert the fund . . . to speculations promising great gain, but sometimes producing great loss. Banking will consequently be in general safest, where capital [meaning national capital] is most largely accumulated."[66] A second danger in banking "had its origin in the system of credit itself." Because bank money was backed in large part by debt, it depended for its very existence on "prevailing opin-

---

[66] *Ibid.*, p. 190.

ion" and "public confidence"; and one criterion for judging the quality of a banking system was its ability to withstand a general panic. The best safeguards against both the misuse of funds and failures brought on by sudden losses of confidence, Rae declared, were large, heavily capitalized firms with many stockholders: first, because owners through a board of directors were better able than note holders and depositors to exercise a restraining influence on loan activities; and second, because a large capitalization caused a correspondingly small portion of a bank's liabilities to be subject to call on demand. He concluded that the best system of banking yet devised was that of Scotland, after which many of the American and Canadian banks of his day were patterned; and his faith was justified by the ability of all the Canadian banks to survive the crisis of 1837. Rae's warning about numerous small banks is interesting, nevertheless, considering the number of unsuccessful firms that were chartered later in the century.

In the years that followed the publication of the *New Principles* Canadian bankers could well have made use of Rae's sound logical arguments when defending the existence of their institutions. His writings, however, except where they touched on commercial policy, were completely ignored in Canada. Rae's statements would not necessarily have caused alteration of banking practices, but they would have helped convince the public of the importance of banks. Instead of being able to explain, as Rae argued, that banks need not be inflationary and are absolutely essential for growth, bankers were forced to fall back on the much weaker defense that their notes were desirable supplements to coined money. It was also unfortunate, perhaps, that Canadian legislators and their constituents lacked knowledge of Rae's theories when assessing the desirability of encouraging banks to enter new territories.

Growth of the Banking System

Slow, steady growth has been the characteristic feature of Canadian banking development. The system evolved gradually with few important innovations, and the signers of the articles of association of the Bank of Montreal in 1817 would not have been surprised at the appearance of their firm a century later. Periods of disturbance occurred and changes were made, but unlike the history of banking in the United States there were no revolutions involving the formation of a National Banking System or a Federal Reserve. Before 1914 proposals were made for sweeping reform, but they were never adopted, and each lack of success inhibited subsequent discussion.

Economic depression and civil rebellion began in Upper and Lower Canada in 1837, and although no banks failed in the stormy years before 1841, most offices suspended specie payments. After Union of the Provinces discussion centered on Sydenham's unacceptable proposal for a Provincial Bank of Issue,[67] the one result of which was a tax on notes in excess of a bank's specie, legal tender, and government securities. Bank charters were revised under the Sydenham administration and several more stringent provisions were inserted, including double liability of stockholders; greater uniformity and clarity of charters were obtained after a Select Committee of the Legislature prepared a concise statement of desirable restrictions.[68] During the 1840's several banks were permitted to enlarge their capital, but the waning influence of the essentially conservative Colonial Office still acted as a restraining force.

An interesting departure from chartered banking occurred in 1850 with the passage of a Free Banking Act. This act stated that any group which complied with certain stipulations and which deposited an amount of government securities equal to, or greater than, $100,000 with the Receiver-General could issue the same amount of their own notes and carry on a banking business in one place. The principle of "free banking" introduced in New York State had been discussed in Canada as early as the 1830's, and in 1836 the position of its advocates was summarized as follows:

Our arguments in favour of free banks are—1st. That we believe the security to the public is greater than under any other system. . . .

2nd. We are against all monopolies. . . .

3rd. We believe that a Free Banking system would have the effect of bringing British Capital into the Province.[69]

---

[67] See above, pp. 77-79.

[68] *Journals of the Legislative Assembly of the Province of Canada*, 1841, Appendix O. The Committee described earlier charters as "complicated and unintelligible."

[69] *Thoughts on the Banking System of Upper Canada and on the Present Crisis* (Toronto, 1837), pp. 3-4. See also Bray Hammond, *op. cit.*, p. 666.

By 1850, after the steady increase of "free banks" in the United States, the strongest supporter of the scheme in Canada, William Hamilton Merritt, was able to make it an important issue—particularly in small towns where there were no chartered banks. Opposition came from two directions as the Colonial Office distrusted American precedent and the chartered banks feared increased competition. Few new firms took advantage of the Act because issuing notes by depositing government securities in an amount equal to note issue, and in addition holding specie reserves sufficient to assure convertibility, resulted in rewards that were not highly attractive.[70] A member of the Legislative Assembly remarked in 1854:

The failure of the Free Banking law arose from the fact that it did not give so great facilities as are enjoyed by the chartered banks; banks established under it could not compete with them; and the result was that the Free Banking law, which was intended to give bank facilities to every body, took them from every body but the chartered banks.[71]

For the chartered bankers the Act had served a purpose, as hereafter they could point to the "failure" of free banking in Canada. The only real concession to reform was a requirement passed shortly after that every bank had to hold one-tenth of its capital in government securities.

In the 1850's banks were permitted to enlarge their capital (and hence their notes and deposits), to invest in speculative securities, and to hold mortgages on real estate and personal property. As a result, reserve ratios fell, and during the financial panic of 1857 banks were forced to reduce sharply their loans and discounts, seriously restricting trade. William Brown of Montreal expressed dissatisfaction felt by many when he wrote:

Our present credit system rests . . . upon the treacherous foundation of a paper currency, such as note, bill, bond, or mortgage. Such being the case it was no difficult matter to foster a fictitious demand by means of a fictitious supply.[72]

---

[70] See Bray Hammond, *op. cit.*, p. 667.

[71] *Scrapbook Debates*, Oct. 24, 1854 (filmed by the Canadian Library Association).

[72] "Remarks on the Value of Money: and on the Principles which Regulate its Demand and Supply," *Hunt's Merchants' Magazine and Commercial Review*, XLII (1860), 410.

During the depression of the fifties even the bankers realized the need for improvement of some kind, and in 1859 they conceded for the first time that compulsory reserves against notes and deposits, as well as government supervision, might be desirable.[73] However, public attention was partly distracted by proposals for an irredeemable paper currency, and as was so often the case, when the memory of depression faded so did enthusiasm for the reform. Criticism of banking was not rekindled until failures of the Bank of Upper Canada and the Commercial Bank in 1866 and 1877 brought the subject up for discussion at Confederation.

The British North America Act of 1867 placed currency and banking under the control of the Parliament of Canada, and acts passed shortly after Confederation extended bank charters and the Provincial Note Act of 1866 until 1870 to provide a temporary status quo for discussion. During this period two plans were suggested, representing sharply conflicting schools of thought. The first proposal was for increased government control with legislation similar to the National Bank Act of the United States;[74] it was supported by E. H. King, General Manager of the Bank of Montreal, who envisaged a profit for his firm as government issue agent, and by John Rose, the Minister of Finance, who foresaw a ready market for the national debt and a uniform currency for the Dominion. Under the plan banks would have only indirect issue power and a compulsory reserve requirement: each would receive notes printed in its name by the government after deposit of government securities with the Treasury, and would hold specie equal to 20 per cent of its notes and one-seventh of deposits not paying interest. The plan was similar to the Free Banking Act of 1850; in its currency provisions it differed from Sydenham's plan in 1840 and Galt's proposals of 1860 only in that the determination of the extent of the issue and obligation for specie payment would rest with the banks rather than the government. Replying to charges that his scheme would destroy desirable flexibility, Rose argued that bank deposits could provide ample adjustments in the money supply over seasonal fluctuations.

[73] See "Proceedings of the Special Committee on Banking and Currency," *Journals of the Legislative Assembly of the Province of Canada,* 1859, Appendix 67.

[74] This act, passed in 1863, had provided for a uniform currency issued by the Treasury on the deposit of government securities. See Bray Hammond, *op. cit.,* pp. 725-727.

Bankers and some businessmen were, as usual, strongly opposed to any extensive government issue of paper money, but recognizing that reform was in the wind, asked that improvements be made in the existing system. A Select Committee of the Senate reported in 1868 that, in the opinion of bankers:

. . . it would be for the general interests of the country, to return to the banking system as it existed before the passing of the Provincial Note Act, with additional guarantees for the certain redemption of bank-notes on demand; limiting the issue of the same, providing greater security to depositors; recommending that an improved Form of Return be made by the Banks; suggesting a Government inspection, and other amendments.[75]

The bankers realized that a government currency might be introduced over their objections and explained that if this should happen they would prefer the National Bank System of the United States to an extension of the Provincial Note Act or an issue of irredeemable paper. The Senate report continued:

. . . if the financial requirements of the Dominion should induce the Government to desire the introduction of a new system, including the taking possession of the currency of the country (which your Committee would strongly deprecate), then your Committee would recommend that the issue of the paper currency be based upon the deposit with the Government of public securities of the Dominion, under a system somewhat analogous to that of the National Bank system of the neighbouring United States, but redeemable on demand—the Government regulating the issue under the authority of Parliament; the banks through which the notes are issued, being responsible for their instant redemption.[76]

In 1869 bankers made specific proposals to the House of Commons as an alternative to government currency, including a larger capital requirement, greater shareholder liability, closer government supervision, compulsory reserves in specie against liabilities, more limited note circulation, and a stipulation that notes would be a first charge on assets. Bankers emphasized the inflexibility that would accompany a bond-secured currency, the disastrous financial loss they would in-

[75] *Journals of the Senate of Canada*, I (1867-1868), Appendix I, 32.
[76] *Ibid.*

cur, and the monopoly position that would be secured by the Bank of Montreal.[77]

The plan for a National Bank System was defeated in Parliament in 1869; Rose resigned from the Cabinet and Sir Francis Hincks, the new Minister of Finance, achieved a workable compromise between the conflicting viewpoints. Two acts in 1870 and 1871 set forth the powers and obligations of the banks, which considering changes that had been seriously contemplated were remarkably like the terms of the expiring charters.[78]   The only concession to reformers was that all notes under four dollars were to be issued by the government and held as a fraction of the commercial banks' reserves.[79] The Bank of Montreal was replaced as redemption agent by branches of the Receiver-General's Department, and the tax on bank circulation as well as the requirement that government securities be held in a stated proportion to bank capital were discontinued. Charters were required for every bank and were to be revised every ten years.   The stipulated minimum capitalization was $500,000, of which $100,000 had to be paid up immediately and another $100,000 within two years of the start of operations.   Shareholders could increase the capital at any time, but were liable for double their holdings in the event of failure.   The clause in former bank charters which had limited the liabilities of any bank to a multiple of the paid-up capital plus specie and government debentures was replaced by a statement that notes could not exceed total paid-up capital; still, no legal reserves were required.   Banks were permitted to make loans on the same type of security they had accepted before 1867—including warehouse receipts for personal property—and in addition on "shares in the capital stock of any other bank, the bonds or de-

[77] "First Report of the Committee on Banking and Currency," *Journals of the House of Commons of Canada*, 1869, Appendix I.

[78] Between 1868 and 1870 bankers organized themselves as an effective lobby, and in 1869 alone submitted sixty petitions to Parliament "praying that no change of a fundamental nature be made in the present system of banking." *Journals of the House of Commons*, 1869, index, p. 15. Prosperity after Confederation, moreover, permitted the bankers to relax their vigilance. Most of the discussion of banking legislation enacted under Hincks took place quietly between bankers and the government and there was little opposition in parliament. See G. Hague, "The Late Mr. E. H. King," *J.C.B.A.*, IV (1896-1897), pp. 25-28, and R. M. Breckenridge, *op. cit.*, pp. 245-254.

[79] Dominion notes were convertible into gold, and henceforth saved the banks expense in holding specie.

bentures of municipal or other corporations, and Dominion, Provincial, British or foreign public securities."[80] Restrictions were principally against the appearance of small, shaky institutions rather than against any instability in the system.

Seven years of prosperity followed Confederation, and by 1874 twenty-eight new bank charters had been added to the twenty-eight in 1867. Danger signals began to appear when the proportion of gold and Dominion notes held against bank notes and demand deposits fell from almost 44 per cent to slightly more than 26 per cent.[81] In the depression which began in 1874 several banks failed and lending was sharply contracted. Suggestions for public inspection and for a reserve of government securities against notes were again put forward, but discussion of public policy in the 1870's centered on changes in the tariff; the first decennial revision of the Bank Act in 1880 made only minor adjustments.

During the 1880's the banks went through a boom and another collapse, and at the Bank Act revision of 1890, G. E. Foster, the Minister of Finance, proposed legal reserve requirements of specie and Dominion notes against bank liabilities, restriction of the note issue to a fraction of a bank's capital, and an independent public audit. The result of the proposals was the same as in 1841, 1860, 1869, and 1880. On all points Foster was persuaded to alter his position by the following arguments of prominent bankers: first, that reserve requirements were ineffective and crippling to the banks; second, that bank issues were too seasonably variable to permit any additional restriction of total quantity; and finally, that public auditors would not be competent judges of bank safety and might create either needless concern or unjustified complacency.[82] The Bank Act of 1890 did embody several new provisions, the most important of which was the establishment of a "Bank Circulation Redemption Fund" equal to 5 per cent of the note circulation of all the banks, making them mutually responsible for their issue.

The Canadian Bankers' Association was formed in 1891 to protect the interests of the bankers, a function which had in fact been effectively performed for many years by individual bankers and in-

---

[80] *Act Relating to Banks and Banking*, 1871 (34 Vic., cap. 5).

[81] C. A. Curtis, *Statistical Contributions to Canadian Economics: Statistics of Banking* (Toronto, 1931).

[82] See A. B. Jamieson, *Chartered Banking in Canada* (Toronto, 1953), pp. 26-30.

formal committees. The organization was incorporated and empowered to publish a journal, to establish subsections, to maintain clearing houses under the supervision of the Treasury Board, and to take charge of suspended banks.

After 1890 and before 1914 amendments to the banking system were of a minor nature. Provision was made for mergers (seventeen of which took place before World War I), and authority to make loans on goods in production was gradually extended. Seasonal fluctuations in the need for funds, particularly after settlement of the West, led to the increase of Dominion notes and permission for the banks to issue their own notes above the amount of their paid-up capital. After the repeated failures of past demands for reform, the banks' critics, faced with the increasing size and stability of the system, in this period seldom voiced proposals for fundamental change.

III. SUMMARY AND CONCLUSION

The most important monetary discussions have been outlined in this chapter against the background of history; it has not been intended to suggest here in the comfort of retrospect a monetary policy which might have been best for Canadian development. Metallic coinage was never highly controversial; a gold standard with American units of account was adopted in 1853 after little argument. Throughout the period under examination the relation of banks to the paper currency was the most often debated monetary topic. Banks were started in 1817 by merchants and struggled to retain their distinctly commercial character. Bankers claimed that they should facilitate trade, and in the public interest resist vehemently both attempts by farmers and others to obtain credit on collateral other than commercial paper (or later goods in production), and endeavors by government to impose restrictions. However, bank notes and deposits were not always a safe medium of exchange, were heterogeneous in character, could not be used as an instrument of public finance, and experienced frequent expansions and contractions. As a result bankers repeatedly were compelled to defend their institutions against persistent demands for an issue of government notes, and for other reforms—notably minimum gold reserves against liabilities.

Criticism of banks was almost exclusively of their note issue and seldom of their large unit size or branch operations. At first complaint came from farmers who argued that bank notes were necessarily inflationary and from others who said their supply was inadequate. Later, a succession of prominent statesmen contended that for both monetary and financial reasons the government should issue a national currency, which would be redeemable in specie and backed by gold and public securities. Some critics, particularly those who found themselves unable to procure bank credit, called for an issue of irredeemable notes. Bankers on the defensive replied that the financing of raw-material production required a money supply that was not tied either to gold or to government securities; they argued that to insure crop sales more notes were needed at some seasons than at others. This position, that a changing quantity of money was needed for a fluctuating volume of trade and could be provided only by unrestricted corporate banks had more widespread appeal than did the claim that a fixed money supply could be "adequate" at all seasons but might cause fluctuations in the price level and interest rates. Would-be reformers asserted that with a fixed government note issue, deposits would provide adequate seasonal monetary flexibility, and any remaining constancy in the money supply would be less injurious than would a business cycle aggravated by corporate-bank contractions and suspensions. Nevertheless, bankers triumphed in all their conflicts with critics; bank spokesmen even had to give their sanction before the government could issue small bills and take precautions against the growth of weak firms.

The strong position held by merchants, bankers, and financiers in the Canadian community partly accounts for their ability to dominate the determination of monetary policy. However, banking and currency were seldom important political issues and were considered less urgent than questions of commercial policy and national development. Monetary theory was a subject which laymen could not master easily, and the paucity of writing indicates the absence of sustained interest. Before professional economists were present in universities and government the bankers themselves were the best qualified experts on banking. Except in the depths of a depression, even an influential finance minister had little chance to enact reforms, faced as he was with formidable opposition from bankers and apathy from an uncomprehending public.

With the single exception of John Rae, who examined the significance of banks for economic growth but was totally unappreciated in Canada, no one wrote at length and with ability about monetary matters. To some extent the influence of different schools and traditions was evident. Bankers defended the existence of private note-issuing corporations with arguments taken from the English "Banking School" and Adam Smith. Some bank critics supported the "Currency School" principles of Samuel Loyd and Sir Robert Peel, adhered to by the Bank of England after 1844; they favored a single state-controlled bank of issue with notes, other than a fixed quantity issued to the government, backed entirely by gold. Other critics suggested adoption of banking innovations from the United States (free banking, the National Banking System, and greenbacks), and were familiar with the appropriate American arguments.

Not until after World War I did Canadian academic and government economists make the first imaginative and original approaches to domestic monetary problems and make significant contributions to the literature.[83]

[83] See Irving Brecher, *Monetary and Fiscal Thought and Policy in Canada 1919-1939* (Toronto, 1957).

PART TWO

Economic Thought and Economic Science

The second half of this study deals with the acceptance and development of economic science in publications, in government, in learned societies, and in educational institutions. The general position of economics in intellectual life is examined in Chapter 4 together with writings on economic topics not included in Part One. The teaching of economics in universities, course contents, and texts are described in Chapter 5. The writings of senior professors who were the first Canadians to devote a major portion of their careers to the science are covered in Chapter 6.

4

The Development of Economic Science

I. BEFORE THE NATIONAL POLICY

Before the industrialization and westward expansion which began after 1879 and made possible urban development and strong universities, economics had a small place in Canadian intellectual life. There were no "economists" as such, and the few persons who were interested either in theory or in analysis received little encouragement from the public and the press. Apart from discussion of land settlement, banking, currency, and commercial policy described in Part One, noteworthy writing on economics was confined to a single journal, *The Canadian Monthly*, and to one semi-learned society, the Canadian Institute. John Rae, the most able economist the country produced in the nineteenth century, was hardly recognized in Canada and published his major work in Boston.

Position of Economics

Interest in economics was not sufficient to have it generally accepted as a science. Libraries contained few books on the subject, and there were not many public lectures or avenues of publication to which would-be economists might bring their work.[1] The only classes, outside the universities, were given in mechanics' institutes principally by lawyers and clergymen.[2] Many people associated the

---

[1] The Mercantile Library of Montreal in 1844 contained only 15 books on economics out of a total of 1,160 items. See *Act of Incorporation, Rules and Regulations, and Library Catalogue of the Mercantile Library Association of Montreal* (Montreal, 1844). The only three persons I have discovered who gave public lectures on political economy before Confederation are J. A. A. Belle, a Montreal lawyer, the Reverend George Bourne of Quebec City, and the Reverend W. T. Wishart of Saint John, New Brunswick. See H. J. Morgan, *Bibliotheca Canadensis* (Ottawa, 1867), pp. 26, 45, and 400.

[2] In the mechanics' institutes of Upper Canada "Political and Social Economy" was ranked number sixteen among twenty-six subjects with one class in principles

term "political economy" with the increasingly unpopular commercial policy of free trade, which initially implied abandonment of profitable imperial preferences and later denial of self-imposed protection of domestic industry. The fact that free traders for a long time made frequent references to the theory and literature of economics helped strengthen this impression. For example, writers in the *Canadian Economist* defending free trade in the 1840's, quoted liberally such authorities as Smith, McCulloch, Malthus, Lauderdale, Say, Torrens, Storch, Sismondi, Garnier, Whately, and Bastiat; after outlining the pronouncements of one authority, a writer concluded smugly "those principles are founded in truth, and susceptible of the most rigid demonstration."[3] Etienne Parent, a vocal advocate of free trade in French Canada, explained: "The study of political economy is necessary and therefore obligatory for everyone."[4] After Confederation the Liberal party, in opposing the National Policy of high tariffs, treated political economy practically as revealed truth. It is easy to understand why for most people there was no distinction between the study of economics and a policy of laissez faire.

Economics suffered as a result of this identification of the subject with free trade from an early date. George Young told of the frigid reception accorded his economist-father "Agricola" by the Nova Scotia legislators in the 1820's:

. . .whenever he referred to Political Economy,—a science in which he was profoundly versed,—some of the leaders of that day invariably rewarded him with a sneer; and he was told it was a science not fitted for a young country,—in other words, that "we were not old enough to be wise."[5]

---

and another to provide "some knowledge of the Commercial, Financial and Statistical History of the United Kingdom and of Canada." The texts were *Elements of Political Economy*, by James Mill; *Principles of Political Economy*, by John Stuart Mill; *The Phenomena of Industrial Life*, edited by the Dean of Hereford; and Whately's *Lectures on Political Economy*. The course listing explained carefully: "N.B.—The Principles of Political Economy, by John Stuart Mill, need be studied only by those who aspire to a first-class Certificate." *Journal of the Board of Arts and Manufactures for Upper Canada*, I (1861), 10.
  [3] *Canadian Economist*, I (1847), 339. See also above pp. 60-62 ff.
  [4] "L'Importance de l'étude de l'économie politique," *Le Répertoire National*, IV (1850), 37 (translation). See above, p. 64, and below, pp. 145-147.
  [5] G. R. Young, *On Colonial Literature, Science and Education; Written with a View of Improving the Literary, Educational, and Public Institutions of British North America* (Halifax, 1842), p. 45.

The disillusioned authors of a protectionist pamphlet in 1849 declared with bitterness that political economy was "a science which is yet in its infancy and the terms of which are used by different eminent writers to express different meanings."[6]   For a few years after 1850 some protectionists viewed political economy with mixed feelings when leaders such as Isaac Buchanan and Sir John A. Macdonald were able to cite authorities in support of high tariffs; but many believed that any recourse to "theory" weakened their case, and absolute condemnation increased as discussion became more acrimonious.   Walter Arnold, a protectionist writer, described both free trade and political economy as "simple nonsense," and J. B. Hurlbert criticized all teaching of the subject, adding that "the opinions of protectionists should, at least, be taught side by side with those of free trade."[7]   A Conservative member of Parliament in 1876, exasperated by the frequent references of Liberal members to political economy, explained his understanding of the science.   His ludicrous statement may not unfairly be considered representative of much contemporary opinion:

It will be found that the whole system of political economy in England rests upon three great pillars.   Smith's Book, written a hundred years ago, is the first pillar of the system; then Menlkins' [Malthus!] system of population which was the second great discovery in this science; and Mr. Ardles' [Ricardo!] discovery of the system of rents is the third.   Through the whole system of political economy these three principles run.   Menlkins lays it down that the population increases so fast that the production of the necessaries of life cannot keep pace with it.   This does not apply here.   We have abundance of land, and we want population to till it, so that it is a fallacy.   There they have reduced free-trade to a science.   I find it asserted in the London *Times* that those who do not believe in free trade are simpletons, and those who dare to dispute it are not entitled to be heard at all.   A very great many people will dispute it, notwithstanding what the *Times* says.   I believe that political economy is not a science.   I deny to it the right to be ranked among the sciences.   You will find no two of its exponents agree on its principles.[8]

[6] *The Policy of Free Trade*, in a series of published letters addressed to the Honourable L. H. Lafontaine, Attorney General for Canada East (Montreal, 1849), p. 6.
[7] W. Arnold, *Money and Banking* (Ottawa, 1880), p. 6; and J. B. Hurlbert, *Protection and Free Trade with Special Reference to Canada and Newly Settled Countries; History of Tariffs and What They Teach* (Ottawa, 1882), p. 43.
[8] *Debates*, 1876, p. 143.

What work there was on economic topics, apart from that discussed in Part One, was largely technical in nature. John Young in Nova Scotia wrote the famous *Letters of Agricola* on scientific farming,[9] and other writers, in particular Professor James Robb of the University of New Brunswick, were well acquainted with contemporary agricultural literature and were influential in bringing about reforms;[10] however, interest in agriculture was in improved methods and not in economics.

Politics usually counted for more than economic logic in the development of Canadian transportation, therefore few persons theorized on this subject. One noteworthy exception was Thomas C. Keefer, who, himself engaged in transport construction, sketched the history of canals and provided a rationale for the railway boom of the 1850's.[11] Stressing the value of local lines more than trunk routes, he emphasized the civilizing effects of improved transport and the possibility of unifying the independent provinces. He attributed to railroads an almost divine purpose and urged governments to subsidize them with cash and guaranteed loans.

Nothing would be a more powerful antidote to this state of primitive, but not innocuous simplicity, than the transit of Railways through our agricultural districts. . . . Poverty, indifference, the bigotry or jealousy of religious denominations, local dissensions or political demagogueism, may stifle or neutralize the influence of the best intended efforts of an educational system; but that invisible power which has waged successful war with the material elements, will assuredly overcome the prejudices of mental weakness or the designs of mental tyrants. It calls for no co-operation, it waits for no convenient season, but with a restless, rushing, roaring assiduity, it keeps up a constant and unavoidable spirit of enquiry or comparison; and while ministering to the material wants, and appealing to the

[9] See J. S. Martell, "The Achievements of Agricola and the Agricultural Societies 1818-25," *Bulletin of the Public Archives of Nova Scotia*, II, No. 2.

[10] See J. Robb, *Agricultural Progress. An Outline of the Course of Improvement in Agriculture Considered as a Business, an Art, and a Science, with Special Reference to New Brunswick* (Fredericton, 1856). Robb was active in the New Brunswick Society for the Encouragement of Agriculture, Home Manufactures and Commerce. See the *Report* of this body (Fredericton, 1851).

[11] William Kingsford in 1865 described Canadian canals and advocated a deepwater passage from the Great Lakes to the Atlantic; however, he stressed the inherent profitability of transport facilities rather than their external economies, and he made a less convincing case than did Keefer. See William Kingsford, *The Canadian Canals: Their History and Cost* (Toronto, 1865).

covetousness of the multitude, it unconsciously, irresistibly, impels them to a more intimate union with their fellow men.[12]

Because water routes were frozen in the winter, Keefer explained, only railroads could make the Canadian economy prosperous by providing a year-round link with the rest of the world.

Nothing would tend more to the extension of manufactures, particularly the numerous and valuable ones of wood,—the only description we would for some time export,—than the existence of Railways; nothing would more rapidly build up, what every country should have, *a home market*—place the consumer near the producer—keep our surplus population at home—promote the growth of wool, the cultivation of hemp, the settlement of waste lands, the employment of our unlimited water power, and the expansion of national enterprise.[13]

Although the ideas put forward by Keefer were not original, he was the first in Canada to organize and set them down.[14]

Several early statesmen expressed interest in economic science, and in their writings and actions indicated a firm grasp of basic principles. Three of these were Francis Hincks, Alexander Galt, and John Langton. Hincks, Minister of Finance both in the 1840's and the 1870's, mastered banking and tariff theory; and when faced with such a difficult question as government aid to public utilities, made an extensive study of European and American experience. He was called by Goldwin Smith "our greatest economist and financier."[15] Galt, railroad promoter, diplomat, and Minister of Finance in the 1860's, explained and supported the economic arguments for Confederation; his ability to analyze and interpret data was exemplified in his best known writing, a pamphlet entitled *Canada 1849 to 1859.* Professor O. D. Skelton has compared Galt

[12] T. C. Keefer, *Philosophy of Railroads* (Montreal, 1850), pp. 8-9, and *Canals of Canada* (Toronto, 1850). See also D. C. Masters, "T. C. Keefer and the Development of Canadian Transportation," *Canadian Historical Association Annual Report,* 1940, pp. 36-43.

[13] *Philosophy of Railroads,* p. 15.

[14] Israel Andrews, in his notable Report to the United States Senate in 1852, on the "Trade and Commerce of the British North American Colonies," acknowledged a substantial debt to Keefer for "his contributions respecting the resources, trade, and commerce of Canada." 32d Congress, 1st Session, *Senate, Executive Document No. 112* (Washington, 1853), p. 13.

[15] R. S. Longley, *Sir Francis Hincks* (Toronto, 1943), pp. 160 and 362. See also Francis Hincks, *Reminiscences* (Montreal, 1884), p. 220 and above, pp. 78-82.

to David A. Wells in the United States as "a man much after his own heart in breadth of view and lucidity of expression."[16]   Langton, who was successively a member of the Legislative Assembly, Auditor of Public Accounts in the Province of Canada, Vice-Chancellor of the University of Toronto, and Auditor-General after Confederation, was a pioneer in higher education and in the civil service, as well as a lucid exponent of conservation of natural resources.[17]   Hincks, Galt, and Langton were all conditioned by their surroundings, and they made no contributions to the science of economics.   In another climate they might have put their minds to more theoretical and less prosaic matters; but theirs were active times with the frontier never far from hand.

Economic History and Statistics

Descriptions of the colonial economies were sketchy and were contained principally in works on general history.   Joseph Bouchette, Surveyor-General of Lower Canada, completed three books including much valuable statistical material; but he carefully avoided any critical or even analytical comments, presumably fearing the loss of his job or of the market for his writings.   Regarding the economic progress of the colonies Bouchette modestly observed:

In what manner their internal situation can be most beneficially improved, their population most speedily increased by the encouragement of industrious settlers, and particularly the cultivation of hemp and flax supported, which may, in fact, be pursued to almost any extent, belongs to the sagacity of the political economists to point. . . .[18]

Before Confederation Thomas Chandler Haliburton, author of the popular tales of Sam Slick, John McGregor, an Englishman who

[16] *The Life and Times of Sir Alexander Tilloch Galt* (Toronto, 1920), p. 391.

[17] See John Langton, "The Importance of Scientific Studies to Practical Men," *Canadian Journal,* II (1854), 201-204; and "On the Age of Timber Trees, and the Prospects of a Continuous Supply of Timber in Canada," *Transactions of the Literary and Historical Society of Quebec,* V (1862), 61-79.

[18] *A Topographical Description of the Province of Lower Canada, with Remarks upon Upper Canada, and on the Relative Connexion of Both Provinces with the United States of America* (London, 1815), p. xi; see also *The British Dominions in North America; or A Topographical and Statistical Description of the Provinces of Lower and Upper Canada, New Brunswick, Nova Scotia, the Islands of Newfoundland, Prince Edward, and Cape Breton. Including Considerations of Land-Granting and Emigration. To Which are Annexed, Statistical Tables and Tables of Distance, &c.* (London, 1832); and *A Topographical Dictionary of the Province of Lower Canada* (London, 1831).

spent some years in the colonies, and J. C. Taché, a physician and member of Parliament, all wrote useful works.[19] Later as Chief Officer of the first census of the new Dominion, Taché made a remarkable contribution in gathering and re-publishing statistics of all the censuses from 1665 to 1871.[20] In 1867 Arthur Harvey, founder of the *Year Book and Almanac of British North America*, the predecessor of the *Canada Year Book*, wrote a brief account of the prospective new province of British Columbia.[21] The apathy which greeted a work of this kind, however, is indicated by the fact that Harvey twice petitioned the House of Commons to purchase copies for the Parliamentary Library, and was unsuccessful both times.[22] Economic history and description at Confederation were typified by a collection of articles entitled *Eighty Years Progress of British North America* by well-known authors[23] whose object was, in part, to collect information—which could have been accomplished better by a government body—and to interpret the data. Although not uniform in purpose or in quality the collection was valuable as a guidepost to future effort.

In commemoration of the general meeting held at Montreal in 1884, the British Association for the Advancement of Science published a volume entitled *Canadian Economics*, consisting of papers by Canadian and American authors and designed to "effectively illustrate

[19] T. C. Haliburton, *An Historical and Statistical Account of Nova Scotia* (Halifax, 1829); John McGregor, *Historical and Descriptive Sketches of the Maritime Colonies of British America* (London, 1828), and *British America* (London, 1832); J. C. Taché, *Esquisse sur le Canada considéré sous le point de vue economiste* (Paris, 1855).

[20] *Census of Canada 1870-1871*, IV (1876) and V (1878). For an appraisal of this work see R. H. Coats, "Beginnings in Canadian Statistics," *C.H.R.*, XXVII (1946), 112-113 and 115-119. Taché outlined some of the problems of census takers to a Select Committee of the Legislative Assembly in 1865; clearly he was familiar with the experience of other countries. *Sessional Papers of the Parliament of Canada*, 1867-68, No. 3, pp. 106-107. Professor Saint-Pierre may not have been aware of Taché's enormous statistical labors when he wrote: "He [Taché] was an economist not by vocation but by accident and from obedience. . . . Taché had a horror of statistics. . . ." "La Littérature sociale canadienne-française avant la Confédération," *P.T.R.S.C.*, XLIV (1950), Section I, 72 (translation). Taché aroused the ire of some Canadians when in the Census of 1871 he changed from the *de facto* to the *de jure* method of enumeration, thereby producing more realistic but in some cases smaller counts for urban areas. See Arthur Harvey, "The Canadian Census of 1871," *C.M.N.R.*, I (1872), 97 and 98.

[21] *A Statistical Account of British Columbia* (Ottawa, 1867).

[22] *Journals of the House of Commons*, I (1867-1868), 18, 57, 251, and 397.

[23] H. Y. Hind, T. C. Keefer, J. G. Hodgins, Charles Robb, H. H. Perley, the Reverend William Murray (Toronto, 1863).

the political economy of the Continent."[24] This book marked the end of an era when description and analysis were carried out by interested persons in all walks of life and before there were any professional economists in government and the universities. The twenty-seven articles covered maritime problems, agriculture, natural resources and conservation, vital statistics, banking, public finance, education, and two theoretical subjects. The authors were government employees, parliamentarians, educators, and businessmen; none described himself either as "economist" or "statistician." The papers were generally well written, although documentation was infrequent and methods of approach varied with each writer. A lack of statistical data was often evident, as for example when John Lowe, Secretary to the Department of Agriculture, discussing pauperism was able to say only:

> The very general distribution of wealth in the Dominion; the almost universal extent to which the cultivators of the soil are owners and masters of their acres; the generally high rate of wages paid to the working classes, both artisans and labourers; and the relative cheapness of living;— all these influences are happily inimical to the existence of pauperism in any large degree in Canada.[25]

More than anything else, *Canadian Economics* pointed up the need for organized and co-ordinated investigation of economic matters by trained research workers.

Political Economy in the Canadian Institute

The Canadian Institute, established at Toronto in 1849, was the first scholarly body to encourage discussion of economic subjects. Half way between a mechanics' institute and a learned society embracing many disciplines, it permitted those members who wrote on political economy to publish in its journals.[26] Three of these

[24] *Canadian Economics* (Montreal, 1885), p. 2.

[25] *Ibid.*, p. 224.

[26] The publications of the Canadian Institute comprised five separate journals: *The Canadian Journal* (1852-1855); *The Canadian Journal of Industry, Science and Art* (1856-1878), called after 1868 *The Canadian Journal of Science, Literature and History; Proceedings of the Canadian Institute* (1879-1890); *Transactions of the Canadian Institute* (began 1890); *Proceedings of the Canadian Institute*, New Series (1897-1904). See W. Stewart Wallace, *The Royal Canadian Institute Centennial Volume 1849-1949*, (Toronto, 1949); and *General Index to Publications 1852-1912*, compiled and edited by John Patterson (Toronto, 1914).

writers before 1880 were E. A. Meredith, J. B. Cherriman, and the Reverend William Hincks.

E. A. Meredith, a noted educator and civil servant, in 1856 spoke upon the international adjustment of price levels which followed the Australian and Californian gold discoveries.[27] He carried out his discussion within a framework of classical value theory and a quantity theory of money or, as he stated it, "on general principles and with reference to the admitted truths of Political Economy."[28] The discovery of precious metals, he argued, had increased their supply and reduced their value in terms of other goods; because paper money could be assumed to remain in constant proportion to the metals, inflation was attributable "firstly, and chiefly, to. . .gold discoveries; secondly, and in a lesser degree, to the war and other local and temporary causes."[29] The effects were felt first in the producing countries, but before long in the rest of the world. Meredith compiled tables of new coinage and consumption of gold, and arrived at figures for the net increase of specie, which he identified as the cause of inflation. Despite his careful calculations he was reluctant to suggest any close causal connection between economic variables.

As to the existence of these processes, or as to their tendencies there is no room for doubt. It is, however, absolutely impossible to measure their precise share either individually or collectively in the general result. The forces which come under consideration in the domain of practical political economy (unlike those with which the mechanical philosopher has to deal) refuse to submit to rigid measurement, and we must content ourselves with seeing the general result towards which they severally contribute without hoping to ascertain how much of the effect is due to each force separately.[30]

[27] Meredith was born in Ireland and studied at Trinity College, Dublin, where he obtained among other honors, First Prize in Political Economy. He practiced law in Ireland and in Canada, and in 1846 and 1847 was Principal of McGill University in Montreal. In 1847 he was appointed Assistant Provincial Secretary for Upper Canada. H. J. Morgan, *Bibliotheca Canadensis*, pp. 276-277.

[28] Meredith viewed political economy as part of a larger social science which he described as "although the youngest of the sisterhood of the sciences. . . that one of them all which most immediately and directly concerns itself with whatever tends to advance the happiness and well being of society. It deals with those matters especially, which 'come home to the business and bosoms of men.' It is, therefore, pre-eminently a science from which public benefit may be expected." "An Important but Neglected Branch of Social Science," *Transactions of the Literary and Historical Society of Quebec*, V (1862), 38.

[29] "Influence of Recent Gold Discoveries on Prices," *C.J.I.S.A.*, I (1856), 433.

[30] *Ibid.*, p. 438.

Inflation had more than academic interest for Meredith when in 1873 as a Dominion civil servant he used the paper presented in 1856 to support a plea for higher wages for public employees.[31]

One of the most interesting contributions to the publications of the Canadian Institute was a book review of Augustine Cournot's *Recherches sur les principes mathematiques de la théorie des richesses* by J. B. Cherriman, a graduate of Cambridge and Professor of Mathematics at University College, Toronto.[32] Cherriman regarded Cournot's work as the most outstanding contribution to political economy since the *Wealth of Nations*—"the first attempt, and a successful one, at founding a true science of wealth on the only base of observation and induction. . .";[33] he proceeded to "give an outline of the system followed and some of the deduced consequences." With passages translated from the French, he provided a short summary of Cournot's theories of demand, monopoly, duopoly, and taxation, but being interested chiefly in the highly mathematical portions, neglected other matters. Cherriman showed great perception in recognizing the merit of Cournot's work, although his review at the same time was another manifestation of the widespread contempt for economics as a science. He concluded:

> It may fairly be doubted whether our science of political economy has made one real step in advance since the famous treatise of Adam Smith; yet, admirable in itself and wonderful considering the circumstances of its production, as this treatise is, Smith has done little more than clear away obstructions and trace out the foundations of the building which is to be. . .and if Adam Smith had possessed the calculus, we should not at this day be wearied and perplexed with the prolix circumlocution of Ricard, [*sic*], or the refining complications of Mill.[34]

The Reverend William Hincks, Professor of Natural History at the University of Toronto, was the most frequent early contributor to the Canadian Institute on economic topics.[35] His writings seldom

---

[31] E. A. Meredith, "The Public Service of the Dominion—Considered with Reference to the Present Scale of Prices and Wages," *C.M.N.R.*, III (1873), 1–12.

[32] Biographical material on Cherriman can be found in the *University of Toronto Monthly*, IX (1910), 77. See also above, p. 75.

[33] *C.J.I.S.A.*, II (1857), 194.

[34] *Ibid.*, p. 186.

[35] William Hincks, a brother of Francis Hincks, was born in Ireland and spent his early years as a minister of the Presbyterian Church in England and in Ireland. From 1827 until 1839 he was Professor of Natural Philosophy at Manchester Col-

went beyond a simple and wordy exposition of classical economic principles, but he was an enthusiastic critic of schemes which ran contrary to approved theory and policy. An active popularizer of economics as a science, he often proclaimed his praise with missionary fervor, as in 1860 when he explained:

. . . the more we study it the more thoroughly we believe that, as producers and exchangers of produce, there is one plan which suits us all,—that in peaceful intercourse we may help, but cannot injure each other, and that the intercourse which we are disposed to hold is the appointed means for diffusing the enjoyment of the productions of all climates, and distributing the blessings which flow from arts and industry, as well as those which luxuriant nature freely pours forth.[36]

Hincks scolded Canadians for not memorizing economics like the catechism, and attributed their folly to bad habits copied from the uncivilized Americans.

. . . I think I frequently observe symptoms of the prevalence, to some extent, in this country, of what I must account false, delusive and dangerous notions on great questions in economical science. This is probably not the case amongst thinking and reading men, but if we consider that the works on political economy are not in their nature popular, or in their price very accessible, as they offer no temptation for reprints, and that a very bad influence is constantly though imperceptibly flowing in from a neighboring country where opinions and practices which set at defiance all the conclusions of science are almost universal it really is not wonderful that even intelligent and well-informed men amongst us should adopt notions in general circulation which have a certain degree of plausibility, though contrary to the conclusions which the highest authorities on the subject have deduced from the widest experience by the most

lege, York; between 1842 and 1849 editor of the *Inquirer;* from 1849 to 1853 he was Professor of Natural History at Queen's College, Cork; and in 1853 he was appointed at Toronto. Articles by Hincks in publications of the Canadian Institute on economic subjects were: "On the True Aims, Foundations and Claims to Attention of the Science of Political Economy," *C.J.I.S.A.*, VI (1861), 20-28; "An Inquiry into the Natural Laws which Regulate the Interchange of Commodities between Individuals and Nations, and the Effects of Interference with Them," *ibid.*, VII (1862), 180-190; "Notes on Some Practically Interesting Questions in Economical Science bearing on the Prosperity of Countries Situated as Ours Is," *ibid.*, XI (1866), 96-113. Hincks wrote a number of articles on the natural sciences which are of no interest here.

[36] "On the True Aims, Foundations and Claims to Attention of the Science of Political Economy," *loc. cit.*, p. 26.

cautious reasoning, which have come to be accounted as established truths, and have been practically applied with obvious advantage.[37]

One cannot help wondering after reading the often tiresome and repetitious preachings of Hincks, whether despite his good intentions, he did not weaken rather than strengthen the case for economics in Canada.

Political Economy in the Canadian Monthly

Before 1880 almost all articles in periodicals on economic topics were concerning banks, currency, or commercial policy; and writers seldom expressed admiration for economic science.[38] *The Canadian Monthly and National Review*, similar in form to the British *Fortnightly* and *Contemporary Review*, was the only periodical regularly to contain articles on economics.[39] The editor between 1872 and 1874 was Goldwin Smith, an expatriate Oxford don who came to Toronto via Cornell and was for almost half a century the outstanding intellectual figure in Canada. Smith was undoubtedly the author of penetrating reviews in the *Canadian Monthly* of books in economics. In 1872 he called the second series of *Cobden Club Essays* "instructive to the economist and politician, whether he agrees with them or not," and he found the presence of four foreigners among the essayists evidence of "the cosmopolitan character of political and economical science."[40] When commenting on Thomas Brassey's *Work and Wages* Smith exhibited an early awareness of the importance of labor problems:

Now, especially, that the world is being revolutionized, that the aspect of every department of labour is changing or changed, should we be glad to receive a contribution which, by carefully collating figures bearing on

[37] "Notes on Some Practically Interesting Questions in Economical Science Bearing on the Prosperity of Countries Situated as Ours Is," *loc. cit.,* p. 96.

[38] A contributor of the *Canadian Merchants' Magazine* was an exception when he remarked in 1859: "Political economy has brought to light those fundamental truths which regulate exchange—has disabused the civilized nations of the idea that individual or national wealth could result only from another's loss—has changed commerce from a source of hostility into a bond of peace." "The Relations of Science to Modern Civilization," IV (1859), 65.

[39] See Elisabeth Wallace, *Goldwin Smith: Victorian Liberal* (Toronto, 1957), p. 72. The *C.M.N.R.* began publication in January, 1872, and united with *Belford's Monthly Magazine* in June 1878.

[40] *C.M.N.R.,* II (1872), 92. Smith was a charter member of the Cobden Club and author of its motto. Elisabeth Wallace, *op. cit.,* p. 137.

the subject, points out the direction in which the changes are being, or have been, made. . . . It must be read and re-read, entire, to be appreciated; and we trust that our recommendation of it will not be neglected in this Dominion of Canada.[41]

Reviewing a text in economics by John Macdonell—"a comprehensive, sensible and well written account of the chief topics and problems of Political Economy"—Smith became prophetic when he explained the future importance of economic history: "A great service will be rendered and a great fame will be won by the first writer who treats history economically or political economy historically."[42]

Other writers besides Smith touched on economics in the *Canadian Monthly*. In an obituary of John Stuart Mill in 1873 Nicholas Flood Davin of Toronto wrote: "Thirty years ago the knowledge of Political Economy was confined to the learned; it is widely diffused at this hour"; and he expressed appreciation of Mill's contributions to the science: "Sir James Steuart, Quesnay, and Adam Smith treated Political Economy not as a science but as an art. Mr. Mill condemned this method, and. . .wrote of Political Economy as a positive art, his views of it however as a science being interwoven with his precepts."[43] Two criticisms of economic knowledge in Canada appeared in 1873 and 1875. A writer calling himself "Economist" (possibly Goldwin Smith) condemned the ignorance of basic principles exhibited by officials of local governments:

The materials of which Municipal Councils are ordinarily composed are not such as to lead us to expect in these bodies any profound knowledge of political economy; yet we should probably find in the most insignificant of them all members who believe themselves greater authorities on taxation than Bentham or Mill, Ricardo or Sismondi, and who would think themselves making a poor bargain if they bartered their "practical knowledge" for the speculations of Adam Smith. . . .of political economy the number is infinite who do profess to know everything without having studied anything.[44]

[41] *C.M.N.R.*, II (1872), 472. In an article entitled "The Labour Movement" Smith cited Brassey and gave a sympathetic historical account of the growth of organized labor. Unions, he claimed, placed a worker "on an equal footing with his employer," raised wages, and thereby stimulated "economy of labour" and "invention of machinery." *C.M.N.R.*, II (1872), pp. 513-532.

[42] *Ibid.*, II (1872), 93.   [43] *Ibid.*, III (1873), 515.

[44] "Municipal Taxation," *ibid.*, IV (1873), 388.

James Douglas, President of the Literary and Historical Society of Quebec, after a general indictment of Canada's intellectual achievements, criticized the neglect of economics, which he recognized as an independent field of inquiry:

> . . . it is in the domain of history and political economy that we might have expected much work would have been done; but even here comparatively little has been effected. . . . Political economy likewise is a subject, on which, had there been much intellectual life among us, treatises would have been written; for, by a people trying to create a new nationality and to avoid the errors of the old, the subjects of the tenure of land, the treatment of poverty, and the regulation of the currency deserve much attention.[45]

Partly as a result of Goldwin Smith's loss of interest, and partly because of the growing unpopularity of the laissez faire philosophy which the *Canadian Monthly* upheld,[46] publication ceased in 1878. Its successor—*Rose-Belford's Canadian Monthly and National Review*—endorsed the National Policy and evinced no interest in economic science.[47]

The Economics of John Rae

John Rae's writings merit, and have received elsewhere,[48] more attention than can be given in this survey of economic ideas; Rae made original contributions to theory which were far superior to those of any other writer in Canada. Because his place in the history of economic thought is well recognized and secure, his work will be examined here in little detail and principally for its relevance to Canadian conditions.

Rae was born in Scotland in 1796, was educated at the Universities of Aberdeen and Edinburgh, and came to Canada in 1822.

---

[45] "The Intellectual Progress of Canada during the Last Fifty Years. . .," *ibid.*, VII (1875), 470.

[46] See for example "Free Trade and Protection," *ibid.*, V (1874), 214 ff.

[47] See for example John MacLean, "The Alliance of Democracy and Protection," II (1879), 725 ff.; and A Freelance, "Protection and Free Trade," VIII (1882), 499-508.

[48] See R. Warren James, "The Life and Work of John Rae," *C.J.E.P.S.*, XVII (1951), 141-163; Joseph J. Spengler, "John Rae on Economic Development: A Note," *Q.J.E.*, LXXIII (1959), 393-406; Gilbert Horne, "John Rae: Canadian Economist," *The Business Quarterly* (Fall 1950), pp. 151-156. I have examined Rae's work on banking above, pp. 92-97.

He traveled throughout the provinces and settled finally in Glen-garry County, a frontier portion of Upper Canada where he was employed as a schoolmaster and devoted his spare time to a study of the geography and geology of the country. While in Canada Rae wrote his major work, *Statement of Some New Principles on the Subject of Political Economy, Exposing the Fallacies of the System of Free Trade, and of Some Other Doctrines Maintained in the "Wealth of Nations,"*[49] which was mistaken at the time for an unreasonable denunciation of free trade and was a financial failure. He left Canada in 1848 after a religious controversy with the Church of England, went to California, then to Hawaii, and died in New York in 1872.

In his *New Principles* Rae was one of the first to examine capital theory as a separate topic in economics; and as he remarked, "the solitude and labors of the Canadian backwoods" inspired his studies and "altered their form."[50] Rae described capital as a collection of goods called "instruments" which had three common characteristics: they required labor for attainment, yielded a return, and existed over a time period. Capital goods could be arranged in a series, he explained, with their ranks or "orders" established by their productivity—what he termed "the proportions existing between the labour expended in the formation of instruments, the capacity given to them, and the time elapsing from the period of their formation to that of exhaustion." The series had a form A,B,C,. . .X,Y,Z, with the most productive instrument named "A" and the least productive "Z": "Generally, the proximity of instruments to A is inversely as the cost and the time, and directly as the capacity."[51] At any moment, he stated, the relative scarcity of capital in an economy determined which instruments in the series could profitably be constructed; for example, when capital was very scarce (as it was in Canada) only instruments close to "A" giving immediate, long-lasting, and low-cost returns were practicable. Rae regarded the market interest rate as a "fair measure" of the aver-

[49] Boston, 1834. The book was edited and reprinted in 1905 by C. W. Mixter as *The Sociological Theory of Capital*. The development of Rae's ideas in Canada and abroad can be traced through a series of minor writings published both before and after the *New Principles*. These will be contained in a forth-coming book entitled *The Life and Works of John Rae, Political Economist*, by R. Warren James.

[50] *New Principles*, p. iv.

[51] *Ibid.*, p. 108.

age productivity of capital in an economy and therefore indicative of the point in a series beyond which new instruments could not lie. In this analysis Rae obviously came close to a supply and demand theory of the interest rate and was groping for a concept of the margin.

After Rae had outlined characteristics of capital goods he examined the process of their creation, and he suggested four factors which determined the rate of capital formation:

1. Quantity and quality of available raw materials.
2. Strength of the desire to save.
3. Wage rates.
4. Progress of invention.[52]

The quantity and quality of materials and wage rates, he argued, influenced the costs of producing instruments; a wage reduction or an increase in the supply of materials made possible greater returns from a given investment and permitted construction of a larger range and number of instruments. The only ways in which capital could actually be increased, however, were through the last two factors: saving ("accumulation") and invention ("augmentation"). Rae explained:

1. *Accumulation* of stock or capital, is the addition made to these, through the operation of the accumulative principle.

2. *Augmentation* of stock or capital, is the addition made to them, through the operation of the principle of invention.

3. Increase of stock or capital, is the addition made to them, by the conjoined operation of both principles.[53]

Economic progress, Rae emphasized, required continued invention in addition to saving; so long as technology remained constant capital accumulation brought new instruments to progressively lower orders of productivity and increased total income little.[54]

Rae believed that the strength of the "effective desire of accumulation" and the propensity to invent were conditioned by two circumstances: (1) the state of the "social and benevolent affections"

[52] *Ibid.*, p. 109.
[53] *Ibid.*, p. 264.
[54] Often Rae illustrated his theory with simple rural illustrations. For example, he observed that in the threshing of grain, after the initial fashioning and construction of flails, investment in a multitude of flails (more than one per person) barely increased total product. It had been necessary to invent a mechanical threshing machine before new capital could profitably be invested in this industry. *Ibid.*, p. 20.

and "intellectual powers" of the citizenry, and (2) the degree of social and political stability. Both saving and invention were encouraged when people were charitable, looked forward to providing an inheritance for their children, and were accustomed to "reflection" and "prudence." A paradoxical relationship, however, held between economic progress and social stability; although a sense of personal security induced persons to save, it also discouraged them from inventing:

Whatever disturbs, or threatens to disturb, the established order of things, by exposing the property of the members of the society to danger, and diminishing the certainty of its future possession, diminishes also the desire to accumulate it. . . . On the contrary, they excite the inventive faculty to activity. The excessive propensity to imitation, which is natural to man, seems the only means by which we can account for this diversity of effects.[55]

If a government wished to maximize the rate of a country's economic progress, Rae asserted, it should concentrate on facilitating additions to total capital. From his study of capital theory he then concluded "it would seem that its increase is advanced:

I. By whatever promotes the general intelligence and morality of the society; and that, consequently, the moral and intellectual education of the people makes an important element in its progress:

II. By whatever promotes invention;

    1. By advancing the progress of science and art within the community;

    2. By the transfer from other communities of the sciences and arts there generated:

III. By whatever prevents the dissipation in luxury, of any portion of the funds of the community.[56]

Several of Rae's policy proposals were as follows: he recommended reduction of disparities in social and economic status so that the poor could refrain from seeking attention by displaying their "ability to spend" thereby wasting their income, and so that the "self-denying morals" of the lower classes would overcome the "luxury, extravagance and attendant evils" of the wealthy.[57] He proposed

[55] *Ibid.*, p. 222.

[56] *Ibid.*, p. 362.

[57] Rae's views on the importance of social mobility were similar to those of Vilfredo Pareto, *Manuel d'économie politique* (Paris, 1909), pp. 380-434.

that the state defray costs of education because the creation of a skilled labor force benefited the entire community; he believed government should encourage any industry in which there was a comparative disadvantage but in which methods could be expected to improve making domestic production profitable.[58] Legislators legitimately could impose a protective tariff, Rae declared, if they were able to answer in the affirmative any one of the following three questions:

1st. Will the duty so levied, by directly or indirectly effecting an improvement in the arts, increase the absolute capital of the society?

2d. Will it prevent future waste, by the transfer of an art producing useful commodities, the supply of which is liable to sudden interruptions?

3d. Does it fall partly or altogether on luxuries, and is its real effect, consequently, not to diminish, by so much, the annual revenue of the society, but only to apply a part of it, which would otherwise have been dissipated by vanity, to supply funds for the necessary expenditure of the legislator?[59]

Indirectly, Rae had an important influence in Canada because his writings, popularized by John Stuart Mill, provided one of the central arguments for imposition of the National Policy tariffs of 1879. As noted above,[60] Sir John Macdonald cited Rae in a celebrated speech before Parliament to show that comparative costs were not fixed; and John MacLean used Rae's statements in a widely distributed protectionist pamphlet. However, apart from this application of his theories to commercial policy, Rae's studies of capital, economic development, and the role of the state in the economy were ignored; undoubtedly Canadian statesmen in the nineteenth century looked more toward the long-run increase of national capital than to an immediate maximization of exchange values, but they lacked the guidance and support that could have come from Rae's brilliantly clear and closely reasoned arguments.

The *New Principles* won worldwide acclaim late in Rae's lifetime and thereafter. Nassau Senior read and praised it, and J. S. Mill

---

[58] *New Principles*, pp. 61 and 74. Rae listed cases in which the transfer between countries of productive modes had altered comparative cost relationships. *Ibid.*, pp. 253, 353, 363-367.

[59] *Ibid.*, pp. 384-385.

[60] P. 57.

wrote, "in no other book known to me is so much light thrown, both from principle and history, on the causes which determine the accumulation of capital."[61] Ferrara translated the work into Italian in 1856, and it was influential as far afield as Australia.[62] In later years Böhm-Bawerk, Veblen, Taussig, and others received much from Rae,[63] and in 1907 Irving Fisher dedicated *The Rate of Interest* "to the memory of John Rae who laid the foundations upon which I have endeavored to build."[64] Today Rae can have few challengers as Canada's greatest master of the social sciences.

II. AFTER THE NATIONAL POLICY

Economics developed with the economy, and the most pronounced changes in both occurred after the coming of industrialization. Canada at Confederation was dependent largely upon the production of a few staple raw materials, and in 1871 more than half the population were classified as "farmers, lumbermen and fishermen," with service, construction, and unskilled laborers making up most of the remainder. Workers in manufacturing and handicrafts accounted for only 13 per cent of the total; four-fifths of the population was rural, and Montreal was the largest city with about 100,000 inhabitants.[65] For seven years after Confederation there were prosperity and expansion, and therefore little reason to criticize this economy; but after 1874 when exports declined with foreign demand depression caused great hardship.[66] In 1878 the prevailing government philosophy of laissez faire was rejected when the Conservative party under Sir John Macdonald came to power

[61] *Prinicples of Political Economy* (London, 1940), p. 165. See also James, *op cit.*, pp. 156-163.

[62] Professor J. A. La Nauze writes: "It is interesting to find that Henry Parkes [Australian statesman, author, and journalist] had apparently been reading Rae in the original at the time (1859-60) of his temporary conversion to Protection. . . ." *Political Economy in Australia* (Melbourne, 1949), p. 15.

[63] See Joseph J. Spengler, "John Rae on Economic Development: A Note," *Q.J.E.*, LXXIII (1959), 394; and "Veblen and Mandeville Contrasted," *Weltwirtschaftliches Archiv*, LXXXII (1959), 48.

[64] New York, 1907, frontispiece.

[65] *Report of the Royal Commission on Dominion Provincial Relations* (Ottawa, 1940), Book I, Table I, p. 22.

[66] Total exports of Canadian produce rose from 48.5 to 76.7 million dollars between 1868 and 1874, and fell to 62.4 million in 1879. *Ibid.*, p. 53.

with a platform of economic nationalism termed the "National Policy." One of the Conservatives' objectives was diversification through tariff protection to manufacturing industry, and after 1879 the economy underwent substantial modification. Although in the decade 1881-1891 the population increased only 11.5 per cent, employees in manufacturing industry rose 40.6 per cent.[67] In the 1890's settlement of the West provided markets for the factories built under the National Policy, and industrialization continued until World War I.

After protective tariffs became established, commercial policy was discussed less frequently and attention turned to such questions as the distribution of income, causes of depression, the nature of capital, and evils of monopoly. With new problems posed by industrialization there was also increased recognition of economic science in the government, in journals, and in learned societies.

Questions Arising from Industrialization

Distribution of Income. The industrialization of a rural society inevitably brings problems as new economic relationships are made significant, a wage-earning and an urban middle class comes into being, and entrepreneurs play an important role. Most Canadians, however, having watched with frustration a century of American advance, regarded industry as an unmixed blessing and were concerned less with its problems than with means to obtain it. The earliest discussion of possible ill effects from industrialization was in journals operated by or in sympathy with the first trade unions. Writers, often with insight and ability, condemned "monopoly" and "vested interest," and favored state intervention and sometimes socialism.[68] They were acquainted with the writings of radicals in other countries but, with the exception of the supporters of Henry George,[69] were less interested in strictly economic matters than in over-all social and political reform.

The sort of garbled economics that occasionally resulted when one of the labor movement's enthusiastic but untrained writers attempted to analyze the difficult question of income distribution was

---

[67] *Fifth Census of Canada,* 1911, VI, Table 1.

[68] See F. W. Watt, "The National Policy, the Workingman, and Proletarian Ideas in Victorian Canada," *C.H.R.,* XL (1959), 1-26.

[69] Examined above, pp. 32-38.

illustrated in a work entitled *The Conditions of Modern Labour and Modern Civilization.* The author, John McCormick, combined communist with religious doctrines and explained: "Labour is the source, the *alpha* and the *omega* of all wealth"; adding, Christ "tells us more than once how difficult a thing it was for a rich man to enter into the kingdom of heaven." Private property, he concluded, lay at the root of all evil: "Every thoughtful man knows full well that plutocracy or moneyocracy, is the meanest, most exacting, sordid, grinding, heartless, soulless, and most hateful of all despotisms of which we have any knowledge." He demanded that all the product of industry go to labor "on the principles of justice and equity" and claimed that "the results of labour or production, except an infinitesimal portion, is [*sic*] not distributed to the worker. . . ." McCormick attributed the depression of the 1870's to underconsumption which resulted when all national product was not given to labor:

If the masses of the people had the money to supply their wants, the warehouses and the stores of all America would be emptied tomorrow, and their contents would be found to fall infinitely short of the quantity wanted. Over-production, as a cause of our five or six years' misery and depression, is exploded.

He criticized "Our Malthusian philosophers, if we dignify them by such a name" because "they impiously maligned God, and said to Him, in effect, that He had botched His work. . . ." Finally McCormick dismissed economic science with an amusing attack on Adam Smith:

We know that Adam Smith, a Scotchman, who wrote his book, called the "Wealth of Nations," held a sinecure from the Government; and probably only for that fact we might not have heard so many platitudes about "supply and demand," buying in the cheapest market and selling in the dearest; and such puerile phrases that Usurers and Hard Money men are so fond of quoting as gems of wisdom.[70]

McCormick endorsed the principles of the Socialistic-Labor party in the United States, sympathized with the land reforms of Parnell in Ireland, praised the issue of greenbacks, and criticized the national

[70] *The Conditions of Modern Labour and Modern Civilization* (Toronto, 1880), pp. 4, 5, 9, 11, 17, 21, and 22.

debt. He appears to have gathered his ideas from a large variety of sources and to have been unable to assess and integrate them.

Witnesses before the Royal Commission on the Relations of Capital and Labor in 1886 expressed discontent with the division of income resulting from industrialization, and indicated some knowledge of socialist theories. John Smith, an immigration agent, claimed that laborers could find greater opportunity in the northwest than in the east "for the simple reason that there is unearned increment in the North-West, which we have not here" and because in the east "capital has become more concentrated, and poor men have not the same chance to enter into competition with capitalists."[71] When asked, "Can you give any reason how it occurs that while workingmen have gone forward in their intellectual capacity their condition has not advanced materially?" John Hewitt, rating clerk at a city waterworks, blamed monopolies:

I believe the reasons rest nearly altogether upon the economical laws that rule civilized society. We find one of the most notable features of the advance of civilization, especially in new countries, is to centralize and monoplize, and centralization and monopolization are always antagonistic to the interests of the working classes, and will continue to be so.[72]

Hewitt was confused as to the distinction between money and capital—"the portion of the products of labor that goes to capital and land is altogether controlled by the power of money to accumulate, and I think in that one particular the work of legislation should be brought to bear in the interests of the working classes. . . ." He claimed that monopolies resulted from the centralization of wealth and in turn caused a maldistribution of income; he predicted that "monopolies will become so oppressive in the not distant future that the masses will rise up and wipe them out."

When collective bargaining was discussed before the Royal Commission, employers were uncertain whether unions gave workers a monopoly position. One builder said they did and that a single workingman, bargaining alone, stood on an equal footing with his employer; but another businessman was willing to tolerate unions so long as they did not coerce members, and he maintained

[71] *Report of the Royal Commission on the Relations of Capital and Labor* (Ottawa, 1889), Ontario Evidence, p. 759.
[72] *Ibid.*, Ontario Evidence, p. 300

that organized labor could not alter wage rates: "It is only an opinion, and I do not know that it is worth very much here—it is that it is simply a matter of supply and demand. . . ." The Secretary of the Canadian Manufacturers' Association expressed the opinion that neither employers nor unions had substantial economic power: "I think the law of supply and demand is just as applicable to labor as it is to the purchase of commodities."[73] Labor leaders themselves justified unions more on social and cultural grounds than for their economic strength, but their temerity may be attributed to the fact the Commissioners were openly unsympathetic.[74]

Nature of Capital. The growth of factories after the National Policy caused several writers to examine the economic effects of an increased use of machinery. In a paper to the Canadian Institute in 1887 Charles Levy explained correctly the essential similarity of all factors of production; but moralistic language and ignorance of familiar terms made his reasoning difficult to follow. He said, in part:

. . . capital is of two kinds, vital and separate, vital capital being the expectancy of the life, as it would be estimated by the usage governing the sale of life annuities; separate capital being everything attaching to the life. The Creator of all things is the first and greatest capitalist. . . . The terms capital and labour are misleading, inasmuch as they do not explain the relationship between the persons to whom they are applied. The distinction is one of tense only, "separate capital" being the exponent of past labour, "vital capital" the exponent of present labour. Vital capital is lent for a consideration to be paid in separate capital. Interest on vital capital [wages] is of the nature of a life annuity, the purchase price of which corresponds to the total "vital capital" upon which the interest [wages] is paid. Neither class of capital is productive, nor is it safe in the absence of the other. The employer borrows, the workman lends, vital capital. Both are capitalists, one producing present, the other expending past labour.[75]

The seriousness with which the effects of capital accumulation were viewed by some persons was indicated by the extensive questioning

[73] *Ibid.,* Ontario Evidence, pp. 120, 181, and 704.

[74] For example, Thomas Towers, a district master of the Knights of Labor, was closely cross-examined by the Commissioners regarding the purposes of that organization.

[75] Charles Levy, "Capital," *Proceedings of the Canadian Institute,* VI (1887-1888), 29-30.

of witnesses before the Royal Commission on the Relations of Capital and Labor. Several workers believed that machinery displaced labor and reduced employment permanently; one even suggested that Parliament "pass a law prohibiting the manufacture of any machine for the next twenty years," adding that "over-production of machinery had caused a great many men to be thrown out of work."[76] Manufacturers were naturally more optimistic about the effects of capital accumulation, and one replied to the proposal that no machinery be produced by saying: "We would simply go back about 100 years if that were the case." He denied that imported machinery caused unemployment because "the increased demand gives a much greater purchasing power than the increased power of the imported machinery." Generally industrialists were willing to to concede that machinery replaced workers in certain positions, but asserted that the displaced labor would be employed elsewhere.[77]

William Houston, a journalist and author, explained to the Canadian Institute in 1890 how capital was accumulated and in what way it could be more evenly distributed.[78] He criticized the abstinence theory of saving formulated by Senior and Mill and the surplus value theory of Marx, and suggested that large fortunes had resulted from "(1), Monopoly of opportunity, and (2), the law of inheritance." He believed that: "The sociological conditions of the community are improved [more] by having a large number of moderately wealthy persons than by having a few enormously wealthy in the midst of a mass of poor people." He proposed as remedies for the concentration of wealth a "single tax on opportunity" (meaning the possession of any natural resource) and a "succession tax on bequests or inheritance."[79] Houston did not arrive at any

[76] *Report*, Ontario Evidence, p. 472. The witness J. K. Dickson, a real estate agent, continued: "I would suggest that the electric light be done away with, because I think it is injurious to the eyes, and prevents labor from getting employment."

[77] *Ibid.*, Ontario Evidence, pp. 673, 677, and 983; and New Brunswick Evidence, p. 184.

[78] William Houston was born in Lanark, Canada West, in 1844 and received his B.A. degree from the University of Toronto in 1872 and his M.A. in 1874. He worked on the Toronto *Globe* and other Canadian newspapers, and from 1883 to 1922 was librarian of the Legislative Library, Toronto. He was editor of a source book of Canadian constitutional history, *Documents Illustrative of the Canadian Constitution*, Toronto, 1891. See *Encyclopedia of Canada*, III, 205-206.

[79] "Genesis and Growth of Capital," *Transactions of the Canadian Institute*, II (1890-1891), p. 40.

startling or original conclusions, but he approached logically and with a knowledge of relevant theory a subject which was of increasing concern at the time he wrote.

Causes of Depression. Most writers made no attempt to explain the business cycle, and with an occasional suggestion of overproduction accepted periodic bad times as inevitable. William Johnson, manager of a large mercantile agency in Montreal, illustrated what could result when an untrained amateur, without the benefit of critical discussion and not having read the work of others, attacked this question. In a volume unworthy of detailed examination Johnson attributed the depression of the 1870's to "the fact that *private expenditure* has been kept up in a ruinous proportion to the actual income from gains," "*intemperance,*" "next to intemperance the fiend of *speculation,*" "want of *method and regularity.* . .coupled with want of concentration," "irresolution upon matters small or great," "*the lust for political prominence,*" and "*losses through endorsation* of a friend's or relative's paper."[80]

Hugh Bowlby Willson, engineer, inventor, railroad promoter, and newspaper editor, gave a monetary explanation of depression.[81] He asserted that when banks issued currency instead of simply making loans from deposits they caused inflation and subsequent collapse. He outlined his theory to an American Congressional Committee in 1879 as follows:

The effect of the expansion of bank credits. . .is to stimulate the overproduction of goods, which presently leads to a glut in the markets and

[80] William Wickliffe Johnson, *Sketches of the Late Depression; Its Causes, Effect and Lessons, with a Synoptical Review of Leading Trades during the Past Decade* (Montreal, 1882), pp. 22-27. An equally inept attempt to make use of economic analysis was a temperance tract by the Reverend William Burgess of Listowel, Ontario. He cited numerous authorities and prepared over forty statistical tables and diagrams to illustrate the evils of "the most enslaving of all capital-controlled interests—*the Distillery, the Brewery, and the Saloon.*" Depressions, Burgess claimed, were attributable, not to overproduction, unequal income distribution, or monopoly in land, but to "the demoralization and crippling effects of the liquor traffic." *Land, Labor and Liquor: A Chapter in the Political Economy of the Present Day* (Toronto, 1887), pp. 72-117.

[81] Willson was born in Winona, Upper Canada, where his father was a prominent political figure and Speaker of the Legislative Assembly. He may have been a pupil at the Gore District Grammar School when John Rae was headmaster, and C. W. Mixter reports: "There is abundant evidence in Rae's papers that Willson was his best friend," *The Sociological Theory of Capital,* p. xxvii. Willson studied law at Toronto and became a real estate agent in Hamilton. He lived for some time in the United States and contributed to periodicals in that country and in Canada.

a fall of prices. There then happens the reverse of what took place when values and prices were going up. Then the wages of labor rose, and the competition among buyers was brisker than among sellers, and everybody fancied they were growing rich, and an era of reckless extravagance set in. Ignorant folly strutted forth in all its short-lived grandeur and laborers squandered their abundant earnings. Now, however, after the panic has come, and the sources of capital, largely fictitious, drawn from bills discounted, are dried up, there are more sellers than buyers of goods and houses, and the painful process of a reduction of the luxury of living and in the wages of labor, simultaneously begins. Cheap goods necessitate cheap labor, and thousands of laborers are turned adrift, and an army of so called "tramps" is the result.[82]

A second cause of business crises, Willson explained, was distortion in the economy brought about by tariff protection. Artificial stimulation caused temporary "over-consumption" in some sectors, chiefly of capital, but also of consumer goods.

. . . protection first checked the development of agriculture, stimulated manufactures, by attracting capital and labor in an unnatural manner from other callings, and then, causing a plethora of such unnaturally fostered products, utterly broke down, inflicting immense and long-continued suffering on the whole community, but more particularly on the laboring classes; and then, by an equally logical result, unduly drove an excessive amount of capital and labor back into agriculture. It first produces very high prices, and then, by its break-down, creates very low prices; while true economic science teaches that steady employment in all pursuits, and equability in prices of goods and labor, are most conducive to general prosperity, and the happiness and advancement of society.[83]

Willson's writings were published in the United States, and it is difficult to discover the extent to which he was influenced by distinctly Canadian conditions. His concern over a bank-financed, excessive growth in one sector, however, may have reflected his participation in the railroad boom of the 1850's; and his indictment

---

[82] "Testimony before the Select Committee of the House of Representatives relative to the Causes of the General Depression in Labor and Business," 45th Congress, 3rd Session, *House of Representatives Miscellaneous Document No. 29* (Washington, 1879), p. 647.

[83] *Currency, or the Fundamental Principles of Monetary Science* (New York, 1882), pp. 276-277. Other works by Willson on this subject were *A Plea for Uncle Sam's Money; or Greenback versus Bank Notes* (New York, 1870), and *The Money Question Considered Scientifically and Practically* (London, 1874).

of high tariffs as a cause of crises came just after introduction of the "National Policy."

Economic Science in Government

Government before World War I made little use of economic science, and research by experts in the field was seldom contemplated. Investigations of economic problems involved merely interrogation of witnesses by members of parliament and appointed commissioners, and usually neither the questioners nor the respondents had more than a cursory knowledge of the subject. Hearings produced only unreliable evidence and little or no plan for reform. Inquiries into questions of commercial policy, banking, and currency have been mentioned above and those on "The Relations of Capital and Labor," on "Combinations in Business," and on the "Cost of Living" are reviewed in this section. Finally, the collection of economic statistics by the government will be described.

Labor Problems. As a result of increasing worker unrest after the National Policy, a Royal Commission was appointed in 1886 to inquire into and report upon

the subject of Labor, its relation to Capital, the hours of labor, and the earnings of laboring men and women, and the means of promoting their material, social, intellectual and moral prosperity, and of improving and developing the productive industries of the Dominion. . . .[84]

The commissioners selected were uniquely unqualified for this sizable task of economic analysis (their professions included: chief justice of a small island in the Caribbean, publisher, printer, boat builder, journalist, carpenter, blacksmith, cabinetmaker, machinist, manufacturer, and teacher); but at the time there were few trained public servants or academic economists who could have taken their places. They made no attempt to compile organized statistics, and their report was little more than a summary of several thousand pages of testimony from hundreds of witnesses. The general conclusion of the Commission was that a diversified economy held out the advantages of a variety of jobs and cheap manufactured goods, but also led to such abuses as child labor and sweatshops. The commission-

[84] *First Report of the Royal Commission on the Relations of Capital and Labor* (Ottawa, 1889), p. 3.

ers decided that because industrialization had been induced by a policy of protection, the state was responsible not only for the good effects but also for the evils.

There was almost no appeal to the literature of economics in the Royal Commission's investigation, and commissioners as well as witnesses seemed unaware of authorities on the topics of discussion.[85] Witnesses made no detailed proposals for reform although a few suggested sweeping changes in the economy, and others recommended social improvements to ease the burdens placed on workers by the factory system. William Houston declared that the government ought to provide free educational facilities:

. . . if the productive power of the community is being made more effective by means of this organization of labor, and if the result is the deterioration of the artisan, then the community can afford to turn round and do something for the artisan by giving him opportunties which he has not got now of leading some kind of an intellectual life.[86]

Roswell Fisher, who called himself an "economist," reiterated Houstin's optimistic views that education and worker prestige would bring an end to labor strife:

. . . the cause of the labor question, in this and other countries, is due to the conditions of modern industry, to the disparity of means in the literary, educational, and social improvement, and political status of the wage earning classes, with their improvement in mechanical education and technical efficiency.[87]

The desirability of factory acts forbidding employment of women and children, minimum-wage legislation, poor relief, and high tariffs on imports from low-wage countries were discussed; and although the pitiful testimony of women and children offered abundant proof

---

[85] William Houston was an exception when he mentioned Adam Smith and reported on the writings of Francis Walker in the field of wage theory. *Report, Ontario Evidence*, p. 231.

[86] Houston added that class warfare could be avoided only if an educated working class were created and given a respected place in society: "It is hard to tell what the individual may do when he finds himself hedged in—cribbed and cabined and crushed by a great industrial Juggernaut; it is hard to say whether he will not, like the worm, at last turn round. . .and do it in a very foolish way, but I say the best preventive of all for these things would be industrial education; it would do what we can never do by any amount of preaching. It would add dignity to toil, ennobling it and making it intellectual. . . ." *Ibid.*, Ontario Evidence, p. 232.

[87] *Ibid.*, Quebec Evidence, p. 578.

of the need for some action, both commissioners and witnesses were unwilling to approve any measures because of their uncertain economic implications.[88]

With astonishing faith in the accuracy of human memory, commissioners asked witnesses to furnish figures for wage rates, employment, prices and production of goods, and even for such quantities as "the aggregate increase of wealth for the whole population"; naturally statistics collected in this manner were unreliable in the extreme. Several persons expressed regret at their inability to use documented evidence, and Archibald Blue, Assistant Commissioner of Agriculture and Secretary of the Ontario Bureau of Industries, appealed for collection of statistics at the federal level.[89] Frederick Nichols, Secretary of the Canadian Manufacturers' Association, when asked if machinery had replaced labor in factories, reported that it was impossible to answer except on pure hearsay:

No person can answer authoritatively such a question; they can only go by general ideas or superficial information, in the absence of proper statistics. One person can speak for one particular trade but not generally; and every day the need of a permanent Bureau of Statistics for the Dominion is becoming more felt. We have no information, no data, upon which we can write or compile evidence on these questions since the last Dominion census.

Nichols believed that if a national statistical service were established it would improve the stability of the economy.

I think, for instance, if we had a Statistical Bureau there would not have been so much over-production in some trades, for example the cotton trade, in which there was such depression and so many operatives thrown out of work. The cause, I think, was more from ignorance of the consumptive requirements of the country than anything else. . . .[90]

The need for a bureau of statistics was most amply proven by the inadequate findings of the Commission itself.

The value of the Royal Commission on the Relations of Capital and Labor was mainly in its negative results. Many economic prob-

---

[88] See for example *ibid.*, Quebec Evidence, p. 580 ff., and Ontario Evidence, p. 167 ff.

[89] Requests for the formation of a federal bureau of statistics can be found in *ibid.*, Quebec Evidence, pp. 308, 465, and 1035; and Nova Scotia Evidence, pp. 121 and 344.

[90] *Ibid.*, Ontario Evidence, p. 185.

lems were discovered and so was the inability of inexperienced and untrained persons to deal with them; the need for organized research, and particularly for statistical compilation, was made abundantly clear. The Labor Statistics Act of 1890 and, more indirectly, the creation of the Department of Labor in 1900 are traceable to this inquiry.

Industrial Combinations. A select committee of the House of Commons was appointed in 1888 to "examine into and report upon the nature, extent and effect of certain combinations said to exist with reference to the purchase and sale, or manufacture and sale, in Canada, of any foreign or Canadian products." N. C. Wallace, supporting the motion for a committee, declared that combinations raised prices and destroyed "public morality and personal freedom of action." He noted that Parliament could find precedents for control in the law of the United States: "After the House of Commons have investigated this matter, if necessary, if we cannot accomplish our purpose in any other way—and perhaps we cannot—we can follow the example set by the United States. . . ."[91] Discussion centered on the relation between tariffs and the growth of combinations, and a Liberal member of the Opposition postulated a three-stage model for the development of a protected industry. First, after imposition of a tariff, domestic firms raised prices and received large profits. In the second stage profits attracted more new firms than could supply the market at the high prices. Cut-throat competition ensued and "the third stage of the protective system at last came on, namely, combines among manufacturers to protect themselves against the public."[92] Conservatives, however, treated combinations as something incidental to tariffs, and one even claimed that protection fostered competition:

It is well known that the advocates of the National Policy in this House and in the country intended not only that it should stimulate manufactures, but also that it should promote competition. . . . There are evils incident to every progressive movement and to every reform, as has been well shown by writers on progressive government and political economy, and it is necessary to watch these evils.[93]

In its investigation the Committee discovered "evils of monopoly" in thirteen markets, but it criticized these more on grounds of

[91] *Debates,* 1888, p. 29.   [92] *Ibid.*
[93] *Ibid.,* p. 31.

inconvenience to firms than loss to consumers. A combine of grocers was found to be particularly injurious because:

Certain dealers are refused admission into its ranks, others are admitted and afterwards expelled, others again are placed under its ban, who, from conscientious scruples or in a spirit of independence, refuse to join them. . . . Thus establishments, which in some cases are the growth of half a century of toil and honourable dealing, and rich in valuable experience and public confidence, are threatened with extinction.[94]

The "plan" of a coal organization was said to be "copied from the American System of Trusts," an undertakers' combination resulted in "exorbitant charges to bereaved families," and a biscuit ring was able to "keep prices at higher figures than are justified by the prices paid for raw material, and altered conditions of trade, brought about by the introduction of new and improved machinery."[95] The Committee reasoned that when any firm sold under imperfect competition prices were too high, although by how much was not determined. The *Report* concluded:

The Committee find that the evils produced by combinations such as have been enquired into, have not by any means been fully developed as yet in this country, but sufficient evidence of their injurious tendencies and effects is given to justify legislative action for suppressing the evils arising from these and similar combinations and monopolies.[96]

A bill was discussed in 1888 to prohibit anyone from joining combinations which would provide "facilities" for members and deny these to non-members, which would enhance "unreasonably" the price of a good, or would "unduly" limit, lessen, or prevent competition. The anti-combinations act passed in 1889, however, was only a modified version of the original bill and set out not to make new law but to point out combinations for prosecution as conspiracies. In debate on the act combinations were assumed undesirable per se, and such factors as economies of scale were not mentioned. In its final form the act had been carefully weakened by such words as "unduly" and "undesirable," and it was invoked only once in the

[94] *Journals of the House of Commons*, 1888, Appendix 3, p. 5. The *Report* contained 732 pages of evidence but only eight of conclusions. Sixty-eight witnesses were called and forty-eight exhibits received.

[95] *Ibid.*, pp. 6-9.

[96] *Ibid.*, p. 10.

1890's. In 1897 tariff protection was denied to combinations, and in 1910 a new Combines Investigation Act was passed. Both of these measures were unsatisfactory also, however, and effective prosecution of combinations did not take place until after World War I. Looking back one wonders whether the long delay in taking positive action against combines cannot be attributed partly to the confusion and absence of careful analysis which characterized discussion of the question.[97]

Inflation. The report of a Board of Inquiry held in 1914 into the rising cost of living indicates that economic research techniques of government investigative bodies had not improved substantially by World War I. Members of the Board questioned many witnesses, but did not refer to the literature of economics or make extensive use of statistics. Inflation was attributed, without evidence, to an increase in the world's gold supply, "non-productive" investment, uneconomic methods of distribution, extravagance, "wasteful methods in the household," luxury, and the migration of people from rural to urban areas, "which has increased the proportion of non-producing food consumers."[98] R. H. Coats, chief statistician in the Department of Labor and a member of the Board, pointed to the future when, in a minority report, he called for systematic statistical analysis of inflation and a new approach to economic problems.

Economic Statistics. Although records of external trade, insurance, and banking were compiled before Confederation, and those of crime and railroads after 1876, the *Statistical Year Book* which began in 1886 was the first annual collection of economic statistics. In 1890 the Labor Statistics Act provided for a bureau to gather social and economic data, but the depression of the 1890's caused this project to be abandoned. The need for a central statistical service increased with the establishment of the Department of Trade and Commerce in 1892, the Department of Labor in 1900, and the permanent Census Office in 1905. Each of these divisions assembled material important to itself with many duplications and omissions. In 1912 six officers from different levels of government were au-

---

[97] See L. G. Reynolds, *The Control of Competition in Canada* (Cambridge, 1940), pp. 131-290; and V. W. Bladen, *An Introduction to Political Economy* (3rd ed.; Toronto, 1956), pp. 214-266.

[98] *Report of the Board of Inquiry into Cost of Living* (Ottawa, 1915), I, 79-80.

thorized to examine the situation. R. H. Coats, a dominant figure on the Commission, has described the investigation thus:

From any general standpoint and notwithstanding excellencies in spots, "imperfections of method," "restrictions of outlook," "lack of unity and co-ordination," were found rampant. The remedy lay, the Commission affirmed, in a central statistical office, "to co-ordinate the statistics of Canada under a single comprehensive scheme," to extend them to meet immediate requirements, and for the future to act as a "central thinking office" on keeping abreast of national development.[99]

Following the Report of the Departmental Commission on Statistics Mr. Coats was named the first Dominion Statistician in 1915, and under his energetic leadership the Dominion Bureau of Statistics was founded in 1918.

Economics in the Learned Societies

The American and British Economic Associations were established in 1885 and 1890, and in the five years between these dates three men called for increased discussion of economics in the learned societies of Canada.

William A. Douglass, a tireless supporter of Henry George, explained to the Canadian Institute that democracy required widespread knowledge of economics, and he pointed to the United States as a nation where ignorance had permitted evil legislation to become accepted. Douglass was convinced a knowledge of economics would convert everyone to the single tax. Discussants of Douglass' paper agreed that the subject was useful but decided that it could be taught at a subuniversity level. Douglass himself recommended that economics be substituted for history and spelling, another suggested that it take the place of "extremes" of history and geography, and a third commented—perhaps tongue-in-cheek—that it might end some embarrassment by replacing physiology in the curriculum of young girls. It was concluded that economics might be taught at any level, and that the decision as to time and place could be left to the

[99] "Beginnings in Canadian Statistics," *C.H.R.*, XXVII (1946), 128. See also R. H. Coats, *A National System of Statistics for Canada* (n.p., n.d., *ca.* 1916), and "Fifty Years of Statistical Progress," in *Fifty Years Retrospect: Canada 1882-1932* (Toronto, 1932), pp. 77-83.

teachers. This discussion in the Canadian Institute indicated that the subject was regarded, not as an intricate science to be studied in universities, but rather as the memorization of basic maxims.[100]

William Houston explained the usefulness of what he called "sociology" to the Canadian Institute in 1886, and included political economy under this term. The social sciences, he declared, should be taught in Canadian universities for their "practical character" and for their "educative value as a means of culture." In 1888 Houston outlined "The Relation between Political Science and Practical Politics," placing political economy this time within the category "political science." He argued that "The facts of political society have to be analyzed, classified, and made the basis of generalization, just as the facts of the physical world are"; but he cautioned against basing predictions on first hypotheses. Remembering, no doubt, how economics suffered from its association with a policy of laissez faire, he emphasized that the social scientist should search for truth, but not take a position on current problems: "When he does this he leaves the domain of political science and enters that of practical politics."[101]

At the ninth annual meeting of the Royal Society of Canada, founded in 1881, John George Bourinot, Clerk of the House of Commons and a leading authority on constitutional law, spoke on the social sciences in Canadian universities. He reviewed their growth throughout the world, and like Houston included political economy under "political science."[102] In Canada, he declared, there were unexploited fields for economic research, and a clear understanding of basic principles was important for every citizen.

Look around us, and do we not see how important it is for Canadians to understand the principles or doctrines which have been laid down by men like Adam Smith, Ricardo, Mill, Carey, and others I need not mention here, who have devoted their lives in Europe and America to a branch of science so fruitful of discussion, and so intimately connected

---

[100] "Study of Economics," *Proceedings of the Canadian Institute*, VI (1887-1888), 27-29. See also above, pp. 34-35 ff.

[101] "The Scientific and Pedagogic Claims of Sociology," an abstract, *Proceedings of the Canadian Institute*, V (1886-1887), 25-26; and "The Relation between Political Science and Practical Politics," *ibid.*, VI (1887-1888), 41-42.

[102] Bourinot had studied at the Johns Hopkins University and had been influenced there by pioneer work in social sciences.

with the industrial and commercial development and the material prosperity and social comforts of a people?[103]

Bourinot urged that political science and economics be introduced into universities as separate fields of study, and that sincere teaching and research replace cursory treatment in courses on philosophy, history, and law. In Canada, and in all new countries where policies and institutions had to be borrowed and adapted, the social sciences were of vital importance.

In no department of study is there more danger of being deceived and carried away by dangerous theories and delusive ideas than that which leads us to consider political, social and economic problems. In attempting to lay deep and firm the foundations of government and society in the Dominion—for remember we are at the basis as yet of our national structure—our rulers and thinkers must carefully study the systems of other countries, for there is always much to learn from them. . . .[104]

There was no professional society of economists in Canada until 1913, when Adam Shortt and O. D. Skelton became the first president and secretary-treasurer of the Canadian Political Science Association. The prospectus of the new organization suggested that debate at regular meetings would add to discussion of economic and political problems in business, the universities, the press, and on the political platform:

. . . would it not be possible to supplement these various agencies of discussion by an association of more general scope, free from the partisanship of parliaments, though with party politicians as well as government officials among its members; less hurried than the daily newspaper, though with newspaper men in its fold; less theoretical than professional economists, though utilizing their services as well; less specialized in view point than the banker or manufacturer or farmer, but including them all?[105]

The Association held one general meeting at Ottawa in 1913, was interrupted by World War I, and was not revived until 1929.

[103] "The Study of Political Science in Canadian Universities," *P.T.R.S.C.*, VII (1889), Section II, 8.

[104] *Ibid.*, p. 15.

[105] *The Canadian Political Science Association* (n.p., 1913), p. 3. See also K. W. Taylor, "Economic Scholarship in Canada," *C.J.E.P.S.*, XXVI (1960), 13. At least six Canadians joined the American Economic Association in its first ten years, 1885-1895, and there is evidence that political economy clubs were organized in the larger Canadian cities about the turn of the century.

Although the Royal Society, the Canadian Institute, and various literary and historical societies provided limited facilites for publication, no journal in Canada before 1914 was concerned principally with the social sciences. Periodicals published by the universities, with the exception of some special studies in specific fields, were primarily literary in character; and the few popular magazines showed little interest in scholarly writing. To fill the need for a journal in 1910 the Departments of History and Political Science at Queen's University began their valuable series of *Bulletins*. In 1928 *Contributions to Canadian Economics* began under the auspices of the Department of Political Economy at the University of Toronto, and in 1929 the Canadian Political Science Association started to publish proceedings of its annual meetings. The first volume of the *Canadian Journal of Economics and Political Science* appeared in 1935.[106]

III. Economics in French Canada

The reasons why interest in economics has been a recent development in French Canada can be found in the history of the people. After the conquest in 1760 French Canadians maintained a high degree of social self-sufficiency; they arrived at the twentieth century with a population largely descended from, and many times the size of, that which had settled on the St. Lawrence over two hundred years before, and they succeeded in preserving their language, church, and educational institutions. French Canadians did not, however, gain control of their economy; a predominantly Protestant, English-speaking minority, small in numbers and not politically dominant, retained a disproportionate share of business power. This failure to achieve economic leadership was partly the result of historical accident—the demoralizing effects of the conquest, the influx of British and American capital and aggressive entrepreneurs, and the heritage of semi-feudal forms from the French colony; but it was also a natural consequence in an active trade area where English, the native tongue of the minority, was universally spoken, and where Anglo-Saxon culture reigned supreme with obvious prejudice to-

[106] See V. W. Bladen, "A Journal is Born: 1935," *C.J.E.P.S.*, XXVI (1960), 1-5.

wards dissenters. With little other choice short of giving up their language and way of life, French Canadians remained aloof from commerce and industry; those who were able stayed on the farms and in the villages, and others emigrated south or grudgingly accepted junior positions in stores and factories. Students in the colleges and universities were guided into the church and the professions, and were taught to associate economics and other sciences with business and "Les Anglais." Gustave Lanctot has summarized the situation:

The colleges taught classics, philosophy, and history, and boasted of shaping the "honest man" in the obsolete manner of the great century [the seventeenth!] which they still did not dare foresake, except with timidity. As for the practical sciences, the professors proclaimed a condescension which may be formulated thus: for us, fine literature, for the British, the business life.[107]

Etienne Parent, the brilliant and rebellious editor of the journal *Le Canadien,* was in the 1840's the first French Canadian to express publicly an interest in economics.[108] In his paper and before the *Institut Canadien,* a literary society at Quebec City, he took pride in a knowledge of the science, and even argued that national development had been retarded "in particular because we have not had among us men who are profoundly versed in the study of political economy and in the enlightened application of the principles which it teaches."[109] A representative of the British Colonial Office, after talking with Parent in 1835, was impressed enough to remark that the French Canadians' "understanding of political science is superior to that of the men by whom they have been so arrogantly despised."[110] Parent himself made no contributions to economics, and he was often inconsistent in appraising the work of others, as for example when he endorsed at the same time complete laissez faire and doctrinaire socialism. He also had a weakness for utopian schemes, such as compulsory education for legislators and

---

[107] "Rétrospective d'économie sociale au Canada français 1882-1932," in *Fifty Years Retrospect: Canada 1882-1932,* p. 49 (translation).

[108] Parent was editor of *Le Canadien* from 1822 until 1825, and from 1831 until 1842. In 1867 he became Under-Secretary of State for the Dominion.

[109] "L'Importance de l'étude de l'économie politique," *Le Répertoire National,* IV (1850), 22 (translation).

[110] Cited in Mason Wade, *The French Canadians, 1760-1945* (London, 1955), p. 154.

the creation of a privileged intellectual "classe des lettres"; the attention he gave to these dreams detracted from his more realistic
discussion.[111] Nevertheless, before any of his contemporaries in English Canada, Parent lectured on the history of economic thought,
giving a prominent place to French and other Continental writers.
He explained to the Institut Canadien:

> Everywhere this science is new, seeing that it appeared in the form of
> a complete doctrine for the first time in England in 1776 in the work of
> Dr. Smith, the *Wealth of Nations*; in France in 1803 in the *Traité d'éco-
> nomie politique* of J. B. Say. In 1758, indeed, Quesnay published in
> France a work entitled "Tableau économique. . ." in the shadow of which
> was formed a school of economists or physiocrats. McCulloch, a dis-
> tinguished economist of our day, even attributes to Quesnay the merit of
> having been the first to give political economy a systematic form, raising
> it to the status of a science; and he acknowledges that the work of French
> economists have helped substantially to accelerate the progress of economic
> science. But their theory founded on this axiom "land is the only source
> of wealth" has been rejected by more recent economists, so that today
> one doesn't look for the oracles of the science beyond Smith in England
> and Say in France. It is necessary, at the same time, to give Italy the
> credit for beginning political economy; for as early as the sixteenth century
> Botero took up this science and he was followed by many other Italian
> scholars.[112]

Parent chided his countrymen for devoting themselves to literature
and fine arts when they ought to be discovering means of building
a sound economy. In a new country, he said, "the time for painting
and sculpture comes later." He related with regret that nowhere in
Quebec City had he been able to purchase a copy of J. B. Say's
Treatise on Political Economy—"a work which ought to be in the
hands of all our learned men, young and old, the essential com-
panion for whosoever takes part in the public affairs of our country,
was a work which didn't sell." He concluded "the science of political economy which explains wealth is the science of progress *par
excellence*."

[111] See Etienne Parent, *Discours* (Quebec, 1878); and A. Saint-Pierre, "La
Litterature canadienne-français avant la Confédération," *P.T.R.S.C.*, XLIV (1950),
Section I, 82-94.
[112] "L'Importance de l'étude de l'économie politique," *loc. cit.*, pp. 22-23
(translation).

In contrast to other French Canadians Parent expressed glowing admiration for the ambition and enterprise which he considered characteristic of Britons and Americans:

. . . this desire for gain in the Anglo-Saxon race, a desire let us note in passing which has only been strengthened in the American branch of this race, is destined to form an epoch in the history of mankind, an age of industry, of material improvement, of positivism, and of the glorification of labor.[113]

With respect in place of his countrymen's customary fear of economic change, Parent made a plea for industrialization on the ground that a distinct culture could be preserved only in a strong economy.

If we wish to preserve our nationality we must secure a social power equal, at least, to that which will oppose it.   In vain have we cut ourselves off behind treaties; in vain have we made a bulwark of all the principles of public morality, of natural rights, and the rights of men; there is a right which, in the world and above all between peoples, almost always has precedence over all other rights, and this right which is the most powerful is almost always the same, the right of the most capable. . . .   I come to pray you to honor industry; to honor it not only with words but with deeds, and by a conduct completely opposite to that which we have maintained up to the present time, and which explains the inferior position in which our race finds itself in our own country.[114]

Parent deplored French-Canadian disdain for business and urged parents to steer children into commerce and industry and out of crowded professions.

If we have children who show talent for some form of industry, let us encourage them to devote themselves to it.   The more often we consider their interest and give industry a respected position we give our nationality a guarantee of permanence as strong as we could procure.[115]

Etienne Parent was a prophet and reformer who called for action in direct conflict with the values of his society, and he was therefore

[113] *Ibid.*, pp. 26 and 43 (translation).

[114] "L'Industrie considerée comme moyen de conserver la nationalité canadienne-français," *Le Répertoire National*, IV (1850), 8-9 (translation).   See also M. Cadieux and P. Tremblay, "Etienne Parent, un théoricien de notre nationalisme," *L'Action Nationale*, XIII (1939), 203-219 and 307-318; and F. Ouellèt, "Etienne Parent et le mouvement du Catholicisme social 1848," *Le Bulletin des Recherches Historiques*, LXI (1955), 99-118.

[115] "L'Industrie. . .," p. 19 (translation).

doomed to failure. It required the excitement of western expansion and discovery of Quebec's great economic potential a half century after he wrote to convince French Canadians that they should share in the new prosperity and modify accordingly their philosophy and policies.

While English Canadians watched impatiently the steady progress of the United States during the nineteenth century, and with the exception of a few heretics, awaited eagerly results of the National Policy, many French Canadians viewed the future with alarm and predicted dire social consequences from economic growth. J. Desrosiers admitted to the *Union Catholique* at Montreal in 1879 that industrialization might indeed bring prosperity, but with it, he added, would come widespread "luxury" (defined as "the spirit of enjoyment carried to an extreme"), commercial crises, moral corruption of women, small families, drinking, smoking, card playing, regattas, boxing matches, cock fights, and a host of other evils. To guard against the passion for luxury, Desrosiers advised opposition to economic change and retention of spiritual ahead of all other values:

Luxury, we have seen, is above all the evil of nations which have sacrificed the spirit to material things, and desire no other end than leisure and well-being. But our young country sets its sights higher and cherishes more noble aspirations. We know ourselves to be the children of saints. . . .[116]

Finding solace in the colonization movement, Desrosiers advised French Canadians to work hard and cultivate the land: "By encouraging colonization we are able to counter-balance in part the bad effects of luxury."

French Canadians had little sympathy for radical economic ideas, and despite their unfamiliarity with all economic theory, attempted even to defend the existing economic system. Abbé M. H. Bédard explained to the Montreal *Cèrcle Ville Marie* in 1893 that Karl Marx had set out to "disregard the rights of the human being, to pervert nature instead of guiding it, to worsen things with the appearance of bringing a remedy." Avoiding a discussion of Marxian

---

[116]"Le Luxe, principe d'avilissement et de decadence," *Revue Canadienne*, XVI (1879), 345-348. For similar statements see Hubert LaRue, "Luxe et vanité," in *Mélanges historiques, litteraires et d'économie politique* (Quebec, 1870).

doctrine, he argued with evident sincerity that socialism had been nurtured by Jews and Freemasons and had gained strength from the "materialism of science and modern political economy, the ungodly and radical press, the shameless theatre, infamous books, obscene pictures and slanders against authority and religion, atheistic laws, secular schools, civil marriages and closed convents." Social problems, he declared, could be solved only by the Roman Catholic Church:

They have searched very thoroughly for a remedy in political economy, but political economy is not a complete science and it has not been able to resolve the principal problems which have been debated in the course of this century, such as pauperism, the abuse of human power, the evils of competition, the displacement of workers by the preponderance of machines and the extension of commercial communication, etc., etc.

No, all these problems insoluble for all the socialists and economists of the world have only one solution; and that solution is found in the true church of Jesus Christ, in Catholicism, and there alone.[117]

Some French-Canadian priests were particularly concerned with questions of income distribution; but despite frequent mention and condemnation of economics and economists, they only barely comprehended the basic principles involved. Abbé Bédard informed owners of productive factors that income shares had to be determined by "the sound philosophy and doctrine of Saint Thomas" and the encyclicals of Pope Leo XIII; I Ruhlmann, a Jesuit, explained in 1892 that the just wage should take into consideration the needs of the worker rather than mere productivity and added: ". . .wages may not, with justice, be given over to fluctuations in supply and demand, contrary to a theory which has become almost general among modern economists."[118] As indicated by these statements, economics as a science, distinct from moral philosophy, was still not accepted in French Canada by the 1890's.

A change in the attitude of French Canadians toward commerce, industry, and at the same time economics, occurred at the turn of the

[117] "Le Socialisme," *Revue Canadienne*, XXX (1894), 83, 84, 87, and 89. For similar statements, see A. Cambray, "Le Socialisme, religion nouvelle," *ibid.*, nouvelle série, I (1906), 379-396; L. Perrin, "Le Socialisme," *ibid.*, nouvelle série, V (1910), 415-424; VI (1910), 30-44; VII (1911), 431-443.
[118] "La Question du juste salaire," *Revue Canadienne*, XXVIII (1892), 201.

century prompted by unprecedented prosperity and the writings of Errol Bouchette, a nationalistic civil servant. Like Etienne Parent, Bouchette believed that the survival of French Canada depended on economic strength: "We must," he declared, "take an active and energetic part in the great industrial contest for which men of experience predict an early arrival and which will certainly come." Beginning in 1905 Bouchette wrote a series of "social and economic studies of Canada" which outlined his policy position, and which in his own words "created a movement of opinion, was studied in colleges, and was discussed in the journals and indeed in the heart of the legislative assembly in debates on the establishment of forestry and technical schools, and above all the school of higher commercial and industrial studies."[119]   He urged the provincial government to take part in development, and insisted that such action would lead not to the dreaded socialism but to co-operation between men of different interests and races, and to cultural strength through material prosperity.

Improved education was an important part of Bouchette's prescription for reform. French Canadians, he said, "lacked neither aptitude nor capital, but only business training and customs." To understand the "social and economic needs of Canada" they had to study economics, and he added, "it is not sufficient to read, it is necessary above all to think for ourselves."[120]   Bouchette's enthusiasm for economics, coinciding with widespread optimism over Canada's economic prospects, was picked up by French-Canadian educators and by such groups as the *Société d'économie sociale*, established at Quebec City in 1905. The immediate support this latter society received from the Church and from the public may serve to indicate that at last economics had attained not only popularity, but some measure of respectability.[121]

[119] *L'Indépendence économique du Canada français* (troisième ed., Montreal, 1913), p. 3 (translation). This book was a collection of Bouchette's contributions to *Revue Canadienne*.

[120] "*L'Indépendence économique*. . .," p. 26 (translation).

[121] See Sister M. A. Gaudreau, *The Social Thought of French Canada as Reflected in the Semaine Sociale* (Washington, 1946), p. 3. See also Maurice Tremblay and Albert Faucher, "L'Enseignement des sciences sociales au Canada de langue française," *Royal Commission Studies: A Selection of Essays Prepared for the Royal Commission on National Development in the Arts, Letters and Sciences* (Ottawa, 1915), p. 191.

IV. SUMMARY AND CONCLUSION

When Canada comprised a few struggling colonies, isolated from each other and exclusively dependent on external trade, economic discussion was limited mainly to the subjects of immediate urgency examined in Part One. Educated immigrants debated tariffs and banking and remembered the pronouncements of old-country authorities on these matters; but they seldom visualized political economy as a science and rarely adapted economic principles to their new environment. The study of economic problems was a pastime for anyone interested, regardless of training, and most people looked on economic theory as a collection of impractical moral laws, akin to religion and ethics and always doctrinaire laissez faire. Occasional lectures were given and a number of brief studies were published, but with the exception of Rae's brilliant work these seldom contained original or even careful thought.

Beginning in the 1880's protection of domestic industry and western expansion brought urban development, industrialization, and a new interest in problems of economic growth which, in contrast to tariffs and banking, could not be discussed using the literature of other countries. Empirical studies and formulation of appropriate theory were called for. Initially the intellectual activity which resulted did not produce encouraging results; more confusion than reason marked early examinations of income distribution, monopoly, collective bargaining, mechanization, inflation, and the business cycle. Nevertheless, by World War I economics came to be accepted as a science by government, the press, and learned societies. Collection of statistics at the federal level was co-ordinated in a single bureau and the increasing number of professional economists organized their own association. In French Canada economics was recognized and encouraged as a means of gaining a strong base for the perpetuation of a distinct culture.

5

Economics in the Universities

Universities were established in Canada in the first half of the last century but for a long time maintained a precarious existence. Most of the pioneer population was too concerned with survival to provide either funds or students for education past the elementary level. As late as 1880, according to R. A. Falconer:

The universities had no contact with one another. Most of them had been conceived, born, and nourished for sectarian purposes, and all were very poor. Because they were poor they were ill-nurtured, and were as a rule at odds with one another. Professors were badly paid, libraries were meagre, laboratories were few and scantily equipped, museums hardly existed. The provincial treasurers, harassed by other demands for which they were afraid to tax their constituents, took advantage of the divided interests of the colleges to refuse aid impartially to all.[1]

University development reflected the influence of both environment and foreign precedent. A close affiliation of the universities with church and state often resulted in bitter sectarian and political conflicts and largely explains the perpetuation of small, weak institutions.[2] Academic forms were provided by recent immigrants and the Scottish example was most important. During the crucial years of formation the universities of Scotland, led by Edinburgh, ranked with the best in Europe, and Scotch professors were eagerly recruited for service in Canada. With the large settlements of their countrymen there, scholars were not averse to emigration. As important as the ethnic connection and the quality of Scottish education was the ease with which methods were transferred to Canada. The tradition in Scotland of intense study in specific fields and organization along faculty rather than college lines suited the new country well.

[1] "The Intellectual Life of Canada as Reflected in its Royal Society," *Fifty Years Retrospect: Canada, 1882-1932* (Toronto, 1932), p. 10.
[2] See W. C. Murray, "University Development in Canada," *P.T.R.S.C.,* Third Series, XVI (1922), Section II, 77-105.

Canadians believed for many years that they could ill afford the luxury of a "liberal" education.[3] The influence of England, though paramount in the political sphere, was less important in higher education. With Oxford and Cambridge devoted to the cultivation of "a type of character based on the religion of the established church by means of such literature as would promote desirable views of life" it is not surprising that their model was judged unsuited for a country of mixed racial and religious origin, where harsh experience had capitalized the importance of providing a subsistence and developing the nation. English educational forms had greatest influence in the early years when King's Colleges were founded in Nova Scotia, New Brunswick, and Upper Canada, and later when college federations were patterned after the University of London.[4] Before 1900 a distinct American influence was less evident than that of either Scotland or England, partly because American educational traditions in the nineteenth century were little more than a mixed inheritance from Europe. More recently the characteristic spirit of education for the masses, with state sponsorship, a wide variety of general courses, and the "credit" system, has had considerable impact; and American graduate schools have trained a large number of Canadian college teachers. Irish,[5] French, and German traditions had some influence upon the higher education of Canada, but more through individuals than borowed modes.

For purposes of the following examination Canadian universities have been grouped according to three geographical regions: the Maritimes, Ontario, and the West; and two culturally distinct areas: English-speaking Quebec and French Canada. The first professors are mentioned with their courses, texts, and glimpses of their careers.

[3] R. A. Falconer, "Scottish Influence in the Higher Education of Canada," *P.T.R.S.C.*, Third Series, XXI (1927), Section II, 7-20.

[4] R. A. Falconer, "English Influence on the Higher Education of Canada," *P.T.R.S.C.*, Third Series, XXII (1928), Section II, 33-48.

[5] R. A. Falconer, "Irish Influence on Higher Education in Canada," *P.T.R.S.C.*, Third Series, XXIX (1935), Section II, 131-143.

1. THE MARITIME PROVINCES

Dalhousie University, Halifax, Nova Scotia

Dalhousie was founded in 1818 but languished for forty-five years under difficulties of every sort; in 1863, after a major university reorganization, economics was placed on the curriculum for the first time. The subject was taught with ethics in the fourth year by the Very Reverend James Ross, principal and professor of logic, ethics, and political economy.[6] Texts were by John Stuart Mill and Francis Wayland, and the examination questions indicate that an extensive knowledge of principles was expected of the students as well as an ability to discuss such topical questions as the significance of tariffs, the effects of labor-saving machinery, and the desirability of state intervention. In 1871 an honors program was begun with the original single course but with an enlarged reading list.[7]

In 1881 a benefactor of the university established the George Munro Chair of History and Political Economy, and the Reverend John Forrest, a Nova Scotian, became the first incumbent. Forrest announced that his class would be "conducted by means of lectures and examinations on prescribed reading," and would use books by Cairnes, Fawcett, Roscher, and Carey. The course was similar to that given by Principal Ross with a little more emphasis on the history of economic thought and on contemporary discussion, as for example the writings of Henry George. Forrest succeeded Ross as President of Dalhousie in 1885 but continued to lecture until 1912. He offered an "advanced" class after 1888 with a wide range of reading "entering into the principles of Political Economy more fully" than could be undertaken in the "ordinary class";[8] the elementary course was confined thereafter to a study of Mill's *Principles* and "prescribed passages from leading economists and current litera-

[6] *Statutes and By-Laws for the Regulation and Management of Dalhousie College* (Halifax, 1864), p. 3.
[7] Texts recommended at different times after 1871 were: Smith, *Wealth of Nations* and *Theory of Moral Sentiments;* Walker, *Science of Wealth;* Senior, *Political Economy;* Bowen, *Principles of Political Economy;* Fawcett, *Manual of Political Economy;* Perry, *Elements of Political Economy. Calendar and Examination Papers of Dalhousie College and University,* various years.
[8] *Calendar,* 1888-1889, p. 23.

ture" with discussion of "problems of the day: Protection and Free Trade, Trade Unions, Combines, Bimetallism."[9]   That the number of students successful in the examination went from six in both political economy and ethics in 1881 to fifty-nine in economics alone in 1911 indicates that either the subject or President Forrest had growing popularity.[10]

A variety of economics courses were offered first at Dalhousie in 1912 after the arrival of James A. Estey, a graduate of Acadia, Oxford, and the University of Wisconsin.   In his first year Estey gave four classes: economic theory; labour, trusts, and socialism; the state and industry and public finance; money, banking, and international exchange.   In 1913 a fifth course was given by James E. Todd in economic history.

Acadia University, Wolfville, Nova Scotia

Acadia College was established by the Baptists of the Maritime Provinces as an alternative to the Anglican King's College at Windsor, Nova Scotia (later part of Dalhousie).   In 1853, and possibly before, political economy was taught with logic and history by J. M. Cramp, one of the founders and president from 1844.[11]   The connection with history was strengthened in 1875 when Silas Mac-Vane, an Acadia graduate, returned from postgraduate study at Harvard to become instructor in history and political economy. In the 1880's economics was taught by J. G. Schurman with English literature and logic; but in 1890 history regained its affiliation when J. F. Tufts, a graduate of Acadia and Harvard, was appointed professor of history and political economy.[12]   A. B. Balcom, still another graduate of Acadia and student of Taussig at Harvard, received in 1912 the first separate appointment in economics.   Under this series of Harvard graduates, and particularly Tufts and Balcom, the American influence on economics was predominant at Acadia.[13]

[9] *Calendar*, 1898-1899, p. 26.   In 1906 *Principles of Political Economy* by Charles Gide took the place of the text by Mill.
[10] *Calendar*, various years.
[11] R. S. Longley, *Acadia University, 1838-1939* (Wolfville, 1939), p. 71.
[12] *Ibid.*, pp. 85, 86, 88.
[13] *Ibid.*, p. 117, and I.M.M., "Alfred Burpee Balcom," *C.J.E.P.S.*, X (1944), 79.

The University of New Brunswick, Fredericton

The College of New Brunswick received a provincial charter in 1800, was renamed King's College in 1828, and in 1859 became the University of New Brunswick. Political economy was touched upon in the curricula of several subjects in the early days, and lectures were probably given in the 1860's by J. Marshall D'Avray, instructor in modern languages. The first course was not offered until the 1890's and then by W. C. Murray, professor of mental and moral philosophy.[14] A writer in the college paper in 1891 (who may have been Murray) expressed admiration for the new subject but reluctance to act upon its theoretical conclusions:

> No one questions the utility of Political Economy. When trade and labor questions are rife, the value of theoretical discussions of them cannot be overestimated. The only danger here is that too great—not too little— importance may be attached to the teachings of Economics. Men are inclined to regard the laws of this science as practical commands. But economics is nothing more than the servant of the statesman. It merely supplies information in the shape of laws or uniformities about matters in which every one is keenly interested. It imposes no commands.[15]

This defence was undoubtedly an attempt to increase the popularity of economics by dissociating it from all doctrinaire policy positions, and particularly from that of laissez faire.

In 1892 John Davidson, a Scot trained at Edinburgh and Berlin, was appointed to a new chair of mental and moral philosophy and political economy.[16] Davidson, a very popular lecturer and noted author,[17] died prematurely in 1905 a few years after he had

[14] S. M. Wickett, "The Study of Political Economy at Canadian Universities," *Appendix to the Report of the Ontario Bureau of Industries*, 1897, p. 104.

[15] "The Function of Philosophy in Liberal Education," *University Monthly*, Vol. XI (1891), No. 2, p. 24.

[16] Davidson received his B.A. from the University of Edinburgh in 1891, studied at Berlin in 1891-1892, and was awarded the Ph.D. degree in 1897. Upon Davidson's arrival at Fredericton, as was often the practice, a biographical sketch and his references were published in the university paper. A testimonial letter from Professor J. S. Nicholson of Edinburgh said: "Mr. John Davidson was a highly distinguished prizeman in my class in the session 1890-1891. He showed that he had acquired a thorough mastery of the principles of Political Economy and I formed a very high opinion of his philosophical grasp. His work proved that he was a very diligent student and had read widely. I am confident that he will prove a most painstaking as well as interesting and appreciative teacher." *University Monthly*, Vol. XII (1892), No. 1, p. 7.

[17] See below pp. 179-183.

returned to Scotland because of ill health. His immediate successors were I. W. Riley and M. S. Macdonald, two philosophers; in 1907 W. C. Keirstead, Davidson's own student, took over in both philosophy and the social sciences. Keirstead's diversified interests prevented his being a prolific writer; his contributions to economics were nonetheless significant as an inspiring teacher. He is described as "beyond all doubt the dominant figure in the humanities at this university during the first half of the twentieth century."[18]

The University of Mount Allison College, Sackville, New Brunswick

Mount Allison began in 1843 as a secondary school called "The Wesleyan Academy," became a college in 1862, and the University of Mount Allison College in 1886. Political economy was taught in the "Literary and Scientific" course of the Academy from the beginning, probably by the Reverend Humphrey Pickard, principal and "Professor of Mental and Moral Science, &c. &c."; there were thirteen students in the class in 1847.[19] After the college opened in 1862, the subject was taught in the fourth year of the B.A. and the third year of the B.Sc. course by David Allison, "Professor of the Latin and Greek Languages" and later president. The first texts were by Francis Wayland and Archbishop Whately, and later by Perry, Fawcett, Rogers, Mill, and Newcomb.[20] Some indication of the class's popularity may be inferred from the fact that, of the twenty-nine books added to the college library for 1879, six were on political economy.[21] In 1884 a new division of the faculty of arts called "Logic and Political Science" including courses in logic, constitutional history, and political economy was introduced; and a year later "political science" was separated from logic.

The Reverend B. C. Borden became professor of political science in 1888, and continued in this position after becoming president in 1911. Under Borden the political economy class grew in size from seven to nineteen students in 1913 and enlarged its scope. In 1895 he announced that lectures would go beyond standard texts and

[18] Desmond Pacey, "The Humanist Tradition," in A. G. Bailey, ed., *The University of New Brunswick Memorial Volume* (Fredericton, 1950), p. 65.
[19] *Catalogue of the Officers and Students of the Wesleyan Academy*, 1843, p. 9, and 1849, p. 10.
[20] *Circular and Catalogue of the Mount Allison Wesleyan College and Academy*, various years.
[21] These were by Bastiat, Senior, Jevons, and Cairnes.

cover such matters as "Canadian Banking Law, sociology, and the various modern problems of applied economics."[22]   More than a single course in economics was not given at Mount Allison until the 1920's.

II. ONTARIO

The University of Toronto

By the middle of the nineteenth century there were three universities in the Toronto area.   In 1827 the Anglican Church received a charter for King's College, which opened in 1843 and was secularized in 1850, becoming the University of Toronto.   In 1841 Upper Canada Methodists started Victoria College at Cobourg, and in 1851 the Anglicans, led by the energetic Bishop Strachan, who had been undaunted by the disappearance of King's, founded Trinity College in protest to the other "godless" institutions.   Between 1887 and 1889, Victoria and the University of Toronto were federated with several smaller colleges and were joined finally by Trinity.[23]

As early as 1837 when Strachan was planning the curriculum of King's College, he proposed a department of "Mental philosophy; moral and intellectual philosophy; Christian ethics; and political economy."[24]   University College, which replaced King's in name in 1853, began required courses called "Civil Polity (viz., the elements of Political Philosophy, Paley's 'Political Philosophy,' and Mill's 'Political Economy')" with lectures on political economy by the Reverend James Beaven, and after 1872, by the Reverend G. P. Young.[25]   Civil polity was treated as a very minor division of moral philosophy, and readings from texts were required only of

[22] The texts were by Walker and Gide.
[23] See The Librarian, *The University of Toronto and Its Colleges, 1827-1906* (Toronto, 1906), W. S. Wallace, *A History of the University of Toronto, 1827-1927* (Toronto, 1927); C. B. Sissons, *A History of Victoria University* (Toronto, 1952); C. T. Bissell, ed., *University College: A Portrait* (Toronto, 1953); T. A. Reed, ed., *A History of the University of Trinity College Toronto, 1852-1952* (Toronto, 1952).
[24] R. A. Falconer, "The Tradition of Liberal Education in Canada," *C.H.R.*, VIII (1927), 107.
[25] The Librarian, *The University of Toronto and Its Colleges, 1827-1906*, p. 83.

honors candidates.[26] Classes were given at both the University of Toronto and Victoria in the faculties of law as well as arts.[27]

The teaching and study of economics in the early years at Toronto may not be revealed fully by existing records. A number of professors not connected directly with the subject had a marked personal interest in it, and via lectures in other fields undoubtedly passed their enthusiasm on to students. J. B. Cherriman in mathematics, the Reverend William Hincks, and J. B. Hurlbert in the natural sciences have been mentioned above; and J. G. Hume, a philosopher who had studied under R. T. Ely at Johns Hopkins, was a fourth. In 1892 Hume summarized the history of economic thought, and giving an indication of the direction of his own teaching, concluded with a plea for "a closer alliance. . .between the study of Political Economy and Ethics."[28] Toronto graduates, notably the journalist William Houston, in later life often revealed a familiarity with and interest in economics which probably began in their student days.

Before completion of the university federation in 1889, at the insistence of the Hon. G. W. Ross, the Ontario Minister of Education, provision was made for a new department of political science.[29] William James Ashley, a distinguished graduate of Oxford, after interviews with the Provincial Premier and Leader of the Opposition in the Federal Parliament, was given a chair of "Political Economy and Constitutional History." Ashley proved extremely energetic and in his first year offered four courses in both the arts and law faculties, using texts by Walker and Mill with extensive supplementary reading lists.[30] He also organized a volun-

[26] Books recommended by Professor Beaven for 1865-1866 were by Whately, Senior, Smith, and Mill. *Calendar of University College, 1865-1866*, p. 19.

[27] The text in the elementary course in the law faculties was by Whately, and in the advanced course it was Smith's *Wealth of Nations*. See J. G. Hodgins, "Historical Sketch of Education in Upper Canada," in *Eighty Years' Progress of British North America* (Toronto, 1863), pp. 448, 449, 464, and 465.

[28] J. G. Hume, *Political Economy and Ethics* (Toronto, 1892), p. 39.

[29] Ross later described to William Ashley the public-spirited character of his motives: "I was then organizing a department of political science in the earnest hope that I would be able to afford the undergraduates of our University a comprehensive course of training in economics and political philosophy, which would fit them for dealing with the many social and constitutional problems which require particular attention in a rapidly expanding country like Canada. . . ." Anne Ashley, *William James Ashley, A Life by his Daughter* (London, 1932), p. 54.

[30] The four course headings were: (1) "The Elements of Political Economy," (2) "The History and Criticism of Economic Theories," (3) "The History of

tary seminar where papers ranging from "The Greek and Modern Conception of the State" to "Growth of the Factory System and Its Present Appearance in Ontario" were read and discussed.[31] Ashley was an inspiring lecturer and attracted many students to the new courses—twenty-two in his first graduating class and thirty-seven in the second.[32] He recognized the importance of research in Canada and started the University of Toronto *Studies in Political Science.* He was a man of many interests and sympathies, and Professor Schumpeter noted that he "conformed more than any other English economist to the German professional type of that time."[33] In 1892 Ashley went to Harvard to join Dunbar and Laughlin and to pursue his study of economic history, later returning to England, where he helped establish schools of commerce.

James Mavor, a Scot and graduate of St. Mungo's College, Glasgow, became chairman in 1892, and was assisted at different times before 1914 by J. M. McEvoy, S. J. McLean,[34] and S. M. Wickett. Under Mavor's direction the number of courses increased and original research was encouraged even at the undergraduate level. Wickett reported in 1897:

At Toronto the honor economic students are obliged to write as many as four "term essays" on specified subjects. The first of these essays regularly treats of the "Social Conditions and Resources" of the district whence the student comes, and at times furnishes some valuable sociological material, such as typical household budgets, etc.[35]

Some graduate work was offered, and although Mavor's own interests were world-wide, with a special emphasis on Russia, the *Studies in Political Science* were continued.[36]   The thorough in-

Economic Development," and (4) "Modern Economic Questions." *Calendar,* 1889-1890.

[31] The original "Minute Book of the Economics Seminary" conducted by Professor Ashley is preserved in the University of Toronto Library.

[32] *The University of Toronto and Its Colleges, 1827-1906,* p. 262.

[33] *History of Economic Analysis* (New York, 1954), p. 822. See also below, pp. 176-179.

[34] S. J. McLean published his *Tariff History of Canada* in Toronto in 1895. An important study he completed for the Dominion Government was "Reports upon Railway Commissions, Railway Rate Grievances and Regulative Legislation," *Sessional Papers of the Parliament of Canada,* 1902, Number 20a.

[35] "The Study of Political Economy at Canadian Universities," *loc. cit.,* p. 105.

[36] Wickett wrote: "The department is supported by one teaching fellowship, and has attached to it two economic post-graduate scholarships of $375 each, and one of $60, besides five undergraduate scholarships of from $50 to $75." *Ibid.,*

tegration of economics with political science and history, begun by Ashley, was continued and developed by Mavor and reached maturity in the works of such later scholars as Jackman, Fay, Innis, Logan, Bladen, and Easterbrook.[37]

The student of both Ashley and Mavor at Toronto best known today was William Lyon Mackenzie King, later the controversial and durable Prime Minister of Canada. R. MacGregor Dawson, King's biographer, reported that he "found his greatest enjoyment in economics and politics," and even when vacationing at the beautiful Muskoka Lakes buried himself in Ruskin and "our old friend 'Dave' Ricardo."[38] Unfortunately for King, his enthusiasm for study was not matched by his professors' confidence and affection; despite his desire to become the first Ph.D. in economics from Toronto, Mavor refused him the necessary fellowship. King went on to the University of Chicago, and at least to some extent disproved Mavor's skepticism when in 1906 at the age of thirty-two he was offered a full professorship at Harvard.

Queen's University at Kingston

In 1840 the Presbyterians of Upper Canada obtained a charter for Queen's University and in 1842 opened its doors.[39] The only teaching of economics for some years was with ethics in the department of logic and metaphysics; and although the departmental name was changed in 1886 to Mental and Moral Philosophy and Political Economy, this did not signify greatly increased enthusiasm for the subject.[40] Lectures were given by John Watson, an eminent professor of philosophy, until 1882 when the Reverend Dr. Campbell, a part-time lecturer from Montreal, was

---

p. 103. A list of University of Toronto studies published before 1907 is contained in *The University of Toronto and Its Colleges, 1827-1906*, pp. 254-256. For comments on Mavor's writing, see below, pp. 188-190.

[37] For appraisals of more recent developments in the Department at Toronto see: C. R. Fay, "The Toronto School of Economic History," *Economic History* (A Supplement to the *Economic Journal*), III (1934), 168-171; and W. T. Easterbrook, "Trends in Canadian Economic Thought," *The South Atlantic Quarterly*, LVIII (1959), 91-107.

[38] *William Lyon Mackenzie King* (Toronto, 1958), I, 29, 30, 40, and 41.

[39] See D. D. Calvin, *Queen's University at Kingston: the First Century of a Scottish-Canadian Foundation 1841-1941* (Kingston, 1941).

[40] See O. D. Skelton, "Fifty Years of Political and Economic Science in Canada," in *Fifty Years Retrospect: Canada 1882-1932*, p. 87.

called in to assist. Campbell announced optimistically that his reading list would consist of works by Smith, Roscher, Jevons, Cunningham, and Fawcett, but added that a "minute knowledge" was not necessary.[41]

In 1886 Adam Shortt, a graduate of Queen's and Edinburgh, took over from Campbell and in the succeeding term was named John Leys Lecturer in Political Science; in 1891 he was appointed Sir John A. Macdonald Professor of Political Science and chairman of a new department. Shortt's first action was liberalization of the syllabus, which involved less change of emphasis than broadening of scope. He continued to use the writings of Smith, Malthus, and Mill to provide training in theory, but he prescribed intense and critical study of these works rather than a survey of them. He also discussed current problems and introduced the writings of other authors, for example Walker, Marshall, Cairnes, List, Marx, Brentano, and Bagehot.[42] Students of Shortt were usually well trained and have ranked among Canada's greatest public men.[43] After establishing at Queen's a firm tradition of "applied economics"[44] Shortt left in 1908 for a career of his own in public service. His successor was O. D. Skelton, who ably continued Shortt's work before he himself became Under-Secretary of State for External Affairs.

It would not be correct to attribute the rapid development of economics at Queen's to Adam Shortt alone. G. M. Grant, principal from 1877 to 1902, had many interests close to economics, and as the driving spirit of the university was at least partially responsible for the activity which began in economics shortly after he took office. The major laurels, however, still rest with Shortt and the men who followed him; if one is justified in calling Queen's the cradle of a truly "Canadian" economics, then Shortt may be named the father.

[41] See W. A. Mackintosh, "Adam Shortt 1859-1931," *C.J.E.P.S.*, IV (1938), 166.

[42] See *ibid.*, and examination papers preserved in the Queen's University Library.

[43] C. H. Bland, O. D. Skelton, and Duncan McArthur were Shortt's special protegés, and B. M. Stewart, R. M. Fisher, and W. C. Clark, all of whom were his pupils, went on to become important in government.

[44] See W. T. Easterbrook, "Trends in Canadian Economic Thought," *loc. cit.*, p. 93.

McMaster University, Hamilton

McMaster was formed at Toronto in 1887 from Woodstock College and the Toronto Baptist College, and in 1927 moved to Hamilton. The influence of the larger University of Toronto was evident throughout McMaster's history, and particularly in economics, which was taught from the beginning by the philosophy department in a required course with the Torontonian title "Ethics and Civil Polity." Texts were by Adam Smith, Jevons, and Ely; lectures were by a succession of professors in other fields: T. H. Rand in education, A. H. Newman in history, G. J. Menge and William Dale in classics and history, A. L. McCrimmon in education and sociology, and W. J. Donald in sociology.[45] Not until after World War I, when the university grew in size and changed location, did economics receive the full attention of one man in a separate department.[46]

The University of Western Ontario, London

The "Western University of London, Ontario" was incorporated in 1878 and opened three years later with twelve students. Although by 1903 there were still only thirty-six enrolled in Arts and two hundred books in the library, small classes began in economics with J. M. McEvoy from Toronto as lecturer.[47] Louis A. Wood was named the first chairman of a new department of history and economics in 1914, but the two fields were not separated until 1920.

The University of Ottawa

The College of Bytown was founded in 1848 by the Roman Catholic Oblate Order, had its name changed in 1866 with that of the city to the College of Ottawa, and was made a pontifical university in 1889. From the beginning the Oblates set out to make

---

[45] *Calendar, McMaster University*, various years.

[46] K. W. Taylor reports that "McMaster University between 1908 and 1916 graduated four economists of distinction: D. A. MacGibbon, W. J. A. Donald, N. J. Ware, and H. A. Innis, all of whom went on to graduate studies at Chicago. The first three each in turn won the Hart, Shaffner, and Marx award for the best economic studies by younger economists in the United States." "Economic Scholarship in Canada," *C.J.E.P.S.*, XXVI (1960), 7.

[47] See W. M. Tamblyn, *These Sixty Years* (London, 1938), pp. 16, 43, 106, and 107.

use of the social sciences, recognizing that as a bilingual institution in the national capital they possessed a unique opportunity to influence public affairs. As early as 1859 political economy was placed on the curriculum, and professors gave addresses and wrote comments on economic topics of contemporary interest; the Reverend J. H. Tabaret, a founder of the university, lectured to the public around the time of Confederation and was followed later by the Reverend L. P. Paquin and the Reverend C. Gohiet.[48] After 1875 economics, as a division of "Mental and Moral Philosophy, Political Economy and Social Sciences," was made compulsory in the faculties of arts and civil engineering. The course consisted of "History of Economic Theory—Discussion of Practical Economic Questions—Financial Systems," and used texts by Say and Bastiat, which were available in both English and French.[49] The professors after Tabaret were: The Reverend J. J. Fillâtre (1886-1887 and 1889-1894), the Reverend J. B. Balland (1887-1888), the Reverend C. Gohiet (1894-1899), and the Reverend N. Nillés (1899 until after World War I).[50] Lectures ranged from a detailed study of classical principles to contemporary problems of organized labor, pauperism, bimetallism, and universal suffrage.[51] Emphasis on the link between economics and philosophy was never neglected; Tabaret asked his students to comment on the "philosophical dissertation" that "Moral science, without political economy is incomplete, political economy, not based upon morality, is unsound and injurious to the interests of society," and Fillâtre requested proof that "political economy is but a branch of social sciences, and that it is dependent on morals."[52]

[48] I am indebted for this information to the Reverend L. P. Gravel, Archivist of the University of Ottawa.

[49] *Annual Calendar, College of Ottawa,* various years.

[50] Fillâtre is said to have written a text in economics in the 1890's which apparently was never published.

[51] See for example reprinted examination papers in *Annual Catalogue of the College of Ottawa,* 1887-1888.

[52] *Annual Calendar,* 1885-1886, p. 95; and *Annual Catalogue,* 1889-1890, p. 93. See also Georges Simard, "Le Fondateur de l'Université d'Ottawa," *P.T.R.S.C.,* third series, XXXVII (1943), Section I, 117-121.

III. THE WEST

The University of Manitoba, Winnipeg

The University of Manitoba was established in 1877, and affiliated in subsequent years with five small colleges. Following American precedent, in 1885 a large tract of public land was granted for its support; but rapid growth had to await completion of the transcontinental railways and settlement of the prairies. Political economy was on the curriculum as early as 1882 in a special course entitled "Mental and Moral Science," with one section termed "Industrial Economy" covering price theory and exchange, and another "Social Economy" comprising public finance, international trade, and the "Progress of National Prosperity." Texts were by Smith, Mill, and later by Walker, with books by Say and Hervé-Bazin for French-speaking students.[53] Lectures were given in the component colleges, principally by clergymen; and the university served only as an examining body. Classes, which were conducted both in English and French, were confined to a study of classical principles with some attention in the 1890's to more topical questions such as "the chief causes which influence the efficiency of the individual laborer in the production of wealth," "trade unions and strikes," and (indicating an interest in the Henry George movement) "the nationalization of land."[54] In 1909 A. B. Clark, a former student of Nicholson at Edinburgh, became the first university professor of political economy[55] and ended the desultory teaching in the colleges. He offered classes covering "the leading principles of Political Economy, together with the chief landmarks in the history of Economic Theory, and the outlines of Economic History." In 1912 T. H. Fraser was appointed lecturer in economics, and thereafter a variety of courses was offered.[56]

The University of Alberta

The University of Alberta opened in 1908, and the first classes in economics were given six years later in the department of ac-

---

[53] *University of Manitoba Calendar*, 1882, p. 19.

[54] See examination papers in political economy, preserved in the University of Manitoba Library.

[55] See W. L. Morton, *One University: A History of the University of Manitoba* (n.p., 1957), p. 76.

[56] *University of Manitoba Calendar*, 1912-1913, p. 128.

countancy by A. L. Burt, a lecturer in history. The texts were by Ely and later by Gide. In 1915 a Department of History and Political Economy was formed, but not until after World War I was there a range of courses in economics.[57]

The University of Saskatchewan

When the University of Saskatchewan opened in 1910, three classes in economics were offered; texts were by Ely, Ashley, Cunningham, and Ingram, and lectures by E. H. Oliver, a graduate of Columbia and professor of history.[58]   L. C. Gray, trained at the University of Wisconsin, became Engen Research Professor of Economics in 1914, and began what was to become one of Canada's foremost departments.[59]

IV. ENGLISH-SPEAKING QUEBEC

McGill University, Montreal

McGill College was chartered in 1821 on the strength of a bequest from a Scotch fur trader; like the other early institutions, it developed slowly and did not open until 1843. In 1855 the first mention of economics was by Principal J. W. Dawson who proposed a special diploma course, apart from the regular arts program, to be entitled "Commercial Education" and to include, in addition to a variety of other subjects, "if suitable arrangements can be made, Lectures on Political Economy."[60]   Nothing came of Dawson's proposal; and the subject was given a small place in the fourth year of the arts course with lectures probably by the Reverend Canon Leach, Professor of Moral Philosophy and Logic, Vice-principal, and Dean of Faculty.[61] As late as the 1890's economics received attention

---

[57] Dean W. H. Johns of the University of Alberta, written communication, June 25, 1957.

[58] *Calendar, University of Saskatchewan,* 1910.

[59] See A. S. Morton, *Saskatchewan: The Making of A University* (Toronto, 1959), p. 78.

[60] J. W. Dawson, *On the Course of Collegiate Education Adapted to the Circumstances of British America: The Inaugural Discourse of the Principal of McGill College, Montreal* (Montreal, 1855), pp. 23 and 24.

[61] *McGill College, Montreal, Officers, Professors Course of Study, &c. &c.,* Session 1855-1856, pp. 3 and 15.

only in a course entitled "The History of English Philosophy from Hartley to Spencer."

McGill's deficiency in the social sciences was recognized at last in 1899 when Principal Peterson and Chancellor Strathcona suggested improvements in the faculty of arts and science. Explaining the need for reform, they appealed to the civic pride of Montrealers:

Effective provision must at once be made for those new subjects which are to render the Arts curriculum more varied and attractive; prominent among which is the subject of Economics and Political Science. It would be a matter of great surprise in other university circles—including those which flourish, on both continents, in the great centres of commercial and industrial activity—if it were more generally realized that an institution of such high standing as McGill University had been till now destitute of any provision for teaching in a department so universally recognized as indispensable to proper training for citizenship.[62]

The first action taken was the appointment of J. E. LeRossignol, a graduate of McGill and the University of Leipzig, as lecturer in economics and political science. LeRossignol's interests lay principally with philosophy, but a notable achievement in economics while at McGill was his writing of a book entitled *Monopolies Past and Present*.[63] His economics course had an impressive syllabus and an ambitious reading list, however, it ran only until Christmas, and it is to be doubted that either of these received serious consideration.[64]

The social sciences received their first real recognition in 1901 with the establishment of a department of economics and political science, and endowment of the Dow Chair in political economy. A. W. Flux was the first appointee, and S. B. Leacock was named lecturer in political science. Flux, a former student of Alfred Marshall, Fellow of St. John's College, Cambridge, and Stanley Jevons Professor of Political Economy in the Owens College at Manchester,

[62] *Annual Report of the Governors, Principal and Fellows of McGill University*, 1899-1900, p. 2.

[63] New York, 1901. After LeRossignol left McGill he taught most of his life at the Universities of Denver and Nebraska.

[64] The course was listed as "Economics,—Scope and Method of Economic Science; history of economic theory; public and private wealth; theory of value; theory of rent; interest and profits; money and credit; combinations of employers and labourers; speculation; transportation; commercial development and generally the industrial organization of society." Text and reference books were by Hadley, Ingram, Gide, Bullock, Marshall, MacLeod, MacFarlane, and Cohn.

was a frequent contributor to learned journals and an acknowledged authority in several fields.[65]   On his arrival at McGill he gave courses in "Elements of Economics," "History of Economic Theory," "Currency, Banking and Trade," and "History of Industry and Commerce," also a "Seminary in Economics" and an evening class to bankers on "Money, Banking and the Foreign Exchanges."[66] In subsequent years Flux added or alternated courses in "The Theory of Distribution," "Public Finance," "Economic Problems of Great Cities," "Descriptive Economics," "Modern Industrial Progress," and "Labour Problems."   Sheer fatigue may have prompted his return to England in 1908.   Stephen Leacock succeeded Flux as chairman and remained in this position until retirement in 1936.   Except for a few years as a graduate student at the University of Chicago Leacock was Canadian trained; and although a less than inspired economist, he was an interesting and entertaining teacher.[67] J. C. Hemmeon, another Canadian and a graduate of Harvard, was appointed to assist Leacock as lecturer in economics in 1907.

University of Bishop's College, Lennoxville

Bishop's College was chartered in 1843, opened in 1845, and attained university status in 1853.   It was closely associated with the Anglican Church in Canada, but admitted students of other denominations.   Students, in fact, were what the university consistently lacked; in 1889 G. B. Woolcombe, a graduate of Oxford, gave the first course in political economy and the Principal thought him a great success when he attracted four out of the ten students in the second year.[68] By 1893 the college had only thirty students and in 1898 reached a high of sixty-nine; it is not surprising that there was no separate department of economics.   In 1902 a "philosophical honors" program was set up including logic, psychology, and a single "Outline Course" in economics.   In 1914 one man, the Reverend R. C.

---

[65] See below, p. 184.

[66] See *McGill University Calendar*, 1902-1903, and A. W. Flux, "Is the Study of Political Economy Helpful to Bankers in Their Daily Occupation?" *J.C.B.A.*, X (1902-1903), 10.

[67] See below, pp. 190-193.

[68] D. C. Masters, *Bishop's University: The First Hundred Years* (Toronto, 1950), p. 85.

Burt, was still responsible for the three diverse fields of philosophy, economics, and church history.[69]

v. French Canada

Laval University and the Classical Colleges

Higher education in French Canada before 1914 was provided by a single university and a number of smaller institutions which were analogous to present-day American junior colleges. In 1663 Monseigneur Laval, the first Bishop of New France, founded the Petit Séminaire at Quebec City which grew into the Grand Séminaire and was chartered in 1852 as Laval University.[70] Beginning in the late eighteenth century classical colleges (*collèges classiques*) were set up to supplement secondary schools and to provide elementary university classes, principally in the classics. Eventually, most of the *collèges* affiliated with Laval to standardize instruction and insure admission of their graduates to the university.[71]

Several classical colleges offered courses in political economy as early as 1820, but the widespread public controversies over commercial policy and the general unpopularity of laissez faire (with which the subject was associated) discouraged their growth. In the 1840's Etienne Parent, one of the few doctrinaire French-Canadian free traders, praised the *collège* at Ste. Hyacinthe as the first to give political economy an important spot on the curriculum; he also made an eloquent appeal for endowed professorships:

. . . I wish to speak about the introduction of the elements of political economy into the collegiate course of studies, and about the establishment of chairs of political economy in this country, as they have been established in other countries which have less need than us. I believe that at the College of Ste. Hyacinthe, that institution which under its present professors has taken a foremost position among our schools of higher education, they have begun to pay attention to political economy; in this case,

[69] *Statutes, Rules and Ordinances for the Conduct and Government of Bishop's College and of the University of Bishop's College, Lennoxville, Province of Quebec* (Montreal, 1902), pp. 55 and 58; and *Calendar*, 1914.

[70] A branch of Laval was established at Montreal in 1876 and was incorporated in 1920 as the independent University of Montreal.

[71] For a brief account of early higher education in Quebec, see Abbé Camille Roy, *L'Université Laval et Les Fêtes du Cinquantenaire* (Quebec, 1903).

that institution will have had the merit of having been the first to recognize a great and pressing social need. Let us beseech it to continue this useful work; let us pray our other colleges to follow its example. Let us pray also our legislators to furnish for our young students the means of perfecting the study of the science begun in the colleges. Professors, everyone knows, save considerable work and time for the student; they show, at the outset, the route to follow; they point out dangers, make obstacles apparent, and prevent mistakes. It is necessary to learn so many things in a young country such as ours, where the division of labor is not yet as advanced as in old lands, that one cannot save too much of the time of the young. And the money which would be employed to this end could not be appropriated with greater profit. A few hundreds of Louis's voted annually for chairs of political economy, over some time, would save the province hundreds of thousands of Louis's, both in avoided waste and gain occasioned by the diffusion of economic knowledge.[72]

Parent seems to have been almost alone in his views about economics, and as enthusiasm for high tariffs increased after 1850 protectionists in French as in English Canada denounced the science as mere free-trade propaganda. When in a public debate at Laval University in 1859 a speaker merely suggested that French-Canadian students could benefit from study of economics, he received an indignant rebuttal. His critic explained:

I believe that we are able to cut off with advantage the teaching of Political Economy. . . . I don't know, gentlemen, if anyone among you has ever asked what Political Economy is. Assuredly it is not a science! A science is a collection of truths clearly deduced from certain principles—, and, in political economy, or that which exists today, almost everything is arbitrary: one finds there, scattered without order and sequence, the fruits of the observation of several influential men, each in his own way, according to his own ideas, habits, and the customs and interests of his caste or nation.[73]

Support for protection and disapproval of political economy reached a peak after Confederation; and in the 1870's François Langelier,

---

[72] "Importance de l'étude de l'économie politique," *Le Répertoire National,* IV (1850), 41 (translation).

[73] Cited in J. C. Taché, *Notice historiographique sur la fête celebrée à Quebec, le 16 Juin, 1859, jour du deux centième anniversaire de l'arrivée de Monseigneur de Montmorency-Laval en Canada* (Quebec, 1859), pp. 22-24 (translation).

an eminent professor of law, was actually rebuked by the Laval administration for presenting a series of lectures on the subject.[74]

Economics was not given an important place in French-Canadian universities until after World War I. Edouard Montpetit (examined in the next section) lectured on "Économie Politique et Sociale" in the faculty of law at the Montreal division of Laval, but this was subsidiary to his work at the School of Higher Commercial Studies. A school of social sciences opened at the University of Montreal when that institution was formed in 1920; a similar school grew out of the department of philosophy at Laval in 1932.[75]

L'École des Hautes Études Commerciales

As part of an awakening provincialism which included demands for the discovery of new ways to preserve and strengthen French-Canadian culture, a school for "higher commercial studies" was established at Montreal in 1907 by the Quebec Government to provide university instruction for students headed into business or civil service. The school opened in 1910 with 30 students and by 1920 was attracting 340;[76] to achieve this growth, however, faculty members throughout the decade spent most of their time as propagandists. Henry Laureys, Director of the school, explained to an audience in 1920 the difficulties that he and his colleagues faced.

You have all heard a father, badly disappointed at the progress his son is making in school, say: "Bah! I'm going to send him into business!" The reasoning behind the thought is clearly that for this career he has made enough. This is a serious error. . .the prejudice is deeply rooted. It is necessary to destroy it at any price, above all if we wish to achieve in the future the predictions of commercial and industrial prosperity, which are correctly made about Canada.[77]

Political economy was an important part of the school's cur-

[74] S. M. Wickett, *op. cit.*, p. 104.

[75] See Maurice Tremblay and Albert Faucher, "L'Enseignement des Sciences Sociales au Canada de langue française," *Royal Commission Studies: A Selection of Essays Prepared for the Royal Commission on National Development in the Arts, Letters and Sciences* (Ottawa, 1951), pp. 193-198.

[76] L'École des Hautes Études Commerciales became the faculty of commerce for Laval University at Montreal in 1915.

[77] *L'Education commerciale: facteur de notre expansion* (Montreal, 1920), p. 25 (translation).

riculum and was taught by Edouard Montpetit, a French Canadian trained at the École Libre des Sciences Politiques and the Collège des Sciences Sociales in Paris. Like the first professors in English Canada, Montpetit was forced to lecture in a number of other fields, and as he reminisced twenty-eight years later, there was little time for contemplation or research:

> It was necessary to adapt to French Canada the lessons learned in France and to form a discipline out of them. Furthermore, it was not only necessary to do this for political economy! I had to apply the same method to other courses of which I had been put in charge to justify the honor of being a career professor: public finance, commercial policy, statistics, public law, and indeed the elements of public, commercial and industrial law, all of which were more or less new to me.[78]

Montpetit used *Principes d'économie politique* by Charles Gide as a text, but told of the extreme scarcity everywhere in Montreal of books on economics in French.

Beginning in 1911 L'École des Hautes Études Commerciales published a journal, *Revue Économique Canadienne,* with articles principally by Laureys, Montpetit, and A. J. De Bray, another professor who wrote mostly in defense of commercial education and research.[79] This publication marked the beginning of systematic economic writing by French Canadians.

VI. SUMMARY AND CONCLUSION

Economics was taught in most Canadian universities from their beginning, but was not widely accepted as a science worthy of separate departments and the undivided attention of scholars until after World War I. Three periods may be discerned in the history. For some years after the first college formations, racial, religious, and geographic divisions caused a proliferation of small, weak institutions

---

[78] Edouard Montpetit, "Les Canadiens Français et l'économique," *P.T.R.S.C.,* Third Series, XXXII (1938), Section I, 56 (translation). See also below, pp. 194-195.
[79] A. J. De Bray, "L'Enseignement commerciale au Canada," *R.E.C.,* I (1911), 4-19; "L'Enseignement de la statistique," *ibid.,* 228-232; "La Réforme des statistiques canadiennes," *ibid.,* III (1914), 261-267; "Pourquoi des hautes études commerciales?" *ibid.,* pp. 333-341; and *L'Essor industriel et commercial du peuple canadienne* (Montreal, n.d.).

in which a minimum number of courses were offered and professors were burdened with heavy loads in several fields. Political economy was regarded as a distasteful, tedious, and non-essential division of moral philosophy—an easy preparation for any faculty member and particularly well-suited for a busy administrator. By 1886 the subject had been taught by at least six heads of colleges, eight clergymen, three historians, three linguists, one teacher of education, and one lawyer, not one of whom could have called himself "economist."[80] The purpose of the course was intellectual discipline and lectures for the most part were dull and unrelated to local conditions; important texts were by John Stuart Mill, Francis Wayland (an American Baptist minister), and by Archbishop Whately. Teachers never undertook research, and students were not encouraged to go beyond their first uninspiring contact with the subject.

In the 1880's and 1890's a combination of circumstances gave life to economics. Industrialization, westward expansion, and a new national consciousness resulted in unprecedented public awareness of economic problems; at the same time controversies over commercial policy (which for over fifty years had made economic science unpopular) abated, and attention focused on labor legislation, land taxation, industrial combinations, and a government currency. By the turn of the century powerful social groups which formerly had regarded economics with distrust as an obstacle to tariff protection came to view the science with approval because it provided arguments against trade unions and government intervention.[81] The universities, in some instances after reorganization or federation, became relatively secure and contemplated expansion of their curricula. Interest in economics in Europe and the United States,

[80] Evidence in this chapter does not support the statement by Professor C. B. Macpherson that "Economics and political science got their start in Canadian universities in the 1870's and 1880's, but until the 1920's. . .was [sic] taught. . . usually by imported professors," "The Social Sciences," Julian Park, ed., The Culture of Contemporary Canada (Ithaca, 1957), p. 185. The statement by K. W. Taylor that "The first university course in political economy to be offered in Canada was in 1878 when the Department of Philosophy at Queen's University introduced a course of lectures based on Adam Smith, Mill, and Jevons" also requires some qualification. "Economic Scholarship in Canada," C.J.E.P.S., XXVI (1960), p. 6.

[81] See above, p. 131. An official of the Canadian Manufacturers' Association whose predecessors in the 1850's had termed economics "simple nonsense" was anxious to explain in the 1880's that wages, where there was no collective bargaining, were the result of "supply and demand" and were therefore "just."

aroused by economic historians and the marginalists, was carried to Canada; as Principal Peterson of McGill explained before making his first appointment in 1901, the science had at last become "universally recognized as indispensable."

Since Canada possessed no facilities for advanced training in economics, the first professors had to be educated abroad. They represented most of the significant academic traditions of the day: Davidson, Mavor, and Shortt, the Scotch political economy of economics linked with philosophy; Flux, Cambridge theory; Ashley, German economic history; Montpetit, French empiricism; and Leacock, the training of American graduate schools. The new men introduced a variety of courses to replace the old classes in "principles," and they enlivened ancient reading lists with the writings of contemporary authors (particularly Böhm-Bawerk, Ely, Fawcett, Ingram, Jevons, Marshall, Roscher, and Walker). After several years they began to use local institutional material in lectures and to work in a modest fashion on Canadian problems. But when they attempted to move from economics as taught in other countries to an indigenous discipline these pioneers were for some years effectively thwarted. University administrations saw no purpose for economics beyond filling a gap in the curriculum and, mindful of the subject's recent affiliations, continued to require economists to teach in other fields. Lecturing was emphasized above research, and five or six class preparations were not regarded as unreasonable. When John Davidson described himself in 1898 as a "scholar in exile," he might have added "at hard labor." The first economics professors found limited attractions in Canada, and either like Ashley, Davidson, and Flux they soon left the country, or like Leacock, Mavor, and Shortt spent their energies in more rewarding occupations.

A third period in the development of academic economics was only taking shape by World War I, and is mainly outside the scope of this study. Scholars with an interest in the Canadian economy increased in number and made contact with each other through the Royal Society, the Canadian Political Science Association, and the civil service. Growing public awareness of economics was evidenced by mounting class enrollments and new employment opportunities in government and industry. Raw economic data became available to professors from the Dominion Bureau of Statistics, and avenues of publication opened in scholarly journals and sympathetic university presses.   In this favorable environment the historical tradition introduced at Toronto by Ashley and Mavor was continued and greatly expanded by C. R. Fay and Harold Innis, the founders of the "Toronto School" of economic history.   The association of economics with history and its application to public policy, established at Queen's by Shortt, was continued by Skelton, Mackintosh, Curtis, and Knox.   At the other universities strength in economics eventually replaced weakness, and full recognition of the discipline was a-chieved.[82]

[82] Canadian economics in this century has been treated in two articles by W. T. Easterbrook, "Trends in Canadian Economic Thought," *The South Atlantic Quarterly*, LVIII (1959), 91-107; and "Recent Contributions to Canadian Economic History: Canada," *The Journal of Economic History*, XIX (1959), 76-102.   K. W. Taylor has covered the same ground in "Economic Scholarship in Canada," *C.J.E.P.S.*, XXVI (1960), pp. 6-18.

6

The First Academic Economists

In this chapter the chief interests and most important writings of the first university economists will be examined. Because all these men either devoted but a part of their careers to economics, or lived but a portion of their lives in Canada, some of their best-known works lie outside the scope of this study and will not be treated here. The economists have been placed in three groups: Britons who emigrated only to return home after a few years, English-speaking native Canadians together with immigrants who spent the largest part of their lives in Canada, and French Canadians.

i. British Immigrants Who Later Returned Home

William James Ashley

William Ashley taught at the University of Toronto for only four years but during this time was able to establish a tradition which developed eventually into the distinctive "Toronto School" of economic history. His appointment as an economic historian to the first chair in political economy was not accidental. When Ashley came to Toronto, economic theory, particularly as applied to commercial policy, had been a source of bitter controversy for almost half a century; undoubtedly it was hoped that with his background in history he would not assume any doctrinaire theoretical position. Ashley quickly made his stand clear on this matter and did not disillusion those who had appointed him. During his inaugural address in 1888 he argued that economics as a science really began in the 1870's with the first work of economic historians. Before that time political economy in universities had comprised untested hypotheses and was taught only to women and "pass" students "who certainly found it the easiest course in which to 'get through' "; elsewhere the subject "stank in the nostrils of intelligent working men. Mechanics' Institutes had been fed up on it for half a century to show artisans that everything in the industrial world was for the best; or, at any rate, that it could not be improved by combination, or by the interference of the State." Gladstone spoke for numerous disgusted politicians when he remarked "the principles of Political Economy must be relegated to the planet Saturn." The British Association had with good reason talked of doing away with its Economics Section, and in the United States "professors were free traders or protectionists according to the state in which they taught."[1]

The revolution in economics, Ashley explained, began in Germany, where candidates for the civil service were taught without "the prejudice against Government action which was natural to an English or French Liberal," and where scholars were influenced by "what has been the great achievement of German thought in the last fifty years,—the discovery and application of the Historical Method." In England Cliffe Leslie, Ingram, and Arnold Toynbee followed the Germans in attempting to discover "a Political Economy. . . which shall be of real value to society; in it the old doctrines will be shewn to be not untrue, but to have only a relative truth, and to deserve a much less important place than has been assigned to them. . . ." Pointing out the path that would be followed by Toronto economists for generations, Ashley explained that "the direction for fruitful work" was "no longer in the pursuit of the abstract deductive method which has done as much service as it is capable of, but in the following new methods of investigation— historical, statistical, inductive."[2] For example, when making a study of agriculture in Ontario "the economist will not aim at ending with a 'law of rent' or a 'law of production' based on Ontarian facts, but with a picture of Ontarian agriculture, and of the influences that affect it." Only a careful student of Canadian economic history, and not a mere expert in theory (that "neat little body of compendious 'laws' and maxims"), could qualify as an advisor on public policy.

Ashley's experience in Canada, in addition to its profound effect

---

[1] *What Is Political Science? An Inaugural Lecture Given in the Convocation Hall of the University of Toronto, 9th November, 1888* (Toronto, 1888), pp. 10-13.

[2] *Ibid.*, p. 16.

on the Department at Toronto, had an impact upon his own interests, and his attention shifted somewhat from historical to contemporary problems. In Canada he wrote a series of *Nine Lectures on the Earlier Constitutional History of Canada*, the second part of his *Economic History*, and several lengthy reviews later contained in *Surveys, Historic and Economic;* he also edited a work by Fustel de Coulanges, translated by his wife, Margaret Ashley.[3] As Profesor J. H. Clapham has explained, however, "Four years as a professed economist at Toronto, with history reserved for summer resorts in long vacations, had done their work in linking him to the exciting American economic life."[4] Ashley became particularly concerned over the fate of the British Empire, and proposed holding it together with economic bonds. In 1903, eleven years after leaving Canada, he advocated intercolonial tariff preferences, admitting "the starting point of my thought in this matter is the conception of the British Empire as it may be."[5] Like so many other immigrants, Ashley had come to believe that Canada was in dire peril of being absorbed, or at least overwhelmed, by the United States; and he advocated strengthening the connection with England at any cost.

I recognise to the full that there are some who cherish what they think an equally noble ideal—the ideal of an Anglo-Saxon federation, which shall include all the English-speaking peoples. It was an unanticipated result of my residence in America that in me such a hope soon faded away. . .the peoples still within the British Empire are peoples for whom we are still in a measure responsible; and something better can be made of the self-governing colonies than a set of second-rate States, shivering beneath the shadow of two great empires of the future.[6]

Ashley's thinking with regard to certain elements of the economic system was affected by his stay in Canada. Only a short time after his arrival he explained that he had come into sympathy with "the younger economists" who "no longer accept laissez faire as a general

---

[3] *The Origin of Property in Land* (London, 1891).
[4] "Obituary: William James Ashley," *Economic Journal*, XXXVII (1927), 680. Ashley wrote to Professor Lujo Brentano from Toronto in 1890: "My residence here has . . . given me opportunities to come in contact with business men, and to study the workings of modern financial operations." H. W. McCready, "Sir William Ashley: Some Unpublished Letters," *The Journal of Economic History*, XV (1955), 36.
[5] "The Argument for Preference," *Economic Journal*, XIV (1904), 1.
[6] *Ibid.*, p. 2.

principle"; probably with the recently enacted National Policy and much-subsidized Canadian Pacific Railway in mind he added: "Each case. . .must be decided on its merits, on a balance of advantages and disadvantages. The state may wisely do some things and not others; and it may do things in some countries which in others it ought to be prevented from attempting."[7] Recognizing the dif- ficulty of maintaining competition in an isolated colonial economy, Ashley refused to pass judgment on any monopoly without a hearing. After examining the report of an alleged combination in the Canadi- an sugar industry he enumerated the "good and bad features of this organization," and discovered that as a result of large scale produc- tion sugar prices had risen very little and costs had fallen; few firms had been prevented from entering the market, and the industry generally had been stabilized. Having begun his study with a bias "strongly against all such combinations of trades," Ashley con- cluded: ". . .in my opinion it is impossible wholly to condemn or wholly to praise the sugar combine. The economist must stand by, and see what takes place."[8] Although Canadian conditions did not inspire Ashley to present important new hypotheses, they did lead him to strengthen his historian's skepticism of accepted theory.

John Davidson

During a decade spent at the University of New Brunswick John Davidson wrote in several fields of economics, and consider- ing his heavy teaching load and situation, as he said, "some four hundred miles from any library even half as good as his own," he produced an amazing quantity and quality of work. His best known book The Bargain Theory of Wages (1898) traced the development of wage theory, examining particular theories partly in terms of the social background of their authors. He described the subsistence, wage-fund, and productivity theories, and concluded that all were inadequate under modern conditions. He suggested his own "bar-

[7] "What Is Political Science?," p. 22.
[8] Surveys Historic and Economic (London, 1900), pp. 361-377. Ashley also was not opposed to monopoly in the labor market. He wrote to Professor Brentano in 1892: "I find that I am in a position to influence to some extent public opinion in Canada in the direction of accepting the principle of Trades Unions; and one of the most effective arguments, as I have soon seen, has been to present them as the necessary basis for the successful working of Boards of Conciliation." H. W. McCready, op. cit., p. 37.

gain theory" which he believed proved that neither the supply price of labor (meaning a human subsistence level) nor demand based on productivity determined wage levels:

We must get rid altogether of the idea that there is an economic force which allots absolutely any share of the product, even the smallest, to any of the claimants. There is no absolute minimum and no absolute maximum for any share; and the amount at which the share is finally fixed is determined by a combination of forces.[9]

Wages were fixed, he declared, by a bargaining process within "estimates" set by workers and employers; although he claimed novelty for this theory, it was essentially a description of supply and demand forces in an imperfect market. He explained:

The price of labor is determined somewhere between two estimates placed upon it—the estimate of the employer and the estimate of the laborer. The estimate of the laborer is the resultant of two factors—one positive and one negative—the utility of the reward and the disutility of the labor; and the estimate of the employer is on the whole dependent on the indirect utilities afforded by what he purchases, or rather by the discounted value of the product created by the laborer's exertions.[10]

Davidson examined some of the circumstances of collective bargaining, making almost the only use in Canada of the large Report of the Royal Commission on the Relations of Capital and Labor. He considered the effects on wage rates of new machinery, employer and worker knowledge, labor and capital mobility, and trade unions. Davidson exaggerated his contribution when he claimed to have established a revolutionary new theory of income distribution; however, his work must be appreciated as one of the first descriptions of wage determination in a less than perfect market.

The *Bargain Theory* was reviewed by several journals in the United States, but by none in Canada. Frank Fetter praised the historical exposition and criticized the theoretical pretensions of the author: ". . . there has here been dignified with the name of a theory a shrewd and suggestive discussion of the various practical forces which limit or facilitate competition."[11] Irving Fisher pointed out that Davidson's "estimates" could have been expressed better as schedules of supply and demand, noted "a lack of that precision which we are

[9] *The Bargain Theory of Wages* (New York, 1898), p. 119.
[10] *Ibid.*, p. 140.
[11] *Political Science Quarterly*, XIII (1898), 569.

gradually requiring in economic treatises," but concluded, "As a critical and historical essay his book is full of interest, instruction and suggestion."[12] Sidney Sherwood considered the work a "suggestive and enlightening review, at once historical and critical, of the development of the theory of wages."[13] Davidson must certainly be regarded today as Canada's first "labor economist."

In his second book, *Commercial Federation and Colonial Trade Policy* (1900), Davidson approached a question of perennial interest both in Canada and Great Britain—How could the ties of Empire be strengthened? He rejected intercolonial preferential tariffs such as Laurier's double scale of 1898, on the grounds, first, that the revenue requirements of developing areas made high duties essential, and second, that protectionist sentiments had become permanent.[14] He concluded that "an Imperial Customs Union is, in the strict sense of the word, an impossibility for the British Empire."[15] A second unsatisfactory imperial bond, Davidson explained, was the sentimental tie of patriotism and the flag; trade, he argued, was directed by comparative cost conditions, and the migration of capital and labor by comparative returns. Davidson urged, as the only possible means of strengthening the Empire, that trade be subsidized with grants or loans to railways, shipping lines, ocean cables, and even postal systems.

Closer and mutually beneficial commercial relations are as sure a way of strengthening political relations as any other; and since the grant of responsible government, perhaps the only way available for the mother country. It is a question simply which is the easiest, which is the most practicable, which is the way that leads most directly to the desired end.[16]

Although Davidson's criticisms and proposals were without substantial influence, he injected a realistic note into contemporary dis-

---

[12] *Yale Review*, VII (1899), 110-112.

[13] *A.A.A.P.S.S.*, XI (1898), 403-405. More favorable but less interesting reviews also appeared in *The Dial*, XXVI (1899), 21, and *The Nation*, LXVI (1898), 466.

[14] In 1903 Davidson criticized proposals that a British preference be extended to Canadian wheat for a third reason; he believed a wheat boom would be started which would result in eventual collapse. "Canada's Second Thought on a Preference," *Fortnightly Review*, LXXX (1903), 474-479.

[15] *Commercial Federation and Colonial Trade Policy* (London, 1900), p. 81.

[16] *Ibid.*, p. 94.

cussion of such airy schemes as Imperial Federation and an Anglo-Saxon free-trade area.

Influenced by John Hobson's underconsumption theory of economic crises, Davidson examined the history of life insurance in Canada, and estimated that the total quantity had increased almost 125 per cent between 1884 and 1894, against a mere 40 per cent increase in national wealth. Davidson regarded all savings as a reduction in the demand for goods, and as the initial cause of a decline in income. He explained:

> . . . it is certain that one of the great practical questions of the day is the striking of a better balance between the present and the future. We need for the sake of industry to spend more rather than to save more; for, if we save, we curtail the area of production within which our savings must be invested. Saving implies consumption in the future, but the world already has as much as it wants of the commodities which will be produced if we save. A general increase of expenditure and less saving would remedy many of the evils of industrial depression.[17]

Davidson must be accused with Hobson and other underconsumptionists of failing to recognize that, given sufficient investment, no amount of saving will cause a decline in production. He may have discovered more valid criticisms of life insurance, however, when he pointed out first that if policies were contracted during inflation they might lapse in depression, and second that by investing abroad insurance companies failed to support domestic development. On the last point Davidson concluded:

> The saving hampers the community where we need to be freest; and we have not even the consolation of knowing that our savings are developing the industry of the country. It is a serious question when the citizens of a young community are so timorous of its future that they hand over their savings to insurance companies to invest in securities which ought to be left to the more timid foreign investor. The savings of a young country ought, if they are made at all, to be invested in industrial undertakings for which foreign capital is not so easily obtainable.[18]

As an exercise in demography, Davidson examined the increase of the French Canadians in North America, hoping to discover a

---

[17] "Over-Insurance and Under-Consumption," *J.C.B.A.*, IV (1896-1897), 297.
[18] *Ibid.*, pp. 301-302.

standard rate of population growth, or what he said without evidence, Malthus had called a "natural prolifickness." French Canada, he explained, had been "visited neither by war nor by pestilence" and had enjoyed "normal conditions," i.e., "security of life and property, and freedom of development. . .abundance of good land unappropriated. . .inexhaustible fisheries and unexhausted forests, with developing industry at home and unrestricted freedom of migration. . . ." As a result, "The French population of Canada is an isolated, homogeneous body of which we can observe the true increase, the whole increase, and nothing but the true increase, and from this source it is possible to set up a standard which shall not be arbitrary even in appearance."[19] French Canadians increased between 1765 and 1890-1891 about 30 per cent each decade, less than might have been expected from their high birth rate and adequate food supply. Davidson discovered that a single factor, high infant mortality caused by irregular and excessive feeding explained this relatively low rate. He concluded that, because of constantly changing social factors such as child care, the concept of a standard rate of population growth was meaningless, and "the assumption made by Malthus of a natural 'prolifickness' which is approximately the same the world over, becomes quite untenable."[20]

None of Davidson's writings was of great significance or lasting importance. He was, however, one of the first to recognize the number and variety of problems awaiting the economist in Canada, and he made the earliest use of some of the basic raw materials (e.g., Royal Commission reports and the census returns collected by J. C. Taché). He urged the government to collect and process systematically economic data,[21] and the lack of response to his request may have caused him to return from "exile" (as he described his position at the University of New Brunswick) to Great Britain. At his death Davidson was engaged in writing an economic history of Scotland.[22]

---

[19] "The Growth of the French Canadian Race in America," *A.A.A.P.S.S.*, VIII (1896), 219-220 and 228.

[20] *Ibid.*, pp. 230-231.

[21] See John Davidson, "Statistics of Expenditure and Consumption in Canada," *Transactions of the Nova Scotia Institute of Science*, X (1898-1899), 1-3.

[22] John Davidson and Alexander Gray, *The Scottish Staple at Verre* (London, 1909), p. v.

Alfred W. Flux

A. W. Flux (later Sir Alfred Flux) brought to Canada for seven years the influence of Cambridge theoretical economics and Alfred Marshall. Before leaving England Flux had already established a substantial reputation, and his stay at McGill was only an interlude in a notable career. His writings over a lifetime were numerous and varied, principally on economic theory and statistics;[23] he was the first to associate a linear homogeneous production function with the Euler Theorem,[24] and he carried on an acrimonious controversy with J. R. Hobson over the theory of underconsumption. While at McGill in 1904 Flux wrote a textbook entitled *Economic Principles, An Introductory Study*[25] which was a compilation of accepted fundamentals and included references to most outstanding contemporary authors.[26] Heavy emphasis was placed upon the writings of Mill and Marshall (whom Flux described as "the teacher to whom he [Flux] owes his chief guidance in economic study"), and heretical doctrines received relatively little attention. The book was adequate and conservative, and to the extent that it was representative of teaching at McGill it did justice to the department. Flux's only indication of interest in Canadian economic problems was a short note on "Canadian Banking and the Financial Crisis" written after he had returned to England.[27] Canadians were neither a stimulating nor receptive audience for an economic theorist, and Flux made little impact either upon McGill or upon the country's economics.

[23] Among Flux's most important writings were an edition of W. S. Jevons, *The Coal Question* (London, 1906); *The Swedish Banking System* (Washington, 1910); *The Foreign Exchanges* (London, 1924); and many articles, particularly in the *Economic Journal, Transactions of the Royal Statistical Society,* and *Transactions of the Manchester Statistical Society.*

[24] See G. Stigler, *Production and Distribution Theories 1870 to 1895* (New York, 1941), p. 326.

[25] London, 1904. J. M. Keynes considered this book one of "the leading treatises of the modern classical school." *The General Theory of Employment Interest and Money* (London, 1936), pp. 175 and 176.

[26] Authorities cited by Flux were Bagehot, Bastable, Böhm-Bawerk, Cairnes, Conant, Cossa, Dunbar, Farrer, Fawcett, Giffen, Goschen, Hadley, Hobson, Jevons, Keynes, Marshall, J. S. Mill, Nicholson, Pantaleoni, Schloss, Seligman, Sidgwick, Taussig, Walker, and Wieser.

[27] *Yale Review,* XVII (1908), 93-98.

II. ENGLISH-SPEAKING CANADIANS

Adam Shortt

Whereas Ashley at Toronto linked economics with the study of history, Adam Shortt strengthened at Queen's the traditional Scotch association of economics with philosophy. Shortt's works are too numerous to list here, but they reveal above all a desire to understand and solve social problems through the study of well-documented fact. He was one of the first to recognize the wealth of historical material available in Canada for scholars, and he also saw that it was quickly being lost as a result of inattention and lack of interest. With Arthur G. Doughty he directed extensive compilation and research for the Canadian Archives, and he edited several volumes of selected documents.[28] The pioneer work *Canada and Its Provinces* was his special project, and he wrote a biography of Lord Sydenham for the *Makers of Canada* Series.[29] Shortt was particularly interested in monetary problems, and he produced a notable set of articles for the *Journal of the Canadian Bankers' Association* on Canadian currency and banking.[30] He left Queen's in 1908 to work on a number of boards set up under the new Industrial Disputes Investigation Act, and henceforth the duties of a public servant took most of his time. From 1908 until 1917 he was the first chairman of the Civil Service Commission and after World War I he worked for the International Economic Conference and in the Economic and Financial Section of the League of Nations. In his later years Shortt was again able to devote some attention to research and to the Canadian Archives; his last project was a catalogue of the Baring Papers, which he had obtained from Sir Edward Peacock, a former pupil.[31]

As an economic historian and advisor on public policy Shortt was first rate, and his work stands as irrefutable testimony. He was

---

[28] *Documents Relating to the Constitutional History of Canada* (Ottawa, 1918); *Documents on Currency, Finance and Exchange of Canada under the French Regime* (Ottawa, 1925); *Documents Relating to the Currency, Exchange and Finance in Nova Scotia with Preferatory Documents, 1675-1758* (Ottawa, 1933).

[29] *Canada and Its Provinces* (Toronto and Glasgow, 1914-1917), 23 volumes. *Lord Sydenham* (Toronto, 1908).

[30] See chap. ii above.

[31] For biographical information on Shortt, see W. A. Mackintosh, "Adam Shortt 1859-1931," *C.J.E.P.S.*, IV (1938), 164-176; and A. Haydon, "Adam Shortt," *Q.Q.*, XXXVIII (1931), 609-623.

less adept, however, as an economic theorist and student of the analytical tools developing so rapidly in his day. Like most persons trained in philosophy, he was reluctant to recognize economics as a distinct "science," and he deplored a separation of the study from ethics and politics:

> . . . to take as the basis of an independent science the subject of wealth and the best possible means for its production and accumulation, produces a tendency to regard wealth as in itself a kind of final object. Smith and Mill were not in this respect so rigid as many of their followers. With later economists the desire for scientific exactness has led to the greatest possible exclusion of all considerations as to the proper use of wealth. There is, it is true, in Political Economy an element which admits of rather precise treatment, namely the conditions necessary for the production, exchange and distribution of wealth. It is altogether desirable that this element should receive definite and separate treatment. But it is not so desirable that this treatment should be elevated to the position of a separate science.[32]

Shortt did not appreciate the attempts of the Austrian marginalists to incorporate demand analysis in a theory of price, and he even criticized, with apparent misunderstanding, the logic of Alfred Marshall's demand curve:

> . . . so eminent an economist as Professor Marshall of Cambridge, claims that demand schedules may be made out for individuals and groups. . . . In so doing he asserts to begin with that each several want is limited, which is true only of the simpler animal wants for a given time, but is wholly untrue of the distinctively human wants. Hence he is mistaken in saying quite generally that every increase in the quantity of a thing which a man gets produces a diminishing pleasure. His law of diminishing utility of pleasure, which is so very important in his theory of value, is, therefore, true only of the barest necessities of life and is no general economic principle.[33]

Unlike Ashley at Toronto, who regarded economic theory as largely a collection of untested (and therefore useless) hypotheses, Shortt at Queen's disputed the very reasonableness of theoretical formulation, except in general terms as in moral philosophy. At the two schools the results of the diverging attitudes of the founders were

[32] "The Nature and Sphere of Political Economy," Q.Q., I (1893), 100-101.
[33] "The Basis of Economic Value," Q.Q., II (1894), 72-73.

in one sense similar; strictly theoretical questions were put aside, in the one for full concentration on economic history, and at the other for the study of history as a guide to economic policy.

Perhaps because of his Canadian background, Shortt was not worried, as were Ashley and Davidson, about maintaining economic independence from the United States. In 1904 he concluded that Canada would have nothing to gain from increased integration with the British Empire, and he argued that economic autonomy should be increased—leaving commercial policy unencumbered by foreign commitments.

The fact is that our own national future, with its many problems and possibilities, is opening out before us with such attractiveness and with such responsibilities that, while it is our obvious policy to maintain good relations with all the world, it would be the height of folly to tie ourselves up under any hard and fast obligation, either commercial or political, for, in view of our constantly changing circumstances, these might prove most embarrassing within a very short time.[34]

In his policy proposals as well as his research interests, Shortt exhibited a sincere and refreshing faith in the permanent viability of the Canadian economy.

Adam Shortt was the first native-born Canadian economist, and the first to select the domestic economy as a primary field of interest. Professor W. A. Mackintosh has written:

It would be a mistake to represent Adam Shortt as a great master in the social sciences. There have been but a few, and none in Canada. He achieved no distinctive body of doctrine nor any brilliant synthesis. Yet, he was a journeyman who wrought mightily in his chosen craft, and whose work will have enduring influence in Canada. As a teacher, more than anyone he helped to establish the place of Economics and Political Science in Canadian universities.[35]

A. R. M. Lower said: "Shortt was the only senior economist prior to 1914 to see Canada through Canadian eyes, those at other universities being either old-countrymen, or colonials. He left a school behind him which has had vast influence in Canadian develop-

[34] "Preferential Trade Between Britain and Canada," *Publications of the American Economic Association*, Third Series, VI (1905), 321.

[35] *Op. cit.*, p. 175.

ment."[36] H. A. Innis concluded: "He must be regarded as the founder of the subject."[37]

James Mavor

James Mavor's interests were widespread and his writings voluminous in many areas of the social sciences.[38] When he came to Toronto in 1893 and for some years afterwards he was concerned principally with labor problems; however, he emphasized that he always aimed at description and not reform. He explained in his inaugural lecture:

If we are to build up a science of economics we must do so with our eye on, but with our minds and voices away from, the market place or the hustings. We must have as little emotional interest in this or that theory, or this or that policy, as we should have in the examination of the evolutions of an oyster feeding under a microscope or in the discussion of the succession of the rocks in our neighbourhood.[39]

A Report to the British Board of Trade in 1904 on the Canadian West was Mavor's first important work on a Canadian topic; in it he anticipated some of the problems which were to materialize after the peak of the wheat boom. In 1914 he wrote one of the first texts for use in the growing number of business and commerce courses.[40] Mavor's best-known books, *An Economic History of Russia* (1914) and *The Russian Revolution* (1928, two volumes) were products of years of research outside Canada.

Mavor's thinking was not substantially affected by his exposure to Canadian conditions. He brought with him from Scotland a

[36] "The Development of Canadian Economic Ideas," in J. F. Normano, *The Spirit of American Economics* (New York, 1943), p. 230.

[37] "The State of Economic Science in Canada," *Commerce Journal*, March 1933, p. 6.

[38] For an incomplete listing of Mavor's works, see *P.T.R.S.C.*, Third Series, XX (1926), Proceedings, p. xvi. Mavor's autobiography is *My Windows on the Street of the World* (London, 1922), 2 vols.

[39] "The Relation of Economic Study to Public and Private Charity," Inaugural Lecture delivered before the University of Toronto, February 6th, 1893, *A.A.A.P.-S.S.*, IV (1893-1894), 37. Works by Mavor on labor questions were *The Scottish Railway Strike 1891: A History and Criticism* (Edinburgh, 1891); with J. R. Motion, J. Speir, and R. P. Wright, *Report on Labour Colonies* (Glasgow, 1892); "Labour and Politics in England," *Political Science Quarterly*, X (1895), 486-517; *Report on Workmen's Compensation for Injuries* (Toronto, 1900).

[40] *The North-West of Canada with Special Reference to Wheat Production for Export* (London, 1914), Cmd. 2628; *Applied Economics* (New York, 1914).

strong tradition of laissez faire and he found in Canada many instances of government economic activity to examine and criticize. He concluded from a study of a public telephone company in Manitoba:

> It is possible that only by repeated and costly failures such as the Manitoba Government Telephones, will the public realize that the proper function of Government is not the conduct of industries but the impartial inspection of them under intelligent laws adapted to the character and conditions of the community and the country.[41]

He used the example of the Hydro-Electric Commission of Ontario to prove that state ownership may lead to corruption. He explained:

> Whenever the Government, either as a Government or in the form of an organ created by it and insusceptible of differentiation from it, assumes operation of an industry, especially when to this operation there is added the incident of monopoly, there ceases to be any independent official critic of that industry. Moreover, anyone within the Government industry or outside of it who ventures to criticize the industrial proceedings of the Government or the financial soundness of its enterprises is denounced as an enemy of the people, as an agent of profiteers or of the interests of capital or whatnot. . .a Government which embarks upon a large scale in industrial enterprise encounters strong temptations to act in an arbitrary manner. It cannot afford to have the defects of its administration disclosed. It must close the mouths of critics. In this way, the Government and its enterprises are defended by a reign of terror, varying in its incidents according to the country and to the stage of economic development. Such a reign of terror has been established by the Ontario Hydro-Electric.[42]

Mavor's absolute condemnation of public ownership was not modified by his experience in Canada, where in fact the choice was often between having state enterprise or no enterprise at all. In matters of policy Mavor was much more doctrinaire than either his predecessor Ashley or his contemporaries Davidson and Shortt.

It is fitting to conclude with the tribute of an anonymous obituarist of Mavor:

[41] *Government Telephones: The Experience of Manitoba, Canada* (New York, 1916), p. 164.
[42] *Niagara in Politics: A Critical Account of the Ontario Hydro-Electric Commission* (New York, 1925), pp. 9-10.

No economist of our times could rival him in the encyclopoedic quality of his mind, or was less limited in his survey by the frontiers of time and space. His sympathetic discrimination and his marvelous memory distinguished his descriptive writings, and gave a peculiar intimacy to his lectures and addresses. On the other hand he excelled as a critic and analyst, and his unsparing logic was fearlessly applied to current economic problems and conditions. In this union of wide knowledge and critical insight he resembled his own fellow-citizen, the father of economics, Adam Smith, and his method of presentation reminded one of, though it never merely imitated, that of the author of the "Wealth of Nations."[43]

Stephen Leacock

Stephen Leacock made few contributions to economics. Although he studied at the University of Chicago with Thorstein Veblen and wrote his doctor's thesis on "The Doctrine of Laissez-faire," his writings show little influence of either classical or contemporary theory.[44] Leacock even refused to examine as an economist the two questions that concerned him most before 1914: imperial unity and domestic development. With an emotional fervor that shamed the more coldly rational appeals of the old-country economists Ashley and Davidson, Leacock called in 1907 for colonial tariff preferences, a common navy, and "the pure fire of an Imperial patriotism, that is no theory but a passion." He concluded: "Measure not the price. It is not a commercial benefit we buy. We are buying back our honour as Imperial Citizens."[45] In 1911 Leacock deplored rapid settlement of the Canadian West, not on economic grounds, but because of an influx of "the Slavonic and Mediterranean peoples of a lower industrial and moral status." Preaching a doctrine of racial and class inferiority seldom voiced in Canada, he argued that "mere herds of the proletariat of Europe" were "but indifferent material from which to build the commonwealth of the future." If settled by continental Europeans, he predicted, the Western Provinces would soon join the United States, and it would be "all over with the Confederation of Canada." He made a poetic appeal for exclusion of all but British immigrants from Canada:

[43] *P.T.R.S.C.*, Third Series, XX (1926), Proceedings, p. xv.

[44] See H. A. Innis, "Obituary: Stephen Butler Leacock (1869-1944)," *C.J.E.P.S.*, X (1944), 221. A "Select Bibliography of Stephen Leacock's Contributions to the Social Sciences" is appended to this obituary.

[45] Cited by H. A. Innis, *op. cit.*, p. 220.

The prairies of the West blossomed and withered under the suns of un-numbered ages before the coming of the harvester: the forests of British Columbia have slept in silence for countless winters before the prospector measured them into their billions of feet of timber.   Let them stand a little longer, till we can feel assured that the men who fell them will belong to a nation worthy of the task.[46]

Despite the fact that he seldom worked seriously in the field, Leacock was never backward in criticizing economics.   In 1916 he objected to the use of empirical data on the ground that "economics is being buried alive in statistics and is degenerating into the science of the census. . . ."   At the same time he voiced concern over the state of the subject generally: "When I sit and warm my hands, as best I may, at the little heap of embers that is now Political Econo-my, I cannot but contrast its dying glow with the generous blaze of the vain-glorious and triumphant science that once it was."[47]   By 1936, according to his own account, Leacock had become completely disillusioned: "Forty years of hard work on economics has pretty well removed all the ideas I ever had about it.   I think the whole science is a wreck and has got to be built up again.   For our social problems there is about as much light to be found in the older eco-nomics as from a glow-worm."   His disenchantment culminated in a choleric little work entitled *Hellements of Hickonomics,* intended as a satire in verse and prose upon a variety of economic subjects: state planning, life insurance, Malthusian population theory, bank-ing reform, and Adam Smith.   The book turned out to be a crude ridicule in extremely poor taste.   Leacock seemed unable to under-stand the objects of his criticism; for example, in one place he de-fended protective tariffs on the obviously invalid ground that with-out them the living standards of prosperous countries would fall to the level of the poorest.   He wrote: "We are not yet ready for the Kingdom of Heaven of Universal Free Trade.   In our present world it would tend to force down the wages of all nations to the wages of the lowest.   Not until the sunken areas are leveled up can we have a uniform world."[48]   Economics in the universities came

[46] "Canada and the Immigration Problem," *The National Review,* LVII (1911), 316-327.

[47] *Essays and Literary Studies* (New York, 1916), pp. 88 and 28.

[48] *Hellements of Hickonomics in Hiccoughs of Verse done in our Social Planning Mill* (New York, 1936), pp. vi-ix.

under Leacock's critical eye as part of "the new idea of a practical curriculum." He wrote:

I regard it [the new idea] as very largely a failure. It undertakes to train college men exactly in the way in which men who don't go to college get trained. It substitutes four years in college for one in a workshop. Here belongs in great part, as now taught, the subject of Political Economy, compelled by the outside pressure of mass demand to convert itself into a *vade mecum* of business.[49]

Leacock suggested, and only partly in jest, that economics could be resurrected through an injection of his own humour:

. . . political economy must alter or perish. It needs, if it is to be reformed and reconstructed, the vivifying touch of warm imagination. The ossifying frame of Economics needs a Pygmalion to wake to life the Galatea that was once a living form; or shall I put it more simply and say, It has got to be louder and funnier? This Hickonomics book is an attempt to open the locked door behind which economic scholasticism is drowsing into final oblivion, and to let in a new current of life.[50]

Leacock was never entirely happy in the Canadian academic community, and after a heated argument with James Mavor he resigned from the Royal Society, as he said, "on grounds of personal economy." Enforced retirement from McGill in 1936 made his bitterness toward economics reach a peak; and he described the subject as first "a bright new dogma" and later "a sort of dream, like philosophy itself, bankrupt since Plato but garrulous as an aged patient in a workhouse ward."[51] Leacock quoted a phrase out of context from J. R. Hicks's *Value and Capital* and explained: "The ordinary person can no more read it than he can Chinese."[52] He concluded in perplexed disillusionment:

Take enough of that mystification and muddle, combine it with the continental area of the United States, buttress it up on the side with the history of dead opinion and dress it, as the chefs say, with sliced history

---

[49] *Ibid.*, pp. 81-82.

[50] *Ibid.*, p. 84.

[51] "Has Economics Gone to Seed?" in *Too Much College, Or Education Eating up Life, with Kindred Essays in Education and Humour* (New York, 1940), p. 113.

[52] The quotation, unidentified in Leacock's criticism, can be found in *Value and Capital* (Oxford, 1953), p. 14.

and green geography, and out of it you can make a doctor's degree in economics. I have one myself.[53]

Leacock was more at home with political science than with economics,[54] and he was a competent historian and biographer.[55] It is only because he was chairman of the economics department at one of Canada's largest universities that his work must be examined outside these fields and without considering his principal role as the country's greatest and most successful humorist. Harold Innis wrote:

It is safe to say that Stephen Leacock was the best known Canadian in the English-speaking world. . . . In the social sciences we are grateful for his direct contributions and for his indirect contributions in saving the subject through making major contributions to humour. Stephen Leacock deserved well of Canada.[56]

It was unfortunate both for Leacock and for Canadian economics that he was forced to earn a living from a subject which he disliked, was unable to comprehend, and took time away from areas where he made the best use of his talents.

III. FRENCH CANADIANS

F. A. Baillairgé

Abbé F. A. Baillairgé, professor of philosophy and political economy at Collège Joliette, in 1892 wrote the first text for economics classes in Canada, entitled *Traité classique d'économie politique selon la doctrine de Léon XIII—avec—applications au Canada.* The author explained that his purpose was "to give our teaching colleagues and those who wish to learn about social questions a treatise which is both complete and *elementary;*"[57] he suggested that economics could eliminate many problems of national growth. ("The study of economic science is *indispensable* today because of the im-

---

[53] "Has Economics Gone to Seed?", p. 120.

[54] See for example his work *Elements of Political Science* (Boston, 1906), and "Responsible Government in the British Colonial System," *A.P.S.R.,* I (1907), 355-392.

[55] See *Baldwin, Lafontaine, Hincks,* in "Makers of Canada Series" (Toronto, 1907).

[56] "Stephen Butler Leacock (1869-1944)," *loc. cit.,* p. 226.

[57] Jolliette, 1892, p. viii (translation).

portance of industrialization to social questions.") Baillairgé argued that knowledge of economics would prevent the development of countless difficulties ("it is easier to maintain good health than to cure") and would help to secure "in its own way the reign of God on earth, which ought to be our single end."[58]

The *Traité* followed the conventional pattern for the time of a text in economics, with parts headed Production, Exchange, Distribution, and Consumption. The book was difficult to read because the author employed an annoying literary device of question and answer, giving lengthy quotations in reply to hypothetical queries.[59] He supported classical theory, except where a conflict occurred with religious dectrine; for example he rejected the pessimistic conclusions of Malthus and Ricardo on the ground that "God did not put men on earth to have them die from hunger."[60] Baillairgé described but did not analyze questions of contemporary Canadian interest: tariffs, reciprocity, banking regulation, and inflation. He recommended the doctrine of co-operation in the papal encyclical *Rerum Novarum* as the only solution for conflicts between economic groups. In an appendix, Baillairgé reminded employers of the Thomistic determinants of the "just wage," i.e., commutative and distributive justice.

The *Traité* was not a memorable contribution to economics, but it serves to illustrate an early interest in the subject at the French-Canadian colleges. Baillairgé was the first of his countrymen to have a detailed knowledge both of economics and of religious dogma, and to face the difficulties of reconciliation.

Edouard Montpetit

Before 1914 Edouard Montpetit was the foremost apologist of economics in French Canada. As the first professor at L'École des Hautes Études Commerciales and the University of Montreal he was called upon repeatedly to give explanations of his purpose and

---

[58] *Traité*, pp. vii, x, and 5 (translation).

[59] Baillairgé cited works by the following authors: H. Baudrillart, J. Garnier, P. Guillemenot, F. Hervé-Bazin, Émile de Laveleye, and A. Rondelet. He also referred to several Jesuit writers and to the *Rerum Novarum* of Leo XIII. Listing the most important writers in the history of economic thought, he named a majority of French and other Continental figures. See *Traité*, pp. 10-12.

[60] *Traité*, p. 217 (translation).

method; in the early years, in fact, he was compelled to devote more time to popularizing the science than to making contributions to it.[61] Montpetit was educated in France and drew on the literature of economics in French; describing the development of economic thought he cited Quesnay, Turgot, Say, Sismondi, and more recent authorities such as Rossi, Leroy-Beaulieu, Mesnil-Marigny, Courcelle-Seneuil, Bazin, and Blanqui. In the historical tradition he put little faith in the abstract diagrammatic methods of Pareto, Jevons, and Walras. On this point he wrote:

> Ought one yet to believe that the study of economic phenomena requires a profound knowledge of lines and circles? Not at all. Economics is not essentially an abstract science. It is above all a science of observation. It is very near the life that it endeavors to penetrate. It takes account first of the facts, and if it states principles it is on the condition that they are supported by many and varied observations.[62]

Like other early Canadian economists Montpetit called for empirical research to demonstrate or disprove existing theory before new hypotheses were suggested. After World War I he applied this philosophy in his own work.[63]

IV. SUMMARY AND CONCLUSION

The first generation of academic economists contributed little to economic science; however, it laid the groundwork for later growth of a distinct Canadian discipline. Three professors came from Britain and while in Canada for only a few years continued to work on topics which had interested them at home: Ashley—European economic history, Davidson—wage, employment, and population questions, and Flux—pure theory. James Mavor taught in Canada for most of his life and retained a lasting interest in labor matters and Russian history. After a period of adjustment these scholars did complete studies of domestic problems; Ashley—monopoly control, Davidson—population growth and life insurance, Flux—bank-

[61] See in particular: "L'Économie politique," *Revue Canadienne*, Nouvelle Série, I (1907), 154-168, and 259-268; "Le Mouvement économique—L'Économie politique est-elle une science ennuyeuse et abstraite?," *ibid.*, IX (1912), 138-151.

[62] "Le Mouvement économique. . .," p. 144 (translation).

[63] See for example a representative collection of addresses and essays by Montpetit, *La Conquête économique. . .* (Montreal, 1938).

ing, and Mavor—western agriculture and public enterprise; but they had little contact with each other and developed no synthesis or common approach. The only mutual interest was between Ashley and Davidson, who wished stronger imperial unity as protection against the United States.

Adam Shortt and Stephen Leacock were the two senior, English-speaking, native university economists before 1914. Shortt did pioneer work in monetary history and was the first to appreciate fully the potentialities of the Canadian economy as a subject for study. Although undistinguished as a theorist, he collected energetically, catalogued, and interpreted important documents in Canadian economic history. Moreover, in refreshing contrast to pessimistic old-countrymen, Shortt had faith in the viability of an independent Canadian economy. Leacock was a humorist first and an economist only in name; he made no significant contributions to economic literature and had little but contempt for the science.

Abbé Baillairgé and Edouard Montpetit represented two separate traditions in French-Canadian education. Baillairgé was a cleric, trained in philosophy and with a bent for economics; he outlined in his elementary college text classical principles, gave familiar examples, and urged study of the subject as intellectual discipline. Montpetit, who had been trained in France, regarded economics as a full-fledged science in which the most important task was testing hypotheses; he was the real founder of the university subject in French Canada.

PART THREE

7

Interpretation

Much of the economic thought examined in this study involved the application of borrowed theory to the formulation of domestic policy. Canadians were seldom interested in theory for its own sake. Land problems were examined by two able pioneer writers who had a firm grasp of basic principles, and by several less competent nationalists. During settlement of the West the effects of land ownership on income distribution were described by disciples of Henry George. Many persons discussed commercial policy with well-prepared cases both for and against tariffs, while monetary matters aroused interest principally among bankers and legislators. Before World War I economic "science" in Canada was barely worthy of the name. The colonies made an impressive beginning when two important analyses of settlement, together with John Rae's brilliant book and several imaginative and valuable works by competent authors, appeared within a thirty-year period. For several decades after Confederation, however, economics ceased to develop and the early progress was not consolidated. Colonial universities, when struggling for their very existence, placed economics on their curricula. But in the Dominion separate departments were not established until the 1890's. Finally about the turn of the century the subject began to be accepted slowly, cautiously, and sometimes reluctantly by government, the press, and learned societies.

John Rae was the only outstanding intellectual innovator examined. He made major contributions to the theory of economic growth and provided an important defense for government action. Other individuals, nevertheless, and particularly several who took active parts in policy controversies, are worthy of note. Gourlay and Wakefield wrote about the settlement process with foresight and ability. Tariff debates produced skilful proponents both of free trade (e.g., John Young, David Mills, Sir Richard Cartwright, the Reverend William Hincks) and of protection (e.g., R. B. Sullivan, Abraham Gesner, R. G. Haliburton, J. B. Hurlbert, Sir John A. Macdonald, John MacLean). John Richardson, Lord Sydenham, Francis Hincks, W. H. Merritt, Isaac Buchanan, John Rose, and E. H. King expounded the monetary arguments of various "schools" and traditions. Several statesmen applied a broad command of theory to a number of different areas: Alexander Galt and Francis Hincks discussed currency problems and methods of stimulating national development; Merritt, Buchanan, and W. L. Mackenzie adapted imported radical ideas to local conditions. Numerous writers, many of whom in universities and the civil service might a century later have become professional economists, devoted spare time to economic topics: J. B. Cherriman, E. A. Meredith, the Reverend William Hincks, William Douglass, Arthur Harvey, and William Houston contributed to publications of the Canadian Institute; Goldwin Smith's economic comments appeared in the *Canadian Monthly*. T. C. Keefer and H. B. Willson each published several interesting volumes; and Etienne Parent, J. C. Taché, Abbé Baillairgé, and Errol Bouchette sought to stimulate French-Canadian interest in economics. Among the first academic economists Ashley, Davidson, Flux, and Mavor immigrated from Britain and in varying degrees were drawn to Canadian research topics. After economics had been taught for many years by a succession of Canadian teachers in philosophy, history, and other disciplines, Shortt, Leacock, Hemmeon, McEvoy, McLean, Wickett, and Montpetit were the first natives to give the subject sustained attention.

Economic ideas in Canada came almost entirely from Britain and the United States. Because the intellectual traditions of these countries had common origins and developed together, however, exact debts to each cannot always be determined. When Canadians discussed international trade they employed the abundant British and American writing on the topic: free traders cited classical economists while protectionists referred to Henry Carey and less well-known tariff advocates such as J. B. Byles. The first commercial banks were patterned after Alexander Hamilton's Bank of the United States and were defended with English and American "Banking School" doctrine. Two groups of bank critics used arguments familiar elsewhere for reform of the note issue: the first, a succession of prominent statesmen, outlined "Currency School" theories and called for a government issue of redeemable notes which would vary in response to changes in gold reserves; the second drew inspiration from American experience and proposed an issue of irredeemable notes similar to "greenbacks." In discussions of land policy scarcity of relevant literature in Britain and America, rather than abundance, accounts for the state of Canadian literature. Gourlay and Wakefield in the 1820's and 1830's were the only competent writers to give the subject careful treatment, and Dominion Lands policy after Confederation was copied from American experience with little critical analysis. The few radical economic proposals voiced in nineteenth-century Canada had their origins either in Britain or the United States: the Henry George "Single Tax" was taken intact as were criticisms of monopoly practices, labor abuses, and a maldistribution of income. Finally, the two older countries provided both books and some professors for university courses in economics, and through their journals and professional associations they also made available regular channels for ideas.

The influence upon Canadian economic thought of countries other than Great Britain and the United States was not of great consequence. Several university economists were indebted to German scholars for development of the historical method, and protectionists referred occasionally to Friedrich List. French Canadians cited French classical writers in support of free trade; and the first French-Canadian professors, who were trained in the best continental schools, imported their texts from France.

Most Canadians who wrote on economic subjects before 1914, whether educated locally or abroad, were steeped in the literature of more developed countries; as a result they were slow to observe and to explain theoretically many relationships present exclusively on the frontier. In particular, they tended to overlook benefits and losses which accrued to communities from the activities of members and institutions; and consequently they failed to develop a theoretical rationale for important government activities. For example, the history of land settlement illustrates an obvious failure to perceive and to legislate against the imposition on society by individuals of significant real costs. Canadian landlords, in contrast to their European counterparts, were unable to find satisfactory tenants, and if unwilling to operate a farm had no choice but to hold land idle. As a result, their properties, together with church and state reserves, formed impenetrable barriers to transport and community development. Yet, despite numerous complaints from homestead farmers who suffered personal loss, Canadians seldom examined and discussed this vital issue; apart from the writings of Gourlay and Wakefield, legislators had no scholarly analysis of land problems to which they could turn for guidance and which they might use as support for remedial action. A land policy of laissez faire appropriate for settled countries was introduced to Canada and through the years became accepted so completely that in the end it was seldom challenged seriously by reformers.

Canadian economists were as unable to explain in theory the generation of external economies as the imposition of social costs. In practice, however, legislators who considered these matters manifested a strong intuitive sense. Subsidies for transport construction and protection of manufacturing industry were imposed partly in response to public demands for creation of a viable nation state, but also as a result of widespread practical understanding of the particular significance of these activities for economic development. Ironically, John Rae, writing in Canada but unappreciated, was the only contemporary theorist who explained clearly the distinction and the possible conflict between short run optimum allocation and long run growth. Without passing judgment here on the wisdom of past policies, it can still be said that Canadians would undoubtedly have benefited from acquaintance with discussions similar to Rae's when they assessed the value of practices such as subsidized education, assisted immigration, and industrial protection.

Inability of economists to explain theoretically the role of the state in the economy together with misunderstanding of the distinction between economic science and economic policy account in part for the slow development of the subject in Canada. These factors were crucial in the period roughly from Confederation until the turn of the twentieth century when Canadians came increasingly to believe that without extensive government intervention, dependence on the United States and excessive specialization in the production of a few raw materials would make national survival impossible. During these years the principles of classical economics were generally accepted both in Great Britain and the Colonies, and Canadians were convinced that any use of economic science as a guide to policy would require compliance with doctrinaire laissez faire and subordination of long run economic, social, and political goals to the short run allocation of resources. Legislators were unwilling to subject their policies of tariff protection, railway subsidy, and western land disposal to searching analysis because they feared that examination of means would lead to condemnation of ends. Governments hesitated to consult or to employ professional economists; avenues of publication were closed to amateurs; and in the face of public disapproval universities were reluctant to offer extensive economic training.[1] The ground was fertile in this period for growth of a distinctly Canadian "protectionist" economics, but no Friedrich List or Henry Carey appeared. Not until the 1890's when the National Policy had become firmly established did fear and suspicion diminish enough for economics to resume a stunted growth.[2]

Economics developed slowly in nineteenth century Canada, but the impact of the science should not be underestimated. Canadians could ignore the subject but they could not destroy entirely its influence. Scarcity of statistics and the absence of fundamental research on domestic problems prevented the best use being made of the tools of economics and inhibited analysis of many facets of the economy, particularly matters pertaining to industry, labor, and the growth process. Lack of facilities for advanced training also made it difficult for governments and universities to find and to employ professional economists. Despite these drawbacks and the subject's unpopularity, however, the importance of economics is suggested by many references to it (often indirect) during formulation of com-

---

[1] In the United States in the late nineteenth century association of economics with a policy of laissez faire does not seem seriously to have retarded growth of the science. See Joseph Dorfman, *The Economic Mind in American Civilization* (New York, 1949), III, 80-98.

[2] Professor O. D. Skelton and Dr. K. W. Taylor have suggested that in the early years of the Dominion little attention was paid to economics because people "were too busy in that generation cementing the Canadian nation and expanding it westward." See K. W. Taylor, "Economic Scholarship in Canada," *C.J.E.P.S.*, XXVI (1960), 7, and O. D. Skelton, "Fifty Years of Political and Economic Science in Canada," in *Fifty Years Retrospect: Canada 1882-1932*, pp. 85-89. A complete explanation would require an examination of social and intellectual history beyond the scope of this study.

mercial and monetary policy and in the assessment of radical reforms. Legislators claimed frequently that economic theory was inappropriate for local conditions; but they were compelled to admit in practice that such generalizations as the "laws" of supply and demand, the quantity theory of money, and diminishing returns, were as applicable to Canada as to any country.[3] Although many persons had contempt for economics and few mastered its principles, most had no choice but to consult and act by its findings. Reflecting upon economic science as a factor in economic history, J. M. Keynes concluded: ". . .the ideas of economists and political philosophers, both when they are right and when they are wrong, are more powerful than is commonly understood. Indeed the world is ruled by little else. Practical men, who believe themselves to be quite exempt from any intellectual influences, are usually the slaves of some defunct economist."[4]

[3] Professor P. T. Bauer when discussing the alleged inapplicability of economic principles to non-western countries writes: "Those who dispute the relevance of the propositions of economics to underdeveloped countries usually base their arguments on the differences in attitudes and institutions between the underdeveloped world and western countries. Usually, however, these views reflect incomplete observation or imperfect understanding of economics." *Economic Analysis and Policy in Underdeveloped Countries* (Durham, N. C., 1957), p. 15.

[4] *The General Theory of Employment Interest and Money* (New York, 1936), p. 383.

INDEX